# NECESSARY
# COURAGE

Iowa and the Midwest Experience

SERIES EDITOR

William B. Friedricks,
Iowa History Center
at Simpson College

*The University of Iowa Press gratefully acknowledges
Humanities Iowa for its generous support
of the Iowa and the Midwest
Experience series.*

# NECESSARY COURAGE

Iowa's Underground Railroad
in the Struggle against
Slavery

**LOWELL J. SOIKE**

University of Iowa Press
Iowa City

University of Iowa Press, Iowa City 52242
Copyright © 2013 by the University of Iowa Press
www.uiowapress.org
Printed in the United States of America

Design by Omega Clay

The University of Iowa Press gratefully acknowledges Humanities Iowa
for its generous support of the Iowa and the
Midwest Experience series.

The University of Iowa Press is a member of Green Press Initiative
and is committed to preserving natural resources.

Printed on acid-free paper

Library of Congress Cataloging-in-Publication Data
Soike, Lowell J.
Necessary courage: Iowa's Underground Railroad
in the struggle against slavery / Lowell J. Soike.
pages   cm.—(Iowa and the Midwest experience)
Includes bibliographical references and index.
ISBN: 978-1-60938-193-6, 1-60938-193-9 (pbk.)
ISBN: 978-1-60938-222-3, 1-60938-222-6 (e-book)
1. Underground Railroad—Iowa. 2. Fugitive slaves—Iowa—
History—19th century. 3. Antislavery movements—Iowa—History—
19th century. 4. Abolitionists—Iowa—History—19th century. 5. Iowa—
History—19th century. 6. Iowa—Politics and government—
19th century. I. Title.
E450.S66 2013
326'.80977709034—dc23
2013010116

*For Karen, Beth, Jonathan, and Anthony*

Few were found willing to engage in the dangerous work of assisting in operating the underground railroad. Some there were who favored the idea of immediate and unconditional emancipation, and aided, by pecuniary means, in keeping the rolling-stock in motion; but few, very few indeed could be found with the disposition or the necessary courage to stand by the throttle or conduct the trains.

*—The History of Clinton County, Iowa*

# CONTENTS

# Between Slavery and Freedom

In late May 1848 a young man who had recently arrived in Salem, Iowa, hoping to improve his prospects decided it was time to bring his family to join him. But this man, a sturdy twenty-three-year-old named John Walker, faced much greater obstacles than most, for, as he was later described in court records, he was a "mulatto"— part black, part white—who had recently run away from the Missouri farm where he had been held in slavery by a man named Ruel Daggs.[1] That farm was near Luray in Clark County, twenty miles south of the Iowa border—twenty miles south of freedom.

The elderly Daggs and his wife worked four hundred acres with the labor of sixteen enslaved workers.[2] Among them was Walker's wife, Mary, a small woman, also twenty-three years old, who worked as a cook and spinner, and their four children: Martha, about eight years old; William, a "well-grown" boy about six; George, about four; and a one-year-old child whose name has been lost to history. John Walker aimed to bring them north to join him in freedom. Since arriving in Salem in April, he had found supporters and made what plans he could. The time to act had come, and so he walked south.

Within a few days, John and Mary Walker walked back into Iowa, accompanied by their children and three others. But before they could reach safe haven in Salem, they were recaptured by slavecatchers in the employ of Ruel Daggs. Furious, the town's antislavery residents, many of them Quakers, crowded around the captors and their victims and succeeded in helping some of the fugitives escape again. The people of Salem also demanded that the slavecatchers prove before a justice of the peace that the runaways were in fact enslaved before allowing them to be returned to Missouri. Lacking the proper paperwork and intimidated by the locals' hostility, the slavecatchers were forced to retreat. Enraged, Daggs organized a posse of his neighbors to invade Salem in search of his missing property. He also appealed to the law, suing those he believed had aided or hidden the runaways.

The Walker family's risky flight toward freedom dramatizes the central themes of this book. Their story demonstrates that the conflict over slavery began long before South Carolina forces attacked the U.S. troops garrisoned at Fort Sumter on April 12, 1861. Nowhere was that conflict more urgent and dangerous than in the Midwest, where slave states and free states lay alongside each other. In Salem in the summer of 1848, Americans from Missouri and Iowa, neighbors living within fifty miles of each other, nearly came to blows over the plight of nine people who were risking their lives to seek freedom. People readily took to the courts to enforce their support for or opposition to slavery. As Iowans grew increasingly opposed to slavery during the 1840s and 1850s and more willing to help those who were escaping from bondage, slaveholding Missourians vigorously defended their property rights. American citizens on both sides of the border between slavery and freedom hid runaways in their barns or captured them and returned them to their owners.

This book, the first full-scale history of Iowa's underground railroad operations, gathers the results of my several years of research while serving as director of a federally funded project of the State Historical Society of Iowa.[3] The purpose of the project was to illuminate the historical details of Iowa's substantial role in the abolition movement and, because of its border with slaveholding Missouri, its status as a battleground in the fight for emancipation. Scholars have interpreted the underground railroad story in various ways, from stressing its great role in bringing on the Civil War and destroying slavery to judging it relatively inconsequential to those battles. Related arguments concern how many or how few slaves actually escaped from slave states and crossed into free states, what effects such escapes had on slaveholders, and how formally organized underground railroad efforts were.[4] On one point all agree, however: runaways and those aiding them, especially in border states like Missouri and Iowa, were the reason for the passage of the Fugitive Slave Act of 1850.

The 1860 census showed that Missouri led every state in fugitive slave losses, with those escaping bondage presumably going to Iowa, Illinois, and Kansas Territory. *Necessary Courage* does not suggest that such losses either destroyed slavery or brought on the Civil War, but rather that the frequency of escapes from slavery was a symptom of disintegrating slaveholder control in slave states that adjoined free states and territories along the western frontier, areas where freeholder settlement was increasing. ("Free states" were those where slavery was illegal; "freeholders" were small farmers who owned no slaves.) Despite slave patrols, proslavery associations, and black codes restricting the migration of African Americans into free states, the rising free-state sentiment fostered anxiety among slaveholders, limiting their willingness to settle near border areas. The same circumstances gave enslaved workers, perhaps fearful of being sold south, the confidence that running to freedom might be possible.

In explaining Iowa's involvement in these historical developments, this book underscores the work of various evangelical and other churches, and their members, that supported underground railroad activity even as the majority of Protestant Northern churches continued to tolerate slavery or avoided taking a stand on the issue.[5] With Iowa a young and mostly unpopulated state in the 1830s, its political life had yet to be clearly defined. The rising force of the slavery issue in national politics during the 1840s and 1850s led to arguments over allowing slavery's extension into western territories, making Iowa a political battleground. At the same time, the growing influence of evangelical faiths in the North lent a moralistic tone to political arguments, casting slavery's defenders not just as wrongheaded, but as wicked and immoral. This trend converted a political issue into an inflexible moral dilemma that drove the debaters toward extremes. As Northern activism faced Southern intransigence, Congress passed and the president signed an act to open the Kansas-Nebraska territory to settlement. The ensuing turmoil upended Iowa politics. These developments frame the story told in this book.

At the heart of the struggle over slavery in the Midwest were the slaves who risked everything to be free and the people who helped them, despite increasingly severe laws against doing so. In Iowa, the underground railroad that carried people to freedom was a chancy enterprise fueled by faith, bravery, and desperation. This is the story of some of the few who had the necessary courage to make it work.

# 1

# Iowa and the Politics of Slavery

*Early Settlement in Iowa*

Iowa's first white American settlers arrived during the 1830s, and it became a state only in 1846, so it isn't usually thought to have had much of a role in the tensions leading up to the Civil War. But a closer look at the involvement of Iowans in the underground railroad movement that helped runaways from the slave state of Missouri find their way to freedom in Chicago or Canada, in the battles in Kansas during the 1850s, and in John Brown's famous 1859 raid on Harpers Ferry, Virginia, shows that the state's residents were a crucial factor in the antislavery struggle. To understand why this was so, we must look at who settled the state, especially in its southern border towns, and how their politics changed over time.

In the 1830s Iowa settlers were living on the western frontier of the young United States (see figure 1). Unlike older states such as Ohio or New York, Iowa had few improved transportation routes, permanent buildings, or densely populated towns. Spectacularly endowed with beautiful prairies, streams, and woodlands, the new territory had more trails than roads, and most wended their way to bridgeless stream crossings. Much of the land west and north of Des Moines was swampy and largely uninhabited, except for the few remaining Native Americans, who were forced to cede their lands in 1830, 1832, 1837, 1842, and 1851. But by the late 1840s settlers were filling Iowa's eastern and central stretches, looking to establish a farm, raise a store, start a law practice, or in some other way grasp a chance for success (see figure 2). Ministers joined the arriving throngs, working hard to set up frontier missions for people wanting a preacher of the same faith they had followed back home. And once settled, the fresh-minted Iowans looked for new ways to boost their own status and that of their communities. Politics for these early settlers mostly focused on calling for better roads—and by the 1840s, railroads—so that they could buy and sell goods more easily.

During the early years, most Iowa settlers took slavery for granted, considering it a fact of life in the country's development. The United States had been a slaveholding republic since its founding in the 1780s. Nonetheless, talk was in the air about the future of slavery, the conduct of slaveholders, and the civil rights of free black people. Many Americans were beginning to wonder whether slavery should be abolished, and if it could, whether the freed people should be allowed to stay in the United States or would have to be sent back to Africa, where their ancestors had come from. Slavery was not legal in Iowa, but what its people thought about these questions depended a lot on where they had emigrated from and which church and political party they belonged to.

### The Border between Slavery and Freedom

In 1820 Congress passed the Missouri Compromise, the first major effort to resolve white Americans' growing disagreement over slavery. The act admitted Maine as a free state and Missouri as a slave state, although it prohibited slavery north of the 36° 30' latitude line, which marked Missouri's southern border. The act granted the state an exception so that slavery remained legal there. Where midwestern free states and slave states lay up against one another, the southern counties of free states typically were settled by pioneers from the South before the northern parts were settled by families from the mid-Atlantic and New England regions. Men in the southern counties of free states commonly voted the Democratic ticket and accepted, defended, or tolerated slavery, whereas in northern areas men were more likely to be hostile to the institution and to vote for the Whigs, the other major party of this era. But as long as slavery was not at issue in local or national politics, most border-state Midwesterners focused on the politics of westward expansion and development and ignored the slavery question.[1]

Both national political parties—the Democrats and the Whigs —successfully minimized slavery as a political issue until 1848. Each party had Northern and Southern wings, so keeping the volatile slavery question out of debate was critical for maintaining party unity and thereby winning elections. The Whigs were most successful during the decades when the slavery question was side-lined, and ultimately, the party's failure to confront the issue head-on destroyed the organization.

Although no one in the 1830s could have foretold the demise of the Whigs, attitudes toward slavery were shifting. A person who spoke out against the institution during that decade might have been ignored as an irritating crank or oddball fanatic. By the 1840s, however, supporters of slavery would brand such a person an "abolitionist"—someone who advocated the immediate end of slavery—who deserved a beating, or worse. The increasing visibility and outspokenness of antislavery activists infuriated slavery's defenders and repelled its apologists. As the 1840s closed, few people remained indifferent.

Many factors contributed to the polarization of Americans' attitudes toward slavery. Perhaps most important was westward expansion itself. By the 1810s Americans had come to disagree about whether slavery should be allowed in the newly won territories. At the national level, this dispute was temporarily resolved in the Missouri Compromise of 1820 and its establishment of Missouri's southern border as the northernmost limit of slavery in the as yet unsettled lands of the Louisiana Purchase. Then in 1836 the conflict over slavery flared up again when the Americans (mostly slaveowners) who had settled in the Mexican state of Texas rebelled against Mexico with the aim of becoming part of the United States. They successfully expelled the Mexican forces in 1836 and declared Texas an independent republic.

Over the next nine years, the question of whether the United States should annex Texas got tangled in the struggle over slavery. Opponents of annexation feared that making Texas a state would increase the power of the slaveowning South, upset the balance of free and slave states, and provoke a war with Mexico, which did not accept Texas's independence. Believing that annexing Texas was critical to the nation's continued westward expansion, proslavery Americans agreed that it would also strengthen the South, which they favored. In short, one's position on annexation became a test of sectional (that is, Northern or Southern) loyalty and linked westward expansion to the spread of slavery. The political conflict reached a critical moment in 1844, when the growing division between North and South was intensified by the presidential election of that year. Democrat James K. Polk defeated Whig Henry Clay in part by promising to annex Texas (to appease Northerners, he also promised to seize the Oregon Territory from the British). Eventually, an expansionist Congress voted to annex the southern republic in December 1845. This decision moved the nation ever closer to crisis over the slavery issue.

Against the background of these simmering tensions, some dramatic events sparked further moral indignation. When enslaved blacks overthrew the crew on the Spanish ship *Amistad* off the coast of Cuba in 1839 before it drifted up near Long Island, the press coverage and court proceedings laid the horrors of the slave trade before the public eye. Though the *Amistad* case also dealt with complex issues involving international law and treaties, many saw it for what it was to the enslaved defendants: a story of inhumanity and injustice. One Burlington, Iowa, newspaper editor wrote, "The man who will not groan within himself if these already suffering, wronged and injured beings must be sent back to a bloody death in Cuba, deserves not himself to be free."[2]

### The Rise of the Abolition Movement

More consistently influential than singular events like the *Amistad* case in agitating the public about the issue was the American Anti-Slavery Society, founded by William Lloyd Garrison and Arthur Tappan in 1833. Its members injected the question of slavery into every conversation, whatever its political and social focus, making the issue of human bondage less easy to ignore. Antislavery activists sought to "clank the chains" of slavery in the ears of both Southerners and indifferent Americans from other regions, and to increase public anxiety accordingly.[3]

Through meetings, mass drives for petitions to Congress, mailings of antislavery literature, and field lectures, the organization built a membership of 150,000 people in two thousand local chapters by 1840. The number of antislavery newspapers mushroomed, the most controversial of them being the *Liberator*, established in 1831 by William Lloyd Garrison. This uncompromising radical called for immediate abolition and assailed slaveholders and gradual emancipationists alike. In the terminology of the time, people who shared Garrison's "immediatist" views were known as "abolitionists." "Gradualists"—or those who wanted to limit slavery to the states where it already existed, supported measures to encourage slaveholders to voluntarily free their slaves, and sought to settle the former slaves outside the United States—counted as "antislavery" activists. Antislavery advocates far outnumbered the more radical abolitionists. Garrison scorned the gradualists as people of "timidity, injustice and absurdity," and he accused the federal government of collaborating with slaveholders.[4] Despite his sometimes inflammatory rhetoric, he relied on moral suasion to awaken the conscience of enough people to change public opinion, and he rejected violence.

The emergence of slavery as a moral issue owed most, however, to a Protestant revival movement now called the Second Great Awakening (the first had occurred about a century earlier). This Christian movement matured in the 1820s and 1830s in New England and inspired much social activism. Those "awakened" during these years discarded older Protestant doctrines of predestination and innate human depravity in favor of the belief that individuals could rescue their souls though personal faith and devotional service.[5]

The Second Great Awakening contained a powerful perfectionist impulse. It was not enough for an individual to be uplifted spiritually; the entire society needed to be uplifted through social and political reform movements that would eliminate its flaws and therefore achieve perfection on earth. From this point of view, the charity given by "better people" to comfort the sick and the dispossessed was insufficient. People of religious conviction needed to improve society to reduce or eliminate such suffering in the first place by bringing the social order into accord with God's benevolence. Ending slavery would help do that, thought Northern evangelicals, for it would establish true equality before the law while giving former slaves the chance to improve themselves through education and property ownership. From its origins in New England, the awakening also spread to the South, where itinerant ministers drew many people to camp meetings and fanned evangelical fervor. But the social realities of the slavery system led Southern revivalists to emphasize individual spiritual experience; one's personal conversion and godly behavior was the aim, not social reform.

As antislavery efforts picked up steam in the North, abolitionists felt justified in attacking churches that sanctioned slavery, accusing them of contributing to human misery through their indifference. The idea that slaveholding was not a sin, abolitionists held, was without a scriptural basis, as was the related view that slavery was a secular, not a religious, issue. Under pressure to remove slaveholders from their congregations, several Northern churches gradually became more outspoken about their disapproval of slavery, but the debate caused painful divisions. Some broad national denominations, including the Methodist, Baptist, and Presbyterian churches, fractured into separate Northern and Southern wings.[6] Among Northern evangelical churches, the more radical western Congregationalists, the Hicksites (which had split from the Society of Friends in the late 1820s), the Anti-Slavery Friends (which had split off from the mainstream Society of Friends in Indiana in 1842), and the Free and Scottish Presbyterian sects were the most active antislavery groups. Significant additional support for ending slavery came from smaller churches such as the Wesleyan Methodists, the northern Baptists, and the United Brethren.

## The Proslavery Economy

But not all Northerners were willing to alienate Southern slave-owners. Restraining antislavery efforts were strong economic ties between the Northern and Southern states. It was no easy matter for opponents of slavery to make headway among Northern shippers, for example, whose jobs depended on delivering food and goods to the Southern states, or with eastern merchants and financial institutions profiting from the capital they provided to Southern planters to grow cotton.

Indeed, cotton bound the North and the South together and was one of the country's most important exports during this period. Since the introduction of Eli Whitney's cotton gin in the 1790s, Northern manufacturers and others had earned handsome profits from the success of the cotton economy. The machine, which stripped the sticky green seeds from the white fibers more quickly and efficiently than people could, increased fiftyfold the amount of cotton that could be processed in a day. Consequently, the cotton gin multiplied the demand for enslaved blacks to work the ever-increasing acreage devoted to cotton. A growing number of New England textile mills hummed with machinery weaving cloth from slave-picked cotton brought in by Boston and New York shippers, who also carried it on to Liverpool to feed Great Britain's textile factories.[7]

And yet, Southerners were uneasy. They realized that, despite their cotton-based prosperity and strong commercial ties with Northern merchants and bankers, population and industrial growth in the free states was reducing their own national political and economic power. People in the slave states were keenly aware of their relative economic inferiority. As one speaker before a Southern commercial convention in 1855 aptly put it:

> From the rattle with which the nurse tickles the ear of the child born in the South, to the shroud that covers the cold form of the dead, everything comes to us from the North. We rise from between sheets made in northern looms and pillows made of northern feath-

ers, to wash in basins made in the north, dry our beards on northern towels, and dress ourselves in garments woven in northern looms; we eat from northern plates and dishes; our rooms are swept with northern brooms; our gardens are dug with northern spades and our bread kneaded in trays or dishes of northern wood or tin; and the very wood which feeds our fires is cut with northern axes, helved with hickory brought from Connecticut or New York.[8]

Another writer of the time wrote that even "in the decline of life we remedy our eye-sight with Northern spectacles, and support our infirmities with Northern canes; in old age we are drugged with Northern physic; and, finally, when we die, our inanimate bodies, shrouded in Northern cambric, are stretched upon the bier, borne to the grave in a Northern carriage, entombed with a Northern spade, and memorialized with a Northern slab!"[9] For many Southerners, the most important means of lessening Southern dependence on the North was extending slavery and the slave economy ever westward into new lands.

### Democratic Iowa and
### the Black Laws

All this national ferment and discontent shaped the new society being established in Iowa during the 1830s and 1840s because of where the settlers came from. As New England industrial towns boomed because of their trade with slaveholding states, towns and rural areas there and in western New York continued to feel the pull of an evangelical fervor that cast slavery as a personal sin and demanded that slaveholders be denied membership in churches. When these people migrated to the Midwest, they carried their ideals with them, powerfully influencing the religious and political temper of newly established midwestern states, including Iowa.

That Iowans would embrace antislavery views or abolitionism was not a sure thing at the outset, however. Iowa's earliest migrants did not share the evangelical fervor of many westward-bound New Englanders. Most of them hailed from Kentucky, Tennessee, and Virginia, Southern states whose people were often irritated by the abolitionist evangelicalism of the New England and upstate New York migrants. The initial settlers in southern Iowa townships and counties for a time gave those localities a Southern and politically Democratic cast. The strong presence of Southerners in early Iowa gave them a larger voice in selecting who would sit in Congress or the state legislature, or who would hold the governorship (see figure 3).

Having come from a slaveholding state, however, did not guarantee that a settler was proslavery in attitude. Most new Iowans had no desire to see slavery brought to their new home and had no particular sympathy for its growth elsewhere. But the Southern settlers were accustomed to slavery and accepted it as an expression of natural human inequality. Like Sen. Henry Clay of Kentucky, one of the leading politicians of the period, most Iowans of Southern extraction thought that Northern abolitionists had no right to challenge constitutionally protected property relations in the South. Although the framers of the U.S. Constitution carefully avoided using the words "slave" or "slavery," they did mention persons "held to service or labor" and included a measure stating that the laws of one state could not excuse individuals from the labor or service they owed in another state. Anyone who ran away from such an obligation was to be returned to the state he or she came from.

Iowans' attitudes toward slavery mainly showed up in antiblack sentiments. The Burlington, Iowa, newspaper editor who in 1837 unblushingly declared slavery to be "the best condition" for African Americans uttered an opinion widely shared among whites in states both north and south of the line dividing slave from free.[10] Such attitudes explain the public policies and laws of the time that restricted the migration of black people into Iowa and severely limited the political and civil rights of black residents. These so-called black laws or black codes are evidence of a common white intolerance for black Americans, even in free states.

Such laws spoke to white fears that runaways and free blacks from adjacent slave states might overwhelm whites.[11] Black laws in Iowa initially appeared in 1839 when the first territorial legislature passed An Act to Regulate Blacks and Mulattoes. It required "negroes and mulattoes" (that is, people of both African and mixed African and European descent) to obtain from a court a certificate stating they were free. They also had to post a $500 bond (about $12,500 in 2011) as guarantee of their good behavior. To hire or harbor a black or mulatto person who had no certificate or bond posted could cost the offender a fine of $5 to $100 (about $100 to $2,500 in 2011). Moreover, the act allowed slaveholders to keep their slaves when passing through Iowa Territory, even though slavery was not legal there. Finally, the law stated that any fugitive slaves were to be arrested and returned to their owners.[12]

The territory's 1844 constitution was somewhat more moderate: it did allow African Americans to settle in Iowa, but it denied them the right to vote, to serve in the state militia, or to sit in the legislature. These black laws carried over mostly unchanged into the early statehood period between 1846 and 1851, when the state legislature enacted an exclusion law prohibiting African American immigration into Iowa. Under this measure, those already in the state could remain, but any subsequent migrants were to leave within three days or face a fine of $2 a day (about $60 in 2011) and possible imprisonment.[13]

Black laws, justified by notions of black inferiority and the desirability of white-only settlement, aroused resistance among antislavery activists and those promoting black civil rights, but changing the majority opinion took time. Attitudes began to change in Iowa in the same ways that they changed elsewhere in the nation: through religious and political activism. Few residents paid attention in 1841 when Iowa's Congregational churches called for repeal of the Act to Regulate Blacks and Mulattoes. Also ignored that year were similar petitions sent to the legislature by Salem's Quakers. In 1842 the House judiciary committee defended the 1839 law as "essential to the protection of the white population, against an influx of runaway slaves and out-cast blacks, from adjoining states."[14]

Undeterred, antislavery activists kept sending petitions. Residents of Denmark (Lee County), Iowa, sent in a petition much like that of the Salem Quakers. In 1842 petitions also went to the territorial legislature from Henry, Jefferson, and Washington counties

—all in southeast Iowa. The appeals got nowhere, being referred to legislative committees from which they never emerged. Whatever public protests were made against black law inequities, the territorial and then the state legislators generally ignored them, responding instead to fears of and antagonism toward blacks.[15]

The flow of petitions to the Iowa legislature and that body's refusal to respond to them mirrored the struggle occurring at the national level during the same period. Southern members of Congress, angry over the flood of petitions from Northern church groups and others who judged slavery a noxious weed, took steps to choke off public debate. Between 1835 and 1844 the proslavery interests that dominated the U.S. House of Representatives imposed various gag rules to block the body from receiving or discussing antislavery petitions. Former president and Massachusetts representative John Quincy Adams and others used various stratagems to counter and circumvent the rules, ultimately winning repeal of them in 1844.[16]

In Iowa, Democratic majorities preferred to focus on western development and keep silent on the slavery issue, despite rising concerns about it among some of the state's residents. The party's resolute focus on the issue that most Iowans could agree on—development—doubtless helped it control Iowa during the territorial and early statehood years. Whenever antislavery agitation raised its face, the majority decried it as disruptive, hostile, and inflammatory rhetoric spread by hated abolitionists—using the word to brand even moderate antislavery advocates as extremists. True enough, Iowans agreed, slavery was an abomination, but because the institution did not officially exist in the state, it should not be discussed, to avoid inflaming passions.

Those who dared to openly speak out for emancipation were rejected, or worse. For instance, when Andrew T. Foss, a lecturer from the Massachusetts Anti-Slavery Society, visited Clinton and Camanche, Iowa, in 1859, he found the church where he was supposed to speak closed to his lecture. And at another stopping place, "threats of personal violence were freely made" against him, leaving Foss "glad to escape with a whole skin and unbroken bones."[17]

Hostility toward abolitionists and more moderate opponents of slavery in Iowa during the 1840s intensified along with the national polarization on the issue. Abolitionist talk, many held, would tear at the scab covering the Union's fragile peace. The 1839 comments of the Burlington *Iowa Territorial Gazette* are typical of many: "We are entirely Southern in our feelings, and hold that every attempt to agitate the abolition of slavery that does not come from the slaveholders themselves is an unwarranted interference in their domestic concerns, [and] should receive unqualified condemnation."[18] As one Clinton County abolitionist later put it, before the Civil War, "the boasted free press of the North avoided the antislavery question and the underground railroad as unclean things, and branded their advocates and adherents as wild fanatics and dangerous agitators."[19]

Wishing to be left in peace, newspaper editors, legislators, and other government officials readily connected the aims of abolitionists and antislavery advocates to public fears that free black people would migrate to Iowa. Abolitionists ought not to interfere with Southern states, such men thought, for the "peculiar institution" is "infinitely the best condition for the Negro," providing African Americans with the paternalistic care they needed.[20] In Iowa things were and ought to remain quiet on this question, in the view of many leading men. The *Davenport Gazette*'s editor noted as late as 1844 that the prevailing temper in the West (as the Midwest was then known) was "without the jar and discord that result from the existence of slavery in the Union and the efforts to abolish it. Though we hear the rumblings in the distance, we are spared the bitter word and rankling feeling that the discussion of this vexed question ever produces."[21]

But this claim—clearly an overstatement, given the petitions that some Iowa churches had sent the legislature—would soon cease to be true. The coming of the railroad and telegraph diminished Iowa's frontier isolation and brought the national struggle over slavery closer to home. In 1848, the same year that John Walker and his family made their courageous bid for freedom, midwestern newspapers could report on an event in Washington, D.C., within twenty hours of its occurrence, when a few years earlier they would have had to wait a week or more for the mail to deliver a capital city newspaper containing the report. By the late 1840s people reading local newspapers in Iowa expected to get up-to-date national news via the St. Louis papers, which received it via telegraph.

As a result of these advances in transportation and communications, sensational stories about slavery became more immediate than they had been before. Now, news of kidnappings, killings, beatings, shootings, and other forms of violence associated with slavery spread quickly, ricocheting through Northern newspapers. The accelerated news cycle made possible by the telegraph spurred public argument and drew people's attention to small events of which they previously might have remained ignorant. And the highly charged opinions of commentators outside the Midwest helped to make the quarrels over slavery in Kansas and Iowa increasingly rancorous.

## *The Politicization of Slavery in the 1840s and 1850s*

By the 1840s, as Iowa was shaping its government, an organized antislavery political party had appeared on the national scene. A strong segment of the American Anti-Slavery Society abandoned the organization's earlier policy of avoiding partisan politics and formed the Liberty Party in 1840. Dedicated to political agitation for slavery's abolition, the inexperienced one-issue party initially polled only a small portion of the vote, but its presence could make a big difference in close elections. In Iowa and elsewhere, the Liberty Party hoped to swing the balance of power in tight local elections by attracting all those who saw slavery as the paramount issue.[22]

Salem townspeople formed Iowa's first local Liberty Party in the summer of 1843.[23] In the next election, Henry County abolitionists ran two candidates for the territorial legislature: Samuel Luke Howe, a Congregationalist in Mount Pleasant who operated an academy, and Joel Garretson, a farmer living north of Salem in Jackson Township. Both made the worst showing in a field of five candidates. Over the next three years Liberty Party candidates also ran in elections in Des Moines, Johnson, Lee, and Scott counties.[24] All harvested few votes, but the party did give men a way to vote their convictions, to punish the major parties for ignoring the issue, and to force the Whig Party—which had only a timid antislavery plank and from which voters defected to the Liberty Party—to pay attention to them in close elections.

Galvanizing both antislavery and proslavery activists was a series of national events that made the question of slavery unavoidable. In 1845 Congress voted to make Texas a state, thus bringing into the Union an enormous amount of land where slavery was legal and precipitating a war with Mexico. Antislavery activists quickly responded. Representative David Wilmot, a Democrat from Pennsylvania, proposed what became known as the Wilmot Proviso in 1846. This amendment to an appropriations bill would have barred slavery from any territory conquered in a war with Mexico. Though the proviso was not adopted, it became a flashpoint in the widespread sectional debate that followed. That debate was inflamed by the war with Mexico, which ended in 1848 with the United States appropriating half of Mexico's land, including not just Texas, but the whole of what today we call the Southwest as well as what became the state of California. Here was more land over which proslavery and antislavery Americans would battle each other.

A statewide Liberty Party formed at a convention in Yellow Springs, Iowa, in 1847, in the midst of the war with Mexico and thanks to the efforts of organizer Alanson St. Clair, a former abolition lecturer, fearless Congregationalist, and skilled infighter.[25] The new party endorsed John P. Hale for the presidency, condemned the black laws, and launched a newspaper, the *Iowa Freeman*, under St. Clair's editorship.[26] On May 24, 1848, the members of the newly born Liberty Party met in Salem, Iowa, for their state convention. The party chairman, Eli Jessup, and executive committee members such as Asa Turner and George Shedd of Denmark and Samuel Luke Howe of Mount Pleasant discussed the party newspaper and how to combat the weak stand that the Whig

Party, their former political home, had taken against slavery at its recent convention.[27]

The Liberty Party was short-lived, however. A few days after St. Clair left Iowa for his home near Chicago in July 1848, exhausted from constant field work and lectures, a national convention in Buffalo, New York, launched a more broadly attractive organization called the Free Soil Party. Its platform called not for abolishing slavery, but simply for resisting its extension into new territories. The latter position appealed to far greater numbers of white Americans than did abolition. Iowa's Free Soil Party, officially known as the Free Democracy Party, took over the *Iowa Freeman* and shifted its operation to Mount Pleasant, where schoolmaster Samuel Luke Howe became the editor. Free Soilers attracted disaffected members of both the Democratic and the Whig parties, including William Penn Clarke of Iowa City and Dr. John H. Dayton of Muscatine. It also developed a strong "conscience Free Soil" wing made up of Iowa's former Liberty Party men, many of them from antislavery towns and townships in southeast counties. The Free Soil Party made the slavery issue a regular factor in Iowa politics.

On the national level, to resolve the intensifying crisis over slavery, Congress passed the Compromise of 1850 after long debate. It included several measures intended to lessen the growing hostility between North and South over extending slavery into the territories. The compromise abolished the slave trade in Washington, D.C., and admitted California as a free state to offset the entry of slaveholding Texas. The law also established territorial governments in Utah and New Mexico and settled a boundary dispute between New Mexico and Texas. Finally, to satisfy Southern border states, Congress strengthened the Fugitive Slave Act, which required people in free states to arrest fugitive slaves and return them to their owners. The 1850 Compromise, hailed as the final answer to slavery in the territories, received the vote of Iowa's entire congressional delegation—Democrats all.

In Iowa, Democrat and Whig alike hoped by this grand bargain to quench sectional fires, neutralize antislavery feeling, and allow the state to focus on economic development. But those residents who were strongly opposed to slavery saw it differently. To them, the united vote of Iowa's congressional delegation was an act of Southern conciliation and a win for proslavery forces.[28] It breathed life into Free Soilers, who urged repeal of the Fugitive Slave Act. Indeed, although most Iowans were relieved to see Congress enact the compromise, a substantial number also felt that the act was a lot to stomach. And in fact, a growing number of Iowans decided not to obey the law.

# 2

# Iowa Becomes Antislavery

How did Iowa go from being a strongly Democratic, proslavery state to hosting major stations along the underground railroad and sending money, arms, and men to fight in the mid-1850s battle over whether Kansas would be a free state or a slave state and later in the Civil War? The answers lie partly in the settlement of several southern Iowa towns by people from Ohio, Illinois, New England, and New York who belonged to strongly evangelical and increasingly antislavery churches. And partly the answers lie in the decisions that individuals made when a fugitive came to them asking for help.

## *The Underground Railroad*

A tap comes on the door. It's night, several miles out of town amid a humble settler's fields of wheat, corn, flax, and vegetables and pens holding some hogs, a horse, and a milk cow. Standing on your doorstep are three weary black runaways. They ask for food and shelter as they describe their flight from Missouri to Iowa. You have to ask yourself which direction they came from. You wonder whether the neighbors to the west spotted them, and if so, will they pass word to the slavecatchers who are, inevitably, dogging the fugitives' footsteps?

One of the three runaways says that they crossed the creek from the south, and they came to your door because they heard you were antislavery and might help. It's illegal to help them, and just last year the Fugitive Slave Act imposed stiff criminal penalties on those who harbor fugitives or hinder their capture. Despite living in a free state, most Iowans, even those opposed to slavery, are highly unfriendly to abolitionists and will gladly report runaways. What happens if someone finds out that these desperate travelers are here? What decisions do you make now?

Many Iowans who lived on the state's southern border had to make such decisions in the 1850s. A growing number of them, convinced that slavery was wrong, accepted the risk thrust upon them. In many cases, such as this one, they might have nervously put some leftover biscuits, a few potatoes, and a chunk of cooked meat into a bag for the fugitives and then directed the three to hide in a nearby thicket for the night. The next day they might have given the runaways directions to the farm two miles distant that was owned by a man who, it was said, was willing to help people escaping slavery.

Contrary to popular myths about the underground railroad, in Iowa fugitives were not hidden in caves or tunnels. Most records show that the people who aided runaways commonly hid them in nearby brush or timber, tall grass, a cornfield, or an adjacent outbuilding—a crib, a hay shed, or the occasional small barn.[1] There are only a few examples of runaways being hidden in some spare space of a house, such as an attic or cellar. The tales of quilts containing secret codes for the journey to freedom are likewise apocryphal; all the accounts of the underground railroad in the Midwest indicate that runaways made use only of spoken directions or traveled with the people assisting them on their northward flight.[2]

Fugitive slaves' prospects for a safe journey across Iowa depended heavily on their own ingenuity, on people who spontaneously befriended them along the way, and on the direct, planned help of antislavery residents who were more committed to a "higher law" than to the law of the land. Of course, before runaways even got to Iowa, they had to devise a plan of escape and summon the courage to carry it out, adjusting plans in transit, following hunches about who could be trusted, and appealing for help as needed. Typically, people fleeing from slavery took things a step at a time, having only the name of a single helpful person to inquire after based on directions from a local black resident or abolitionist they met along the way. One contact hopefully led to another on the long, slow journey northeast toward Chicago and on to safety in Canada. Perhaps, if they were lucky, they would run into someone belonging to the loosely organized underground railroad network, who could usually make the escape a little easier. The fugitives' flight expressed a pattern of defiance that bedeviled slaveowners and constantly belied their argument that African Americans were happy to be slaves.[3]

For those who assisted the runaways, the pride of helping someone in desperate need could be mixed with bitter regret if the escape attempt failed. Clark Smith met his first runaway in 1857 when he was just fifteen years old and living with his family in the new settlement of Amity in Page County.[4] He was driving the family's cattle to the fields to graze when "immediately before me out of the high grass arose a tall, black negro." Startled at seeing the twenty-five- to thirty-year-old man, later estimated to weigh about 175 pounds, Smith "banally asked if he had stayed there all night." No, he said, he had "traveled all night" until he saw a house up ahead and decided to hide until daylight "in the tall grass." Unsure what else to say, Smith asked whether the man had eaten breakfast. No, the runaway said, he had not eaten for many days.

"You come with me," said Smith, "and my folks will give you some breakfast." When they arrived at the boy's house, "the colored man sank down upon the woodpile as though more than grateful for this momentary safety and provision." Once breakfast was ready and the boy invited him in to eat, "the negro drew back hesitatingly" until "Mother then went to the door and said gently, 'that's all right. Come right on in, we will be glad to have you.'" Receiving this invitation, "his objections ceased; and the slave sat down to the table along [with] the white folks for the first time in his whole life. And how that poor, half-starved negro did eat! It certainly did our hearts good to see the relish with which his food disappeared, and to feel a gratified sense of our own instrumentality in alleviating to some extent his sufferings." He "told us he had come from more than a hundred miles south of St. Joseph, Missouri; that he had no family ties; and that his master, a young man, had paid twenty-four hundred dollars for him about two years previous." But he noticed that the growing hostilities over slavery in Kansas were "convincing the slave[holding] element there was trouble ahead," and so he feared "his master was about to sell him south" where slavery was more secure. Fearing this strengthening of the chains of slavery, the man "decided to risk running away."

Unfortunately, about two weeks after leaving the Smiths' place, the man was captured. Amity's residents learned that the "slave's owner, accompanied by an officer, had passed through the country on the fugitive's trail and had posted offers of reward at Marysville and at Clarinda." A prominent businessman in Clarinda discovered the slave's whereabouts and "took a rig and followed his trail." Within a day or two he and some friends retrieved him, "turned him over to the civil officer at Marysville and notified the owner by courier where his property could be found," afterwards sharing a $300 reward (about $8,000 in 2011).

In short, the underground railroad was but a rickety, impromptu network of people offering general assistance (see figure 4). Events altered its direction and speed, and operators adjusted their plans depending on how close behind them the slavecatchers were. The length of the runaways' journeys between stations depended on the friendliness or hostility of the residents of each neighborhood, the distance between one safe haven and another, and how often fugitives came seeking help. Distances between stopping points naturally lengthened in the more sparsely settled areas of the Midwest.

### Eastern Iowa Organizes

Given the risks and the bitter consequences of being discovered, why did some Iowans choose to help slaves escape? The answer has to do with where those who settled along the border migrated from and whom they chose to be their religious and secular leaders. The southeastern Iowa town of Denmark is a good example. In the fall of 1837 a group of New Englanders settled in a hamlet they named Denmark on the west side of the Mississippi River in the newly opened Black Hawk Purchase of Wisconsin Territory (soon to become Iowa Territory). The next spring they looked into organizing a Congregational church, and turning to Illinois missionaries for guidance, they invited Asa Turner (see figure 5) and Julius Reed to assist them. With many settlers moving into this forty- to fifty-mile strip of newly opened land, the missionary preachers saw an opportunity to plant the first Congregational church on the western side of the Mississippi.

Early the next May, in 1838, thirty-two people crowded into a twenty-by-twenty-four-foot rustic "shanty sanctuary" to hear Asa Turner, standing before a pulpit built of cottonwood with a walnut board nailed on top, open the church. All pledged to show "satisfactory evidence of Christian character" to meet the test of membership and promised to "maintain family prayer, support the church, keep the Sabbath holy, and to refrain from 'all vain and sinful amusements.'" The new congregation at once asked Turner to be their pastor, and he as quickly accepted.[5] Turner's quick acceptance likely had something to do with his uneasy relationship with the congregation he had left behind in Quincy, Illinois.

For eight years a trailblazer for the Congregational and American Home Missionary Society, he had lectured on antislavery and temperance as he ministered to the needs of his Quincy flock and traveled among the state's scattered frontier settlements. Everywhere he went, he preached, organized new churches, and helped set up antislavery societies—for he was the Illinois state manager for the American Anti-Slavery Society as well as a minister.

Turner's antislavery activism had not been welcome in Quincy. Things took a turn for the worse in the spring of 1836, when Turner befriended and helped protect Dr. David Nelson, the man the proslavery residents in northeast Missouri hated most.[6] Nelson, a one-time slaveowner, had organized the First Presbyterian Church in Hannibal, Missouri, in 1832. Influenced by Theodore Dwight Weld, a noted abolitionist lecturer and an architect of the 1830s antislavery movement, Nelson became an open advocate of abolition. His activities as agent of the American Anti-Slavery Society so angered his Missouri neighbors that a mob broke up one of his revival meetings in May 1836 and sent him scurrying across the river. Two of Asa Turner's church members helped him escape and took him to Quincy.[7] Arriving wet and muddy just ahead of the pursuing mob, Nelson was grateful to get support from Turner's church and others who rallied to him. Undeterred by the violence he had barely escaped, Nelson decided to start a Mission Institute near Quincy to continue his campaign against slavery.

Turner's own activism brought him to another altercation over slavery, this one in Alton, Illinois, in late October 1837, just after his first visit to Denmark. Publisher Elijah Lovejoy, angry after a St. Louis mob destroyed his printing presses and expelled him from the city, had called upon antislavery leaders to meet in Alton. Asa Turner chaired the meeting, which organized the Illinois Anti-Slavery Society.[8] Alton residents grew fearful and angry that Lovejoy, who had been converted to the cause by none other than David Nelson, seemed determined to publish an antislavery newspaper and make Alton a center for abolitionism. Local anti-abolitionists retaliated ten days after Turner's meeting ended. On November 7, 1837, a mob gathered once again to destroy Lovejoy's latest printing press. This time, someone fatally shot him. Walking past his corpse into the warehouse, the mob then threw the press out into the street and broke it into pieces.

Lovejoy at once became a martyr in abolitionists' eyes, but a newspaper editor in Burlington, Iowa, expressed the feelings of most white Americans when he wrote three weeks before the murder: "We are no advocates for mob-law. We set our faces against it in every shape and form, but, we confess, we can feel but little sympathy for the man who will persist in his 'iniquitous doings' in defiance of the public feeling and the public will. Abolitionism is neither useful [n]or desirable in Alton. Its population is not troubled with slavery."[9] Despite the anger, Asa Turner and the Illinois Anti-Slavery Society continued their meetings elsewhere.

Turner remained strongly opposed to human bondage, but he doubtless saw more trouble ahead from hotheads among the majority in the Quincy area who detested abolitionists. This man of immovable convictions is said to have had a respectful and sympathetic nature, and he probably welcomed shifting his work to the less turbulent new Denmark church.

In late summer of 1838, Turner, with his wife Martha and two children, crossed the Mississippi to take up his duties in Denmark. Within three or four miles of this hamlet of a few dwellings and a meetinghouse on green prairie lived a few dozen farming families. The Turners received two out-lots (that is, parcels of land apart from those already designated as part of the town) for a residence, and Turner also bought a tract of land on which to farm. As he had done previously in Illinois, he pursued his calling and kept food on the table by combining ministerial tasks with farming and traveling for the Congregational and American Home Missionary Society. He became a leading figure on this advancing frontier by establishing missions and churches. The extensive travel also kept Turner closely in touch with kindred spirits in Illinois and back East, and he continued to be active in the Illinois Anti-Slavery Society, returning to Quincy in the fall of 1839 to attend the state meeting.

Others in Iowa who felt as he did toward slavery soon joined Turner. In Denmark, staunch support for antislavery and underground railroad activity came from Isaac Field, George Shedd, and Theron Trowbridge. Field, a Denmark merchant, and Turner became the designated Iowa managers of the American Anti-Slavery Society in 1839. Early the next year they and thirty likeminded neighbors established the Denmark Anti-Slavery Society.[10] Physician George Shedd became especially active in antislavery and underground railroad work. He arrived in Denmark at age thirty-two, after having graduated from Dartmouth College and earned a degree at the Medical Institution of Cincinnati, Ohio. A hard-working country doctor who traveled throughout the area, Shedd led an active life and had a bold and stubborn nature. His son described him as "a man of firm convictions, sturdy principles, with a quiet taste for fighting evildoers." He had "something of the Scotch obstinacy and of the Puritan piety and zeal, with perhaps a little of the intolerance of both."[11] The doctor spoke openly about his abolitionist sentiments and joined in antislavery politics. Theron

Trowbridge, a plasterer in town, became the leading conductor of runaways, often taking them in his light rig to Burlington, where others helped them on to Galesburg, Illinois.

A major addition to Iowa's Congregationalist congregations came in 1843 when, in response to Turner's pleas on behalf of the Congregational and American Home Missionary Society, nine new Congregationalist pastors arrived in Denmark from Andover Theological Seminary in Massachusetts. Turner helped them establish new congregations in the territory. Coming to be known as the Iowa Band, these men founded churches and jointly established Iowa College, which began in Davenport in 1846 and moved to Grinnell in 1859. All were antislavery in spirit and actively fostered abolition and temperance activity in the state.[12]

During the 1840s, Denmark and three other settlements, Yellow Springs, Salem, and Washington Village (part of a township in Washington County), became the core antislavery communities in southeast Iowa. Many of the residents were Congregationalists, New School Presbyterians, and Quakers—all denominations with strong antislavery convictions. But the process of community building did not always go smoothly, and sometimes it was the slavery issue that divided new settlers. First settled between 1834 and 1840, Yellow Springs Township in Des Moines County lay fifteen miles north of Denmark. Its mostly Presbyterian residents, especially in and around the town of Kossuth, organized the Round Prairie Presbyterian Church in 1839, the first church of that denomination in Iowa. But within two years numerous families, stirred by the slavery issue, left this Old School Presbyterian church to organize their own, antislavery congregation.

This division mirrored the national split among Presbyterians that occurred after 1837. Old School doctrinal conservatives (mostly in the mid-Atlantic and Southern states) fought the more evangelical New School progressives (mostly in New England, New York, and the frontier West), who had been influenced by Congregationalism and antislavery sentiment. The new Yellow Springs church openly condemned slavery and refused membership to people who owned slaves. Some church members risked taking part

in antislavery and underground railroad activities, among them
William Rankin, the congregation's first New School minister, and
four farmers: Frederick Heizer, John and William McClure, and
Levi Anderson, whose son Jeremiah would die at Harpers Ferry in
John Brown's raid (see chapter 7).[13]

Fifteen miles west of Yellow Springs, another branch of Presbyterians, the Seceders (so-called because they had seceded from
the Church of Scotland), had come from Indiana, Ohio, and Pennsylvania to settle in the southeast quarter of Washington County.
In 1841 the outspoken minister George Vincent organized the Associated Presbyterian Church to serve a Seceder congregation in
the village of Washington (Washington Township), three months
after a local antislavery society started up. During that same period Seceder settlers in adjacent Crawford Township organized a
church and shortly thereafter began antislavery society meetings.
The well-known convictions of people in the area led Washington
Village to host an annual meeting of Iowa Territory's Anti-Slavery
Society in 1844.[14]

Fifteen miles south of Washington and fewer than fifteen miles
from the Missouri border, in southwest Henry County, grew the
town of Salem, where John Walker would go when he escaped
from slavery in 1848. This Quaker community, the first in Iowa,
had entered the Black Hawk Purchase at the same time as the Congregationalists who founded Denmark. Aaron Street, in partnership with his son, Aaron Street Jr., and his daughter's husband,
Peter Boyer, staked out the town site in 1835, naming it for Street's
family place in Ohio.[15] Soon, likely thanks to Boyer's promotional
work, word of the new town had spread to members of the Cherry Grove Monthly Meeting of Friends in Randolph and northern
Wayne counties in northeastern Indiana (the home of Levi Coffin, a famed underground railroad leader).[16] Several Friends rode
on horseback to see the newly founded Salem for themselves and
returned to Randolph with favorable reports. Nine families put together a wagon caravan in the spring of 1836 and, with considerable livestock, made a four-week journey to establish new homes in
Salem. Others soon followed from the same vicinity in Indiana.[17]

Among the Quaker settlers, three became Salem's leading opponents of slavery: Aaron Street Sr., Thomas Frazier (father of the Thomas Clarkson Frazier who would later play a role in the Walker family's 1848 escape attempt), and Henderson Lewelling, whose home would later house the justice of the peace who heard the arguments about whether the men pursuing the Walkers had the proper paperwork. Street, Frazier, and Lewelling and members of their families engaged in nearly every antislavery agitation event that touched the community. Aaron Street Sr., aged fifty-seven when he and his twenty-four-year-old son started promoting the Salem town site, had always been of independent mind and spirit. By the 1840s he was deeply committed to antislavery work, through both writings and involvements outside the Society of Friends.

When the Salem Friends built their first meetinghouse in 1840, Thomas Frazier, who with his family had come from Indiana's Cherry Grove Monthly Meeting, became their first minister. Within two years, a split occurred over slavery in the Orthodox Yearly Meeting in Indiana with which the Salem Friends were affiliated. Frazier was one of eight purged as "troublemakers" by leading Indiana Quaker townsmen from the Meeting for Sufferings of the Yearly Meeting (another of the eight being Levi Coffin). The 1842 break brought forth a new Indiana Meeting of Anti-Slavery Friends, including a chapter in Salem, Iowa.[18] Henderson Lewelling, thirty-four years old and a successful nurseryman in Salem, sided with the breakaway Anti-Slavery Friends and later chaired meetings of the Salem Anti-Slavery Society. The larger story of Salem's antislavery activities is the subject of the next chapter.

## Proslavery Missourians Respond

Friends of slavery in northeastern Missouri did not welcome the influx of new antislavery settlers into western Illinois during the 1840s, especially those from New England. Anti-abolitionist Missourians not only ran Dr. David Nelson out of Missouri to Quincy and then forced Elijah Lovejoy to flee to Alton, both in Illinois, but also in 1841 they caught and helped convict in a Marion County, Missouri, court three radical abolitionists who had attempted to free slaves. Now they saw communities hostile to slavery sprouting in Iowa—Salem, Denmark, Yellow Springs, and one founded by a group from Cincinnati, Ohio, led by John H. B. Armstrong, northeast of Croton in Lee County (see chapter 4).[19]

Adding to Missouri slaveholders' unease was alarm about the unsettled national scene during the 1840s. The storm over admitting Texas into the Union and Wilmot's Proviso calling for a ban on slavery in the new territory acquired from Mexico sharpened North-South divisions. Slave states might ignore the American Anti-Slavery Society as a mere fringe group and pay no mind to unsuccessful Liberty Party candidates, but increasingly many in the Southern border states feared that the old political arrangements might be crumbling.

As the northwestern-most slave state, Missouri was especially vulnerable to challenges to slavery. Its population and geography limited the usefulness of slave labor there, thus constricting its strength in supporting the proslavery cause. Unlike other slave states, Missouri had relatively few large slaveholders. Only 4 percent of those owning slaves in the state had twenty or more, whereas in states farther south, some 12 percent of slaveowners held twenty or more people in bondage. The few large Missouri operations could mainly be found in areas that raised hemp, livestock, and tobacco in the fertile Missouri River bottomlands in the central and western parts of the state, as well as along the tributaries to the Mississippi River. Most slaveholders in Missouri were small-scale farmers rather than planters, and two-thirds of them had only one to four slaves. Overall, Missouri ranked eleventh among the fifteen slave states in the percentage of slaves in the total population in 1850 (see figure 6). Only 12 percent of Missourians were slaves, compared with an average of 33 percent of residents in all slave states. Moreover, the proportion of slaves in Missouri was declining (from 17 to 12 percent between 1830 and 1850) because of the influx of freeholders without slaves. In contrast, the proportion of slaves to free residents held constant in the South as a whole during this period.[20]

The thousands of nonslaveholding immigrants moving to the state and the expansion of St. Louis as a hub for further westward migration were making Missouri as much western in agenda and outlook as it was Southern. Compounding this transformation was the conversion of the growing city of St. Louis into a citadel of free-labor sympathies, populated by people who opposed the extension of slavery. Within the state, the politics of slavery grew more and more antagonistic. While Missouri senator and later representative Thomas Benton tried to avoid the whole issue of slavery by emphasizing and encouraging white immigration, Sen. David Atchison favored slavery and later would prevent Northern migrants from going to Kansas, the main battleground of the 1850s.[21]

All these accumulating influences, national and statewide, worried Missouri slaveholders, especially in counties along the borders with Illinois and Iowa. It took only a few antislavery or abolitionist events to move the slaveholders from mere anxiety to active reprisal. And in the minds of northeastern Missourians in the late 1840s, no one in Iowa was more dangerous than the fanatics in Salem and the surrounding settlements in Henry County. Antislavery residents in that county, on the other hand, saw themselves as a beleaguered minority. As one county resident put it, there is "not enough of the Northern element in our population to give tone to its public sentiment," for "our larger towns are on the river, and their constant intercourse with Southern cities and States prevents anti-slavery from gaining any ground in them." The writer despaired that "we have but two really Liberty towns in the State, Denmark and Salem."[22] Their vulnerability became abundantly clear in the process of John Walker's attempt to lead his family to freedom. Indeed, the events that unfolded after the confrontation in Salem show just how contentious the slavery question had become along the Missouri-Iowa border by the late 1840s.

*The Escape*

When John Walker went back to Missouri to rescue his wife and four children in late May 1848, he found three other people ready to risk the journey to freedom because they had heard rumors that Ruel Daggs planned to sell his human property. Perhaps the most valuable to Daggs was Sam Fulcher, a large man in his mid-forties who served as a tanner, shoemaker, and cooper and who could write and keep accounts. He was well-respected in the rural neighborhood around Luray. Joining him was his forty-one-year-old wife, Dorcas, who worked as a weaver, spinner, seamstress, and cook. The Fulchers' pregnant eighteen-year-old daughter Julia also joined the runaways.[23]

On Friday night, June 2, 1848, the group of nine quietly crept away from the Daggs farm and headed northward to the border. Fortunately, the twenty miles they had to walk was sparsely settled. They made it as far as the lonely farmstead of Richard Liggon, an isolated eccentric who lived with one slave, one free black woman, and her four children, before stopping for the night. A downpour helped hide their tracks, but it also trapped them there until the following night, when Liggon took them to a point just south of Farmington, Iowa, where they could cross the Des Moines River. Running high from the rainstorm, the river forced a delay as the Fulchers and the Walkers searched for, or perhaps built, a raft. On this rude vessel they crossed to the Iowa shore and then hid in the thickets. Sunday morning, some young men driving a covered wagon picked up the runaways. This meeting was no accident; John Walker had planned this part of the escape with the help of some local Quakers before returning to the Daggs farm. The runaways now faced a twenty-mile ride north to safe haven in Salem.

Meanwhile, Ruel Daggs soon discovered his missing slaves and sought help from his sons, William and George. William enlisted the aid of neighbor James McClure to search the farms and houses around the Daggs homestead. In return for McClure's help, the Daggs family promised to cover his expenses. William Daggs and

James McClure rode through the rain on Saturday toward Farmington, Iowa, not far from where the Walkers and the Fulchers were risking their lives to cross the river that same night. In Farmington William Daggs hired a man named Samuel Slaughter before returning home. McClure and Slaughter stayed overnight at the house of a Mr. Way near Farmington.[24]

Sunday morning the two men found "a fresh wagon track, and followed it for several miles when [Slaughter] came in sight of [the wagon]."[25] He spurred his horse after the fast-moving vehicle and finally found it stopped in some bushes half a mile from Salem. Looking inside, Slaughter found a young man who identified himself as Jonathan Frazier and two of his friends, but no runaways. The hired slavecatcher accompanied the three men to town and waited for McClure to catch up.

That afternoon in Salem, McClure recruited two more men for the hunt: twenty-three-year-old Henry Brown, who knew Ruel Daggs, and Jesse Cook. After spending the night in Salem, McClure and Slaughter began searching the brush around town the next morning, Monday, June 5. Then Slaughter decided to go back to where he had overtaken the wagon on the previous day. There, within two hundred yards of the road, Slaughter and McClure "found the negroes in a thicket of hazel brush under and about a large tree near Doctor Siviter's."[26] All but John Walker agreed to surrender. McClure stayed with them while Slaughter hurried back to town to get Henry Brown and Jesse Cook to help overcome the rebellious Walker.

When the slavecatchers returned to the spot of the recapture, they were not alone. Slaughter, Brown, and Cook arrived at the hazel thicket just ahead of about fifty to one hundred Salem residents, many of whom were calling for the Fulchers and the Walkers to be allowed to go free. Undeterred, Brown drew his pistol and demanded John Walker's surrender. Facing the threat of immediate death, the man complied, but the crowd now surrounding the runaways and their captors continued to demand the release of the runaways. Salem resident Moses Pervis shouted that Brown ought to watch how he carried himself. The outnumbered slavecatchers were "pulling and hauling and shouting some for [the captives] to come this way and some that way" as they tried to get onto the road heading to town.[27]

Finally, McClure and Slaughter managed to force John Walker to mount a horse, and they turned their own mounts to take the recovered slaves immediately back to Missouri. But the crowd was not about to let that happen. Elihu Frazier warned McClure that "if [he] took the Negroes from that place [he] must take them over [their] dead bodies."[28] Henry Johnson told Walker to knock down Slaughter if he touched him again. Amid the tumult, McClure and Brown heard one man yell that he "would wade up to his knees in Missouri blood before [the runaways] should be taken back."[29]

## *The Letter of the Law*

Most of the Salem residents, however, insisted on following the letter of the law instead of fighting. Johnson, Elihu Frazier, and Thomas Clarkson Frazier argued that a magistrate in town must decide whether McClure and Slaughter could legally take the Walkers and the Fulchers back to Missouri. Seeing little choice, the two men relented and let the crowd escort them and their captives down the road to Salem. Nearing town, Sam Fulcher persuaded Slaughter to allow two of the women, Dorcas and Julia Fulcher, and two of the Walker children, Martha and George, to rest by the roadside, after assuring him that all would return to Missouri with Slaughter if only Sam Fulcher, John and Mary Walker, and their two youngest children continued into town with the slavecatchers.

A chaotic, highly emotional scene greeted all at the edge of town. The slavecatchers, their captives, and their hostile escort slowly passed through a crowd of a hundred or so people filling the streets at the south end of Salem. Townsfolk directed the riders toward the office of the justice of the peace, Nelson Gibbs, who administered the law from the Henderson Lewelling house, vacated the previous year when the Lewellings moved to Oregon (see figure 7). As the group neared the house fence, Mary Walker, carrying her baby, pulled away and vanished into the crowd. Then John Walker said he was thirsty. When someone pointed him to the open gate through which he could go to get a drink, he too disappeared.[30]

That left Sam Fulcher, who had been wrenched from Slaughter's hold by the crowd back down the road, and little William Walker. The man sat down and held the six-year-old boy as they shared some bread and a drink of water. Coming up to Slaughter and Fulcher, an old woman said a prayer for both. Other women called upon crowd members to pray aloud for Slaughter and the runaways. Not all were so peaceful. One woman shouted to McClure that "if the [Salem] men had the same spirit she had they would take [him] off that horse and grind [him] in the dust."[31] To quiet the angry crowd, Rueben Dorland, a teacher and antislavery man who had joined the throng as it passed by the school, climbed atop a pile of boards and called for the crowd's attention. He urged that everyone should "go before a Justice, and if the negroes were proved to be slaves their claimants should be permitted to take them."[32] Most of the Salem residents seemed to agree with Dorland, and their fury at the slavecatchers momentarily calmed.

In his office across the street from Tunis Tavern, Justice of the Peace Nelson Gibbs launched the inquiry into the legality of taking the Fulchers and the Walkers back to slavery in Missouri. Crowding into the small room were James McClure, Sam Fulcher, William Walker, and Albert Button, a local attorney. It soon became apparent that the office was too small, and at Button's suggestion, all agreed to shift the meeting to the Anti-Slavery Friends meetinghouse located nearby. Accompanied by the townspeople, the four walked east past Tunis Tavern and toward the meetinghouse, a block away. On the way, McClure asked Button whether he would serve as his counsel, but the attorney declined, saying he was working for the other side. He then went up the street with Justice Gibbs to the meetinghouse. Local anger began rising again as the time for the hearing drew near. To the crowd, Elihu Frazier declared, "Nothing short of a decree unsealed from God Almighty can take these negroes back to Missouri."[33]

Walking through the door of the meetinghouse were the four who had been in Gibbs's office, along with McClure's men, Samuel

Slaughter and Henry Brown. Button had separated the slavecatchers from their captives, saying "out with the Negroes."[34] Also present was Aaron Street Jr., who, along with Button, acted as counsel for the Walkers and the Fulchers. Townspeople filled the rest of the room, eager to see whether the justice of the peace would resolve the situation in favor of slavery or freedom.

Button rose first to ask whether the slavecatchers could establish that Ruel Daggs had authorized them to retrieve his runaway slaves. He also asked whether the blacks now found in Salem were indeed enslaved. Slaughter said that McClure's testimony would prove that they had authority to act for Daggs, but when Slaughter and McClure were asked whether they could show a certificate from a clerk of court in Missouri indicating that the Walkers and the Fulchers were escaped slaves, the slavecatchers could not do so. One of the lawyers for the escaped slaves then demanded Sam Fulcher's release, saying, "Gentlemen, make way and let this free man pass!" The attorney then cautioned the onlookers not to let the angry Henry Brown out of the building, but the young man drew his pistol and made his way out the door undisturbed.[35]

Button did not let the matter rest with a victory over the slavecatchers on technical grounds. In addition to requesting that the runaways still in the court's custody be removed from the proceedings, he asked the justice to issue a writ for kidnapping and hold McClure until the writ could be issued. The attorney then followed Fulcher and little William out of the meetinghouse.

Although Justice Gibbs did not act upon Button's call for a writ, the demand had the desired effect. Slaughter and McClure, now thoroughly rattled, lacking legal counsel, and without legal proof that they were Daggs's agents, were appalled to be portrayed as mere kidnappers. They had had enough. Worn out by the day's hostilities, they told the justice that they were willing to back down on their claim to the Walkers and the Fulchers. Justice of the Peace Gibbs then closed the proceedings by finding that, since the supposed runaways had not been brought properly before him, he had no jurisdiction over the matter. He declared that the runaways were "free as himself for all he knew."[36] Not everyone was satisfied with this muddled denouement to the day's long confrontation over slavery. When Sam Fulcher and William Walker stepped out of the meetinghouse, Henry Brown was standing there with his pistol half drawn, grumbling that he would "shoot that d——d son of a b——h."[37] But he did not follow through on his threat.

Outside, John Pickering approached Fulcher and the young boy. Pickering's horses had drawn the wagon that carried Fulcher and his family and friends from the Des Moines River toward Salem. As Pickering watched, Fulcher walked across the road where a man had a horse unhitched, with the reins thrown over its head. Fulcher mounted the horse, and another man passed William up to him. They rode off, following Salem resident Paul Way, who rode a short distance ahead. Within a few minutes they were out of sight. The dispirited James McClure left town immediately, and Samuel Slaughter followed shortly thereafter. But they did not leave empty-handed. They took with them the four runaways who had rested outside town: Dorcas and Julia Fulcher and Martha and George Walker.

## The Invasion of Salem

If Salem's antislavery activists thought themselves and at least some of the runaways victorious in this battle, they quickly learned that the battle was not yet won. To their surprise, two days after the confrontation in the meetinghouse, on Wednesday, June 7, one hundred Missourians, accompanied by a few supporters from Farmington, Iowa, rode into town. It is likely that Henry Brown had rushed ahead of James McClure and his captives to get news of the events in Salem to Ruel Daggs. Whoever delivered the news, it had electrified the slaveowner's neighbors in Clark County. Angered by the actions of the Salem residents and urged on by Daggs's offer of a $500 reward (about $14,700 in 2011) for the return of the runaways, the Missouri men who rode into Salem on June 7 came armed with rifles, pistols, and knives.[38]

Stationing some of their number on each road that entered and exited the town, they divided into groups and began to search every building. Under the threat of violence, the townspeople felt obliged to permit the searches as long as no one got hurt. Yelling, threatening, and keeping their guns ready to hand, the Missouri vigilantes turned the townspeople's houses upside down but came up dry: Sam Fulcher, John and Mary Walker, and the two Walker children were nowhere to be found. During the search, Henry Brown identified certain townsfolk who had prevented McClure and Slaughter from taking the runaways back to Daggs's farm two days before, and the Missourians arrested them. Using a handful of blank warrants received from a justice of the peace at Hillsboro, Iowa, they took into custody John H. Pickering, Thomas Clarkson Frazier, Erick Knudson, Elihu Frazier, Isaac C. Frazier, John Comer, and others. Paying no heed to the men's protests, the vigilantes took them to a hotel and confined them there under guard overnight.

Despite the Missouri posse's efforts to close Salem down, two residents had managed to slip out of town during the search, one riding north to Mount Pleasant (ten miles away) for the county sheriff and the other going east twenty miles to Denmark, Iowa, for help. The sheriff arrived on Thursday morning, June 8, and, finding no legal basis for the Missourians' arrests, ordered the men being held at the hotel to be freed. After releasing the anxious townsmen, the invaders then prepared to sit down for dinner at the hotel, but the sheriff declared that all the Missourians had fifteen minutes to leave town. They grabbed what food they could carry along with their belongings and rode to the village of Washington (by then generally known as Hillsboro), six miles away. There, according to one news report, "they visited a grocery and drank up all the liquor they could find" and "threatened to return to Salem, set fire to the town and hang some of the abolitionists, if they did not recover their negroes."[39] As it turned out, they had gotten out of Salem just in time to avoid worse violence. Not long after they fled, some forty armed rescuers from Denmark arrived. In the end, the only result was that Henry Brown, the local man who had joined forces with the slavecatchers, was forced to leave Henry County.[40]

And where had all the runaways gone? The details reveal as much tragedy as triumph. The editor of the *Chicago Western Citi-*

*zen* stated confidently that the armed Missouri mob would have had to travel "as far as Canada to accomplish their object" of bringing Sam Fulcher and the Walkers back to Missouri and then "go back with fleas in their ears,"[41] but Dorcas and Julia Fulcher and Martha and George Walker had been forced back into slavery. John and Mary Walker, with their one-year-old, had fled into the crowd. Sam Fulcher and six-year-old William Walker had left town on a horse provided to them after Justice Gibbs declared that the slavecatchers' claims could not be verified. Salem resident Rachel Kellum later wrote that as a girl she had helped shelter and feed Fulcher and the boy near the farm owned by her father, Nathan Kellum.[42]

After Paul Way took the two runaways to the Kellums, Rachel writes that they were "taken to an old lime kiln about three miles northeast of town and hidden." They stayed that night and the next day at the kiln, while Rachel and her sisters made fresh clothes for William. Following a brief stay in the Kellum home, Fulcher and the child then hid in a straw rack hastily put together for the two by the Kellums' neighbor, Francis Shelldan, until men from Denmark came that evening to speed them on their flight. Whether John and Mary Walker and their baby joined Sam Fulcher and William in Denmark for the next leg of their journey toward freedom is unknown. What is clear, though, is that freedom for the five came at a very high cost. Sam Fulcher had lost his wife and daughter, while John and Mary Walker lost two of their four children back to slavery.[43]

## Public Response

Initial newspaper coverage of the battle over the fugitives revealed no sympathy for the Salem abolitionists, portraying their acts in helping Mary and John Walker, two of their children, and Sam Fulcher escape from slavery as shameful and criminal. While Missouri newspapers naturally wrote of the "Abduction of Slaves," Iowa papers described the events as a "Riot at Salem," the work of "a gang of felons," a "flagrant outrage" and "foul robbery"—meaning the antislavery activists, not the slavecatchers.[44] The editor of the *Keokuk Valley Whig and Register* expressed disbelief that "the citizens of Iowa could be induced to violate the right of his neighbor," but if the allegations were true, he felt that "he who entices away or conceals a negro slave, so that his master may not get him again, is as criminal, as if he had stolen that man's horse." Certainly, wrote the editor, "We have yet to see a single person who does not condemn the act as a shameless violation of private rights."[45]

After two weeks, less strident but more telling commentary replaced the emotional editorials. To dispel "odious, slanderous and false reports" about what had happened, nine Henry County citizens wrote to explain that there was blame enough to go around and that "a few of our citizens and vicinity suffered their sympathy for the captive slaves to take the place of their better judgment, and on the occasion acted very imprudently."[46]

Meanwhile, Clark County Missourians remained angry about what had happened. Two days after the Missouri mob returned home from Salem, men met in Alexandria, Missouri (a few miles from Daggs's farm), to talk about how to recover runaway blacks and how to prevent future escapes through Iowa. They decided to hold a larger meeting of concerned citizens on June 21 at Farmington, Iowa.[47] There, William Daggs and other Clark County and Farmington residents met at Tom's Mill and adopted seven resolutions to prevent what they called "negro stealing." These they sent to the *Keokuk Telegraphic Weekly Dispatch*, requesting that the paper print them. Among the resolutions were the following: that Clark County slaveholders organize to prevent the escape of slaves, that they band together to ensure the speedy recovery of any escapees, and that slaveholders raise a tax among themselves to reward people who apprehend "felons suspected of negro-stealing."[48]

### Going to Court

But Ruel Daggs was not about to let things rest there. Three months after the events of June 1848, he filed suit against nineteen Salem townsmen.[49] Daggs sought $10,000 (about $294,000 in 2011) for the loss of the runaways' services, claiming that the

Salem residents had prevented his agents from retrieving the fugitives, then harbored and concealed them, and ultimately enabled their escape. However, then as now, lawsuits were not quickly resolved. The suit dragged on from term to term in the U.S. District Court and, because of procedural mistakes, was amended along the way.[50]

Throughout, the Salem defendants did all they could to delay. They questioned legal procedures, filed various motions to test the legal sufficiency of Daggs's case, and claimed irregularities in the collection of witnesses' sworn testimonies outside court in preparing for trial. When the court's June term convened in 1850 in Burlington, the defendants led off by arguing to have the witnesses' depositions excluded. Judge John J. Dyer, who had practiced law for twelve years in Virginia and then two years in Dubuque before President James K. Polk appointed him U.S. District Court judge in 1847, granted the defendants' motion.[51] The depositions had been gathered, he agreed, without obtaining advance court certification of the reasons for their collection, and they had been completed without filing proper paperwork. Immediately the plaintiff sought a continuance in order to bring the deposed witnesses in court. This Dyer denied, and he ordered the case to trial the next day.

Without the depositions, David Rorer—Daggs's counsel, a former Virginian and noted Iowa lawyer—could see his client's chances for success fading.[52] Of the men Daggs had hired to retrieve his fugitive property, James McClure was no longer available, having moved to Rusk County, Texas, and Henry Brown could not be located, since he was on his way to chase gold in California. Without their depositions, Rorer fell back on asking the court for permission to dismiss several defendants from the suit and then immediately subpoenaed them as witnesses.

A jury was selected, and with Burlington's courtroom in Marion Hall packed full of listeners, the first day's trial began June 6, 1850. Rorer's newly subpoenaed witnesses turned out to be less useful than he had hoped, but at the end of the day their testimony lent some support to the charge of harboring and concealing slaves. Testimony came from witnesses Samuel Slaughter and William Daggs and several Salem residents: attorney Albert Button, Jonathan Pickering, Francis Frazier, and schoolmaster Reuben Dorland.

Then came the closing arguments. J. C. Hall, a Mount Pleasant attorney working on behalf of the defendants, described this case as "truly novel—the first suit of the kind ever brought west of our mighty river." In his lengthy statement, he denied that the evidence showed defendants to have harbored or concealed the runaways. Rather, he argued that attorney David Rorer had "counted upon prejudice" that "sought in the signs of the times, for a feeling in your bosoms which would predispose you to convict the defendants. The Union is at stake—agitation is covering the land; rebuke the one and sustain the other. You are called upon for a victim. My clients are demanded for a sacrifice."[53] In short, he argued his case by placing it in the context of the national antagonism over slavery. The members of the jury should not convict his clients just because they don't like abolitionists, Hall insisted; rather, they should render their judgment on the basis of the evidence.

As Rorer rose to give the plaintiff's concluding argument, he agreed that this was an important trial. All the people involved in the escape of the Walkers and Sam Fulcher knew that "every State was bound by the Constitution to deliver up fugitives when claimed." And yet, "here are men who have established a law of their own. Like all fanatics, they assume that there is a moral law, paramount to the Constitution, and even to the oracles of God himself." He did not hesitate to tar the Salem rescuers with the controversial word "abolitionist," and he called the Anti-Slavery Friends meetinghouse the "Abolition Meeting House." This place, whenever not used for worship, he claimed, was desecrated "by the intrusion of abolition sentiments—when converted into the '*Committee Room*' of the 'under-ground rail road' company." All the circumstances of the case and people involved, said Rorer, showed the defendants to be guilty. And he, too, placed his case in the context of national divisions: "The very subject upon which you are called to decide, is now agitating the country from Washington to the most distant borders. It has been a source of contention and distrust among the people of both North and South—of slave-holding and non-slave-holding States. Your verdict will show whether there is just ground for this suspicion, as to us. Whether fanaticism is to be encouraged among us of the North, or the wild and maniac cry of disunion in the South."[54]

Judge John J. Dyer then sent the case to the jury. He acknowledged that it was

a case well calculated, at this time, to create some degree of interest in this community. For, while our whole country is agitated upon the subject of Slavery—while towns, counties and States, have been and are arrayed against each other in an almost warlike attitude, and this great Confederacy is thus threatened with destruction, and the fears of citizens in various portions of the Union are exciting and inflaming their minds, and driving them to acts, which, it is feared, will have soon, if they have not already, brought us to the very verge of Destruction—I repeat, it is not strange that there should be some interest manifested in the result of this case.[55]

Dyer instructed members of the jury that their role was to decide whether any of the runaways "owe service or labor, according to the laws of the State from which they fled, to the person claiming him," whether the slavecatchers were actually agents of Daggs, and whether the defendants knew these facts at the time of the altercation in June 1848. On the charge of "harboring and concealing," the judge said the jury must decide whether statements made by the slavecatchers amounted to sufficient notice for Salem residents to avoid taking steps to "defeat the means of the claimant to secure the fugitives." When attorneys for the defendants and Daggs, the plaintiff, then requested certain additional instructions, Dyer granted a crucial one to Daggs: "That there need not be positive proof to enable plaintiff to recover, but circumstantial proof is sufficient, if satisfactory in the minds of the jury."[56]

Fewer than two hours later, jury members returned a guilty verdict. They found "the defendants, Elihu Frazier, Thomas Clarkson Frazier, John Comer, Paul Way, John Pickering, and William Johnson, *guilty* upon the *first*, *second*, *third* and *fourth* counts of the declaration, and assessed the damages at TWENTY-NINE HUNDRED DOLLARS." As to the fifth and sixth counts, the Jury found the defendants not guilty. (The first two counts were that the defendants had rescued the slaves from Daggs or his agents; the second two, that the Salem residents had harbored and concealed the Walkers and the Fulchers; and the final two, that the accused men had prevented Daggs from recovering his property.) The next morning, June 8, 1850, the defendants argued for a new trial based on lack of evidence for some of the counts. Judge Dyer denied their appeal, stating that although the verdict was bad on the first three counts, it was sound on the fourth, which concerned concealing the fugitives. Dyer additionally ruled that Daggs could collect the costs of the suit from the defendants in addition to receiving the $2,900 judgment (about $86,000 in 2011).[57]

Daggs's supporters and proslavery Missourians doubtless felt vindicated by what turned out to be perhaps the last federal case decided under the Fugitive Slave Act of 1793.[58] The editor of Muscatine's Democratic newspaper praised the result as one that "should convince our southern brethren that the people of Iowa are mindful of their duties under the Constitution, and are ready to maintain the rights of every portion of our fellow-citizens."[59] Joining him was Iowa's Democratic senator, Augustus Caesar Dodge, then in the midst of congressional deliberations on measures that in September would become the Compromise of 1850, including a new, stronger law requiring all Americans to return fugitive slaves to their masters. He believed that the Daggs ruling showed his fellow Iowans' determination "to discharge their constitutional duties" and to make sure Iowa's "laws and its conduct speak a language . . . that cannot be misunderstood."[60]

The editor of the *Burlington Hawk-Eye* saw it differently. Yes, slavery issues aroused strong public interest in 1850, and the trial "created much excitement in Henry, Van Buren and Lee counties in this State, and in Clark County Mo.," but the editor questioned the verdict: "It may be somewhat puzzling to the readers of the evidence as it has been to us, how a jury could find a verdict of 2,900 dollars, with the costs running up to about a thousand more, in favor of the plaintiff. It certainly shows a disposition to give to the South all they can possibly claim; and all this clamor about the necessity of more stringent laws to catch runaway slaves, as far as Iowa is concerned, is all a humbug."[61]

When it came to Daggs's getting the money the defendants owed him, however, the Clark County slaveholder's work had just begun. For the next three years, his attorneys faced one delay after another while paying numerous fees to have their writs served, even as the defendants filed their own affidavits and depositions challenging the efforts to collect. Also, the defendants had little wealth for Daggs to confiscate because, knowing they might lose the court case, they had sold off or transferred most of their assets before and during the trial. Finally, when a chancery court judge on May 16, 1853, found Daggs's supplemental bill to be inadequately supported by the various documents, arguments, and exhibits presented, Ruel Daggs gave up. For all his legal efforts, payment of numerous court costs and attorney fees, and a verdict in his favor, he never collected a dime.[62]

The June 1848 confrontation in Salem clearly signaled to slaveholders in northeastern Missouri that times were changing. Iowa threatened to become a refuge for runaways, and if it did, its proximity to Missouri would encourage more enslaved people to seek freedom. "These enthusiasts," wrote the editor of the *Hannibal Journal*, "these fanatics, as they are called by some, but who deserve no softer appellation than thieves, have commenced their operations in a new quarter." He recognized that "heretofore our only danger has been from Illinois, in which direction we had some safeguard in the fact that the Mississippi River intervened. Now a more dangerous outlet is opened in the North in the facilities of getting to Salem in Iowa, which is said to be the head quarters of these depredators and in which direction there is no similar barrier, the River Desmoin[es] almost at all times being easily crossed by an individual without assistance from others."[63]

# 3

# The Struggle Intensifies

## Jim White's Story

Northeastern Missourians were not wrong to worry. The battle over the Walkers and the Fulchers was just one of many struggles over fugitive slaves during the late 1840s and early 1850s. Often, as in that case, the legal conflict hinged on proving whether a person was enslaved or free. That question was rarely as simple to answer as it now seems. To give an example, about the same time that Daggs's slaves escaped from his farm with the help of people in Salem, a young black man named Jim White arrived in the city today called Muscatine, then a town of about two thousand people and known as Bloomington (until about 1850). In this Mississippi River town, situated on a great bend at which all steamboats landed, White found work at the American House, a hotel owned by James Borland.[1]

Five months later, in early November 1848, Horace M. Freeman arrived from St. Louis and got a room at the hotel. Late the next afternoon, when he noticed a steamboat coming toward the mooring dock, he left his room to check out in the hotel lobby. Paying his bill, he asked Borland whether he happened to know of a black boy named Jim. When told that Borland had just such a young man working for him in the kitchen, Freeman immediately headed there. He spotted Jim working with Borland's wife and grabbed him by the collar. To the accompaniment of Mrs. Borland's startled screams, Freeman began dragging Jim from the room.[2]

James Borland rushed to the kitchen and demanded to know what Freeman was doing. Jim had escaped from slavery in St. Louis, Freeman shouted, and he meant to get the fugitive back to his master there. When Borland demanded to know Freeman's authority to do this, Freeman pulled from his pocket a letter showing that he held power of attorney for Thomas R. Hughes, supposedly Jim's owner. That was not enough, replied Borland, who directed Freeman to turn the boy loose and get out of his hotel. If Jim was in fact a runaway slave, Borland insisted, Freeman needed to get a warrant for his arrest from the justice of the peace based on proven ownership. Freeman bellowed he would "be d——d if he would do any such thing; that he intended to take him to Saint Louis and try him there, and if any man interfered, he would blow his brains out"—all this as he continued pulling Jim toward the door. When Borland stepped in to prevent Jim's removal, Freeman drew a pistol from his pocket, and in turn Borland grabbed a set of tongs.

News that a hotel guest was aiming a pistol at Borland's breast and threatening to shoot him spread through the house and brought two other people running in to help the hotelkeeper. Seeing himself outnumbered and unable to take Jim on his own, Freeman grudgingly backed off and agreed to get a warrant. But Borland arrived first at the office of D. C. Cloud, justice of the peace, where he filed a warrant for the arrest of Horace Freeman, charging him with assault with a deadly weapon. Then in walked a man named Lowry who, acting on Freeman's behalf, wanted a warrant to apprehend an escaped slave. Cloud told him that the writ for Freeman would require that some preliminary steps be taken. More importantly, "he had better get an attorney because, from the feeling that was aroused, he would have difficulty in getting the Slave." Cloud ordered the arrest of Freeman, who posted bail, while Jim was held in jail until trial.

Word of Jim's arrest spread quickly, causing considerable public excitement. The next morning, crowding into Cloud's twenty-by-twenty-six-foot office were as many people as could fit. Many, Cloud remembered, were there not so much to listen as to "take sides for or against 'Jim.'" The trial took two days, and each day at noon and in the evening, proslavery and antislavery friends constantly buttonholed Cloud to persuade him one way or the other.[3]

One friend awakened Cloud (a widower who slept in a room adjoining his office) by rapping at his door at midnight. The man, an old Virginian, asked where the situation stood, and they discussed the matter briefly. Then, turning to leave, he urged Cloud to find that "that nigger is as much property as a *hoss*, and I hope you will not deprive the owner of his property." And hardly had Cloud left his room the next morning when he "was almost besieged by the friends of Jim." That group left unsure about where Cloud stood concerning the young man's fate, so its members went on to see S. C. Hastings—then a judge of the Iowa Supreme Court. They wanted to arrange for a writ of habeas corpus on Jim's behalf in case Cloud ordered Jim into Freeman's custody.[4] (Such a writ would require a court to determine whether the government had the right to continue detaining the prisoner.)

Entering the crowded courtroom to open proceedings, Cloud could see that both parties were well-represented by Bloomington's finest legal talent—Freeman defended by Ralph P. Lowe and Jacob Butler, and the state by W. G. Woodward and J. Scott Richman.[5] Tempers soon flared. Woodward alleged that if Freeman got Jim back to St. Louis and sold him, Thomas Hughes would give him one-half the price received. And he wanted his opinion known: "If Freeman gets any part of this money I hope it will burn up his soul." "Amen," yelled Dr. C. P. Hastings (brother of Supreme Court justice S. C. Hastings). Ralph Lowe retorted, "That Amen came from an Abolitionist." Hastings replied, "You are a liar," and only the tightly packed crowd prevented them from coming to blows.

This being Cloud's first slave-related case, the thirty-one-year-old justice of the peace moved carefully through the facts and legal arguments during the two days of the early November trial.[6] In the end, he had to rely on a single precedent, which had arisen from a case heard by a justice of the peace concerning an enslaved man named Ralph in 1839.

What we know of Ralph's life begins in 1830, when Jordan Montgomery, a northeast Missouri slaveholder, bought the man, a field hand, from his father. Three years later Montgomery struck a deal with Ralph to buy his own freedom. In a written agreement, the slaveowner allowed Ralph, now in his late thirties, to move to

Iowa Territory and work off his servitude for $550 (about $13,800 in 2011) by the end of 1838. But when the contract came due, Ralph had not yet earned enough working in Dubuque's lead mines to pay his way out of bondage. Montgomery, short of money, hired two men for $100 (about $2,500 in 2011) to get Ralph back. The two men requested and received an order from the justice of the peace at Dubuque directing the sheriff to arrest Ralph. Having done so, the sheriff steered clear of town as he brought the handcuffed man down to Bellevue harbor for the agents to deliver him downriver, back into slavery.

The sheriff was wise to avoid going through town, because Ralph was well-liked in Dubuque and his arrest had not gone unnoticed. Lead miner and grocer Alexander Butterworth hurried to Judge Wilson, a local district court justice who also served on the territorial Supreme Court, and successfully pleaded for a writ of habeas corpus so that Ralph would have to be taken before the court to determine whether he had been afforded due process. The sheriff, on receiving the writ, retrieved Ralph from the steamboat.

Within a month the case moved to the Iowa Supreme Court, and arguments were heard on July 4, 1839. Ralph benefited from the rhetorical skills of lawyer David Rorer, the native-born Virginian and experienced attorney who had been living in Iowa Territory for four years and later acted on behalf of Ruel Daggs (see chapter 2). Rorer argued that the conditions of Ralph's case did not fit the laws for reclaiming an escaped slave because the man had not escaped servitude. In fact, he had been allowed to enter Iowa, which forbade slavery, to find work to meet an obligation. Furthermore, Iowa's 1839 Act to Regulate Blacks and Mulattoes, which required blacks settling in Iowa to post a bond of $500 and show evidence that they were free, did not apply here because Ralph had arrived before the law went into effect and, moreover, was not a slave but a worker under contract.

Montgomery's lawyer argued that Ralph should be considered a fugitive slave because he had failed to buy his freedom. But the two-judge tribunal was not persuaded. By day's end, they ruled in

Ralph's favor. Chief Justice Charles Mason wrote that when Ralph entered Iowa for work, it was under a contract for debt, not as a fugitive slave. And since slave property did not exist in Iowa, Montgomery had no basis to assert rights of ownership over Ralph. (The U.S. Supreme Court's Dred Scott decision nineteen years later would reach the opposite conclusion about the status of a slave in a free state.) Ralph continued to live in Dubuque and even struck a valuable deposit of lead, but then he succumbed to smallpox while caring for another at a pest house.[7]

On the basis of this precedent, Cloud rendered the verdict that Jim White should be considered a free man and that Freeman was guilty of assault and battery and must pay a fine of $20 (roughly $600 in 2011) and court costs. The story might have ended there, with the happy outcome of a once enslaved man set free, except that events before and after the trial made it more complicated—and more interesting.

Horace M. Freeman had not, in fact, gone to Bloomington on the off chance of finding Jim. He knew very well that the young man was there and intended to rush him down to the steamboat just at departure time. Since 1844 Jim had been owned by Thomas R. and Sarah Lowry Hughes. He had come to be the Hughes's property through Sarah's side of the family. As a child, Jim had been raised in St. Louis under the direction of Catherine M. Merry, wife of Dr. Samuel H. Merry, a physician. She had had three children by an earlier marriage to a man named Lowry, one of whom was Sarah. By 1844, however, the Merry family had decided to move north to the area around Bloomington, Iowa, where other family members lived.[8] Moving to a free state meant that Catherine Merry had to either free Jim or sell him. She persuaded nineteen-year-old Sarah to buy him for $500 (about $15,500 in 2011), since the younger woman intended to remain in St. Louis after her upcoming marriage to Thomas R. Hughes. Mother and daughter apparently also agreed that Jim would eventually buy his freedom by working on a steamboat that operated on the lower Mississippi between St. Louis and New Orleans.[9]

The plan went awry when Jim quarreled with a steamboat steward and went away from the fight with a severe head injury. The Hughes family sent him upriver to Dr. Merry's at Bloomington for treatment. Not long afterward, the physician decided that Jim was growing insolent and ordered him off the farm, evidently expecting him to return to his stepdaughter, Sarah Hughes, back in St. Louis. Instead, Jim drifted into Bloomington where American House proprietor James Borland hired him. Jim's risky decision to work for himself left the St. Louis family members in a predicament, having neither their slave nor their $500. The Merrys, seeing the Hughes family's continued ownership of Jim at risk, evidently advised them to retrieve Jim. By early November their agent, Horace M. Freeman, was on a St. Louis steamboat making his way to Bloomington, with the results described above.[10]

When Cloud convened his proceedings, Freeman's assault charges came up first. After listening to considerable preliminary discussion among the parties, Cloud decided to refrain from issuing a ruling, wanting to examine first the charge that Jim was a fugitive slave. The main witness for this part of the case proved to be Catherine M. Merry. Her testimony suggested that she alone within the family was Jim's owner. Indeed, it had been her seventeen-year-old son, Samuel Lowry, who went to Cloud's office for a writ to arrest Jim as a fugitive. Catherine testified that Jim had been, and remained, under no one's control but hers both before and after his transfer to the Hughes family in 1844. Admitting to her habit of "interfering between Jim and his mistress, Miss Lowry [Sarah Hughes]," Catherine acknowledged that Jim had accompanied her upriver from St. Louis to Bloomington four months earlier without having the consent of his legal owner, Sarah. Catherine had in fact known where Jim was living in town, and she concluded her testimony by expressing her intent to free him by refunding the $500 Sarah had paid for him.[11]

Because Catherine had known where Jim was the whole time, argued the claimant's lawyers, her testimony proved that Jim had left the Hughes household without permission and therefore was a fugitive subject to forcible recapture. Not so fast, claimed lawyers for the state. Freeman had illegally attempted to take him directly to St. Louis without having had a hearing before a justice in accord with Iowa law. Furthermore, because Hughes knew of Jim's whereabouts thanks to Catherine Merry's actions, Hughes had essentially consented to her decision that Jim could go to Iowa. Justice Cloud agreed with the lawyers for the state and therefore charged Freeman, as noted above, $20 and costs for his forcible and threatening actions. As for Jim, Cloud found that "there was an implied consent on the part of Hughes, if not a direct allowance, that the young man, Jim, might come to Iowa" under Mrs. Merry's authority, and so the young man need not be returned to slavery in Missouri.[12]

Freeman took the decision poorly, exclaiming, "Well this is a hot abolition hole; it is worse than Chicago; I suppose I will have to go to jail." To that, Cloud abruptly replied, "Certainly, unless you pay up." Hearing this, the old Virginian merchant who had made the midnight visit to Cloud's place came forward. "Sa," said he, "you shan't go to jail, I will pay the bill."[13] Not yet ready to give up, Freeman remained in town. Jim, meanwhile, kept out of sight, fearing another attempt to snatch him away. One of Jim's most dedicated protectors was a twenty-two-year-old African American barber, Alexander Clark, who had lived in Bloomington for six years. Ambitious and businesslike, Clark had begun to invest in woodlot properties so he could supply firewood to the passing steamboats. More importantly, because of his eloquence and general likeability, Clark was rising in local esteem and becoming active in civil rights issues and religious and fraternal life.

The newly married Clark hid Jim in the loft of his house following Cloud's decision (see figure 8). Worries about Jim's plight sharpened when a local fellow informed Clark that an elderly man in town named Michael Greene was about to drive his team to Chicago and had offered to take Jim with him. Suspicious of the proposal, Clark came up with a way to avoid antagonizing Greene while at the same time saving Jim from what he thought was probably a trap. He arranged with Greene that, before nightfall, Greene would cross the Mississippi River and wait at a particular spot until dark, when Jim would come across in a skiff.[14]

At twilight two of Clark's friends rowed out on the river and anchored their boat at a point hidden from shore. As nightfall deepened, Clark and Jim pushed off in a skiff toward the Illinois side, and upon arriving where his friends sat waiting mid-river, the two transferred into their boat and let the skiff float down toward the Illinois shore. In the quiet they heard the sounds of other boats crossing, and as they rowed back toward the Iowa shore, the four smiled to know that the slavecatchers would spend hours poking through the Illinois brush in search of Jim. Greene returned to Bloomington the next morning, having decided not to make the trip to Chicago after all.[15]

Meanwhile, Horace Freeman decided to take the steamboat to Dubuque. This time he appealed for and received a warrant for Jim's arrest from U.S. District Court judge John J. Dyer. Returning to Bloomington the night of November 13, he had Jim arrested the next day. Jim's supporters then sought and obtained a writ of habeas corpus from Judge Serranus C. Hastings (also referred to as S. C. Hastings), acting chief justice of the Iowa Supreme Court, who eventually decided on technical grounds against the legality of Freeman's arrest of Jim. He ruled that because Dyer's court had concurrent jurisdiction with that of Justice Cloud in Bloomington under the U.S. code of procedures, Dyer's order could not apply after Cloud had decided the case. Additionally, Hastings denied Freeman's request for an appeal of Cloud's decision, putting an end to further legal action. Shortly thereafter, standing on the steps of the American House, Dr. C. P. Hastings placed his hand on Jim's shoulder and declared to onlookers, "Here is a free man."[16] Once again, antislavery activists had succeeded in using the law to free someone. Thereafter, Jim remained for some time in Bloomington and became a member of the town's African Methodist Episcopal Church.[17]

## Growing Violence

Reports of Iowans' interference with the return of people whom Missourians saw as fugitives invariably soured the attitudes of pro-slavery people toward the state. The year after these 1848 events in Salem and Bloomington, both Missourians and Iowans began to hear tales of more slave escapes and increased violence, reinforcing some people's belief that African Americans had to be held in bondage to keep white people safe. In late October 1849 a chill went through Marion County, Missouri, when a slave named Ben killed two white farm children. A week later an armed posse caught up with twenty-seven people just preparing to escape north to Iowa from Lewis County. After brief resistance, this large group surrendered. And when three months after that a Marion County slave burned down a stable in town before riding off toward Iowa, people became even more alarmed.[18]

A Muscatine newspaper editor, learning about a woman and her child who had reportedly escaped from Dr. W. T. of Monroe County, Missouri, and gone to Iowa along with her husband from another household in a nearby county, lamented that it would "create a panic among slaveholders"—and, he argued, would work against the interests of abolitionists, too. In addition to nourishing "a dangerous feeling of hostility in one section towards another," the editor believed that the unsettled circumstances along the midwestern border between slave and free states meant that "the first 'nigger trader' that comes along can pick up plenty of first rate bargains." He concluded that although abolitionists might gain "the freedom of some negroes," their actions were causing "many more [slaveholders] to sell [the bondspeople] into worse slavery, further South."[19] "As each year passed," writes Hannibal, Missouri, historian Terrell Dempsey, public meetings about runaways and abolitionists attracted more people and "the measures adopted to restrain slaves became harsher." No more did people talk of gradually ending slavery in the state.[20]

## The Pyles Family

Catherine Merry and her daughter and son-in-law were not the only family members to fight over human property. While slavery ripped apart African American families, it also caused no small amount of strife among slaveowners. Five years after the Jim White case took place, a partially enslaved family from Kentucky arrived in Keokuk through Missouri. What happened to the Pyles family became a story well-known in Keokuk.[21]

Harry M. Pyles was a free man of mixed heritage who worked in the harness- and shoe-mending trade near Bardstown, Kentucky. His wife, Charlotta (who was of Seminole, German, and African ancestry; see figure 9), and their twelve children were enslaved to Hugh and Sarah Gordon, whose farm was near Bardstown in central Kentucky. Fortunately for the Pyleses, the elder Gordon and his daughter, Frances Gordon, had become antislavery Methodists. Upon his death in 1834 Hugh Gordon left Charlotta and her children, plus the family plantation, to Frances for life, with the remainder of his estate split among his other children. Then in 1853 Frances's brothers, Joel (a Baptist minister) and William—administrators of the estate—decided to end their father's arrangements. In response, Frances, now seventy-nine years old, undertook to move the Pyleses north and free them in accord with antislavery Methodist teachings. Her brothers would have none of that and connived to block her efforts.[22]

They first kidnapped Benjamin, one of the Pyles's children, and sold him to a Mississippi slave dealer, who in turn took him to Missouri's hemp-raising country. Now alerted that her brothers posed a greater threat to the Pyles's emancipation than she had supposed, Frances rushed to shield the rest of the family by leaving for Minnesota Territory. To foil her plans again, the brothers sued in September 1853, charging that their aging sister had become incapable of managing her affairs. But after she appeared in court and clearly asserted her rights to do with her slaves whatever she wanted, including take them north and free them, the jury agreed that her senses remained intact. Hence, she kept control of her property.[23]

The next month, the brothers, now joined by other relatives, tried again to have the court intervene. They filed another suit on October 22, 1853, this time questioning Frances's ownership and her right to transport the slaves outside Kentucky, questions the court dismissed the following March. By then, however, she and the Pyles family were gone. In the fall of 1853 the group of at least eighteen people (including five of Harry and Charlotta's grandchildren) had left Kentucky in a covered wagon drawn by three horse teams—the household goods in the wagon bed and family members stuffed in around them—with four extra horses tied to the back of the wagon. Led by Frances and assisted by a white Ohio minister named Claycomb, they passed through Louisville, continued by steamboat to St. Louis, and then traveled by covered wagon toward Iowa, crossing the Des Moines River into Keokuk just as cold weather set in.[24]

Deciding to stay in Keokuk instead of going on to Minnesota, Harry Pyles, then sixty-seven years old, began building a small brick house. The winter was trying, though, because the large family found it difficult to make ends meet with only Harry employed as a leather worker and the oldest son as a teamster. Charlotta (age fifty-four) then conceived a way out of their desperate straits that would also reunify two of her daughters with their still-enslaved husbands, who had been left behind. If the sons-in-law were freed, they could contribute to the family income. Charlotta decided to seek $3,000 (about $90,000 in 2011) from helpful antislavery citizens to buy the men's freedom for $1,500 each. With letters of recommendation in hand, she traveled east to deliver her plea to sympathetic audiences, first in Philadelphia, then New York and New England.

Aided by notable antislavery activists over the next six months, this remarkable, uneducated woman traveled through unfamiliar territory, giving speeches and asking for donations. She returned to Iowa with the entire amount needed and then went to Kentucky, where she bought her two sons-in-law out of slavery. The success came with heartbreak, however, for her son Benjamin, whom the Gordon brothers had kidnapped and sold before he could go north with his family, had learned of her fundraising effort and asked her to buy his freedom instead of that of one of the sons-in-law. When she ultimately chose to redeem the two sons-in-law because each had a wife and children while her son was single, she never heard from Benjamin again. Historical records show that he later married, had four children, and lived in Waverly, Missouri.[25]

In the aftermath of these struggles, Frances Gordon spent her final years living with the Pyleses in Keokuk. Two of Charlotta's daughters eventually worked with a Quaker family in Salem, Iowa, in exchange for board and access to schooling; and one of her grandsons, Geroid Smith, became in 1880 one of the first African American high school graduates in the state of Iowa.[26]

### Thomas Rutherford's
### Missing Slave

Despite northeast Missouri's efforts to restrict slaves' movements and suppress antislavery talk, during the 1850s the expansion of settlement in Iowa gave enslaved people new escape routes to the North, and they seized the opportunities, sometimes gaining public notice as a result. When a black stranger rode up to the Western Hotel in Burlington, Iowa, on a quiet midweek evening in June 1855, hotel and boardinghouse loungers turned their heads to watch. Folks near the corner of Fourth Street and Jefferson (the town's principal business street) naturally began to gossip about whether the fellow might be a runaway slave. The next morning, when the man came down and called for his horse, the hotel proprietor refused to release it.[27]

The stranger, now on foot, by and by found someone in town who either suggested he look for Dr. Edwin James or, more likely, took him by wagon up the bluffs surrounding Burlington and to James's stone farmhouse, five miles southwest of town (see figures 10 and 11). The next morning, early risers looking toward the Mississippi

River landing might have seen Dr. James in his open buggy, waiting to cross to Illinois on the ferry. Beside him on this Saturday morning sat the same black fellow who had earlier stayed at the Western Hotel. Once the ferry reached the Illinois shore, James drove his buggy onto the landing and took a less traveled path. At that moment, two men approached. They had likely crossed on the other ferry from Burlington and now blocked the buggy, commanding the driver to stop. James ignored them and started to push his way forward, but when the two men drew revolvers and knives to back up their demand, he was forced to pull his horse to a halt.

The slavecatchers—for that was what they were, two men named William C. Young and Solomon Rose—insisted that the man seated next to James belonged to Thomas Rutherford, a wealthy fifty-year-old Scotchman who had begun farming in Clark County, Missouri, in 1829.[28] James refused to hand him over. The standoff ended only when the two slavecatchers agreed to have the ferryboat operator return everyone to Iowa where they could take up their claim with the authorities. As James drove his rig back toward the landing, another Burlington man who had overheard the rising argument walked up to the group and asked whether the slavecatchers had papers proving they were Rutherford's agents. When Young and Rose could show none, the man declared that James ought to go on his way. But the buggy was already onboard, and the slavehunters quickly persuaded the ferry operator to release the boat tie. Before anyone could disembark, the ferry shoved off toward the Burlington side of the river.[29]

From the Iowa shore James drove up to Jefferson Street. Three blocks farther west he came to a stop at the post office on Third and Washington streets. One slavecatcher and a few likeminded townspeople stood guard over James and his black companion while the other went to find someone who could grant them the legal authority to take the alleged fugitive back to Missouri. Other Burlington residents went in search of a lawyer for Edwin James and the stranger, both of whom remained silent while they sat for an hour in the buggy. Most passersby and those in the gathering crowd sympathized with the unnamed man's plight and wanted to make sure the slavehunters were given no leeway claiming their prize.[30]

James's quiet bearing had become well-known locally in recent years. He had been an active young man, working as a physician, a botanist with the scientific expedition to the West that Stephen H. Long had led in 1820, an army surgeon, and an Indian agent. He was also an author, having translated five English-language works into Ojibwa. Upon leaving public service, he did land surveys and in 1836 established his farm at what was known as Rock Springs near Burlington. But life's disappointments had taken their toll. At age fifty-eight Edwin James lived largely withdrawn from society, a near recluse, with strong political opinions—opposition to alcohol, concern for Indian welfare, and a hatred of slavery—that not many shared.[31]

So when on June 23 the black man walked down the lane that separated a forested ravine from the open prairie toward James's farm, he met an unusual character. Some described James as gentle, "tall, erect, with a benevolent expression of countenance and a piercing black eye." He was also, in the words of Burlington's Congregational minister, William Salter, something of "a mystic, a recluse, an abolitionist," who was "an underground conductor for men 'guilty of a skin not colored like his own.'"[32] This was just the sort of man the black caller needed—but the slavecatchers had caught up with him despite James's help.

The scene unfolding in front of the post office caught the eye of thirty-four-year-old attorney George Frazee. Gazing out the window of his second-story office at the street below, he saw how the excited and growing "crowd hovered about the wagon in which sat Dr. James and the negro, both quiet and cool, seemingly careless as to what was said or what might eventually be done. They did not appear to take any part in the talk that was noisily going around and about them."[33]

The editor for the *Burlington Weekly Hawk-Eye* observed that "most of the spectators were anxious to see the colored chattel run" and protect himself "with the well loaded revolver with which he

was armed." Others declared that the crowd must remain "sound
on constitutional questions" concerning any interference with
slavecatchers retrieving a runaway.[34] Of the townspeople's divided
opinions, George Frazee later recalled that some were eager "to
take sides with the Missourians. Every man in the crowd who was
himself a native of the slave-region, or the son of such a native—and
there were many such in Burlington—seemed to be very zealous
in his manifestations of sympathy with the slave claimants." Although most were "of the class in the South that never owned a
slave" and had "come here to better their condition," they nonetheless "brought with them all their local prejudices and habits, and
especially their imbibed hatred of the negro who chanced to believe that he had quite as good a right to his personal liberty as the
man who claimed to be his master and owner." Any black people
who thought otherwise, such men thought, deserved "prompt and
decisive punishment" for their insolence.[35]

Of the respectable Northerners in the crowd, though few would
have considered themselves abolitionists or would have been inclined to interfere with slavery where it existed, many saw the
black man in the wagon as the victim of a system that was "inhuman" and "obnoxious because of its political influence." Forced to
confront the pernicious institution of slavery in person, they "were
roused to action" and insisted that the slavehunter must "prove his
claim to the fullest extent and in the most strictly legal manner."[36]

Within an hour of the wagon's stopping by the post office, William Young came out of Marion Hall, Burlington's five-year-old
county courthouse (see figure 12). The slavecatcher had been joined
by Milton D. Browning, a strong-featured, "grave and thought-
ful" Kentucky-born attorney and active Whig Party leader. The
two walked down Third Street toward Frazee's office, because he
served as the appointed U.S. commissioner empowered under the
Fugitive Slave Act to review such cases. Entering the small wood-
en building a block away, Young and Browning climbed a narrow
flight of stairs to meet with Frazee.[37]

The two men filed a complaint against the alleged fugitive,
whom they called "Dick." They asked Frazee to issue a warrant

for Dick's arrest on grounds that he had escaped on June 21 from service owed to Thomas Rutherford of Clark County, Missouri. Having pursued the man to Burlington, Young asked that he, as Rutherford's agent, be authorized to reclaim the fugitive and convey him back to Missouri. Frazee issued a warrant and handed it to the just-arrived U.S. marshal, Frederick Funk, directing him to arrest the man alleged to be Dick and bring him upstairs to the office. While doing this, Marshal Funk also confiscated from the man "a huge, old-fashioned pistol, such as horsemen used to carry before Colt invented the revolver" (in other words, before 1836).[38]

Joining the black man at Frazee's office was T. D. Crocker, a young lawyer someone had hastily hired to represent the supposed runaway at this hearing. To keep onlookers from going up to the commissioner's office, Burlington's city marshal stood atop the second-floor stairs and warned the people gathering below to remain where they were and be peaceful, for he "did not want a fight."[39] Straightaway, Crocker requested that Frazee's examination of evidence be put off until Tuesday so that the alleged runaway could find a more qualified attorney, and Milton Browning, Young's lawyer, immediately agreed, probably because the delay might enable the slaveowner, Thomas Rutherford, to attend. The marshal took "Dick" into custody in the county jail until the examination and trial could be completed.

This action left slavecatcher Young in an uneasy position. To reinforce his claim that he had nabbed the right person (and therefore would quickly get his reward after "Dick" was released to him), he had at one point professed to be Rutherford's son-in-law and said that Dick had run away while working for him. But, Frazee recalled, upon questioning it became apparent that Young "was entirely ignorant of [Dick's] personal appearance, and had assumed that the Negro he found with Dr. James must be the Dick he was hunting for," on the basis of Rutherford's description. Perhaps not wanting to risk taking an oath about the arrested man's identity but still wanting to clinch the case, Young hurriedly went back to Missouri to bring Rutherford's son to Burlington so that he could prove that Young's prey was in fact the fugitive Dick, property of Thomas Rutherford.

Meanwhile, leading citizens took steps to defend "Dick." Iowa governor James Grimes, writing from his Burlington home, dashed off a letter to his wife, who was visiting friends in Maine. "Exciting times here," he wrote, and amid all this great excitement "several personal collisions have grown out of it. How it will end no one knows." He assured her, "It has been determined that the negro shall have able counsel, and a resort to all legal means for release, before any other [course of action] is resorted to." He also confessed that "if not in office, I am inclined to think I should be a law-breaker" on behalf of the alleged fugitive.[40] Much had changed in Iowa since the territorial legislature had so easily ignored anti-slavery petitions in the early 1840s.

Grimes and others arranged for Ralph Lowe of Keokuk, a judge and attorney who would himself serve as governor of Iowa in the near future, to come to town on Monday night with a writ of habeas corpus ready, in case Tuesday's trial brought an adverse decision. Also, Grimes revealed to his wife that he had told his "friends and the friends of the slave to be present at the trial," including Presbyterian abolitionists from Yellow Springs and Huron townships. Two leading men in particular joined Grimes to round up support. One was David Rorer, the intense and animated Burlington lawyer who had won Ralph his freedom in 1839 and had represented Ruel Daggs in the 1850 suit against the men who helped the Walkers and Sam Fulcher escape from slavery. The second, Henry Fitz Warren, was a thirty-five-year-old Whig businessman with undisguised contempt for slavery. In fact, he had resigned his assistant postmaster-general position in disgust after President Millard Fillmore agreed to sign the Fugitive Slave Act. Earlier in 1855 he had been in the running for U.S. senator from Iowa.[41]

Tuesday morning, U.S. Commissioner Frazee convened his investigation proceedings at the district courtroom in Marion Hall amid an air of excitement. The case of the alleged fugitive versus the slavecatchers had attracted throngs of people wanting to see the proceedings. The crowd kept the U.S. marshal and the city marshal busy filling the seats and then turning away all those still standing outside who wanted in. Frazee, unaware of Governor Grimes's personal involvement, knew of Warren's work to gather sympathizers at the court. He also knew that Judge Lowe had been summoned. Seated with the slavecatchers was the attorney Milton Browning and next to him an unidentified man. To represent the man accused of having fled slavery, David Rorer had joined T. D. Crocker. Frazee, a reserved man of a scholarly and kindly temperament, called the proceedings to order and waited as the lively assemblage quieted down.

After a few preliminaries, the doors opened to bring the supposed escaped slave into the packed courtroom. Marshals promptly shut the doors, and the mayor remained as guard to keep the crowd outside from pushing in. Commissioner Frazee called upon Browning to bring his witness to the stand. The man identified himself as the son of Thomas Rutherford. Browning swore him in. Frazee recalled what happened next:

> Mr. Browning asked that the negro, who occupied a seat some distance from the witness, might be required to stand up, so that the witness might obtain a clear view of him. Without any hesitation Dick assumed a standing position and boldly confronted the witness. Mr. Browning then interrogated the witness as to the identity of "Dick." The answer was a surprise to all present, quite as much to me as to anyone. Instead of affirming that Dick was his father's, the witness promptly responded that the negro before him was not; that he did not know him and that he had never seen him before.[42]

Rorer at once moved that the man be released from custody, which was done, and a jubilant shout sprang from the courtroom audience, much to Frazee's shock.

The infectious jubilation continued into the street, where some one thousand people accompanied the man who was not Dick down to the levee. He climbed into Dr. James's buggy once again and, along with several others, boarded the ferry, rode across to Illinois, and went on to a rail stop, where he caught a train to Chicago. By the time writs and warrants for kidnapping and assault could be prepared against the two professional slavehunters, they had skipped town, probably also thinking to evade paying Browning's legal fees.

Throughout the proceedings, the behavior and bearing of Dr. Edwin James suggested that he had anticipated this outcome and had counseled the alleged runaway to keep silent, because all he needed to do to guarantee his release was *not* to be Dick. This silence evidently extended to the man's own attorneys, Rorer and Crocker, who both appeared as surprised as everyone else at young Rutherford's testimony. James returned to his life of solitude and seclusion. Six years later he died when he fell from a wagon loaded with cordwood that then ran over him. Today, only ruins remain of his house, although a modern marker inscribed to him stands nearby at Rock Springs Cemetery.[43]

This 1855 case, in which James played such a large part, was the only one heard under the Fugitive Slave Act of 1850 in Iowa. Its outcome gratified Gov. James Grimes. Seeing it as evidence that Iowa citizens were newly disposed to oppose slavery, Grimes wrote his wife the day after the nameless man's release: "How opinions change! Four years ago, Mr. _____ and myself, and not to exceed three others in town, were the only men who dared express an opinion in opposition to the fugitive slave law, and, because we did express such opinions, we were denounced like pickpockets. Now I am Governor of the State; three-fourths of the reading and reflecting people of the county agree with me in my sentiments on the law, and a slave could not be returned from Des Moines County into slavery."[44] Grimes was seeing the benefits of changing public opinion thanks to the increasing number of settlers from the Northeast moving into Iowa and to national arguments over slavery's future in adjacent territories. By 1855 it did indeed seem that Iowans were beginning to think about slavery in new and different ways.

# 4

# A Hole of Abolitionists

*Slavery and Antislavery Sentiment
in South-Central Iowa*

In the winter of 1852–1853, a black Missouri teenager helped to set the underground railroad in motion in south-central Iowa. Only sixteen, this young man had seen his brothers and sisters sold off one by one upon reaching maturity. He and a friend had vowed this would not happen to them and, whenever chance allowed, they would escape north. The opportunity came that winter, when the Clark County slaveholder who owned the sixteen-year-old and his mother received a visit from his own son, who lived sixty miles south. Upon rising the next morning, they discovered that the son's costly horse had gotten out of the stable and presumably headed for home. The father told his slave—the sixteen-year-old— to eat quickly and straightaway take the master's own swift horse to retrieve the missing animal. Seeing his chance for freedom, the young man gulped down his breakfast as he divulged the plan to his approving mother.

With no time to inform his friend, he set out on his own. First riding several miles south, he then turned onto a less traveled road and drove the horse not toward the Mississippi River, but instead toward the less settled northwest. Afraid to stop, he kept going for two straight days until he reached the house of John H. B. Armstrong across the Missouri state line in Appanoose County, Iowa. He and the horse were both exhausted.[1]

Armstrong and his family had just moved to Appanoose County from northwestern Lee County, Iowa, where he had farmed and operated a sawmill for thirteen years. In this new settlement, which would become the town of Cincinnati, he bought two thousand acres of land and built the largest house in the vicinity, a log residence one and a half stories high, soon to have a porch in front and a shed in the rear. How the young runaway happened to come to Armstrong's place is unknown, but it proved blessedly fortunate to this freedom-bound fugitive.

Armstrong took the teenager in, gave him food to eat, and lodged him until the next night. The forty-two-year-old farmer then took him north toward Centerville, where Armstrong's brother-in-law John Calvert lived. While riding along, the young black man suddenly let loose a great laugh. When Armstrong turned sharply to warn him about the need for silence, the young man reportedly explained with a chuckle, "How mas'r will be disappointed when he goes to look for dis chile." Despite the boy's desire to keep his stolen horse, Armstrong and Calvert insisted that the animal be released near the Missouri state border. Someone subsequently found the stray horse and took it to a justice of the peace, who happened to be none other than John H. B. Armstrong. He judged it either stolen or lost, and after being kept a year it was sold to cover the expense of its upkeep.[2]

Armstrong and his brother-in-law were two of a small number of opponents of slavery in Iowa's south-central counties in the 1850s who were willing to help fugitives. Although southeast Iowa counties tended to be somewhat antislavery, the two or three counties west of them had greater percentages of Southern-born settlers who were hostile to those who opposed slavery. Having so many residents who hailed from Kentucky, Tennessee, Virginia, and the southern parts of Indiana and Illinois guaranteed Democratic political dominance in Davis, Appanoose, Wayne, and Decatur counties. In the words of one Davis County pioneer history: "most of the young men growing up, had nursed at the breasts of Southern parents, and imbibed Southern ideas. It never occurred to them that their fathers were wrong, or that there were two sides, or any need for two political parties."[3]

Although Southern migrants to south-central Iowa had no time for those who would meddle in the right to own slaves elsewhere and would not help blacks in any way, they did not necessarily endorse slavery. These conservative Democrats did not want Iowa to adopt the institution, but they did not especially care if it was adopted by settlers in the western territories, as long as residents there approved it. They also strongly opposed free blacks moving into Iowa. In the face of the hostility of the majority, the minority of antislavery-minded settlers in the area became acquainted with each other at church and political gatherings. Drawing on these connections, a daring few, like Armstrong and Calvert, put together a loose network of people willing to risk helping blacks escape enslavement in Missouri.

The historical record offers evidence of few escapes from slavery into the south-central counties, but it is clear that a line of the underground railroad ran through Appanoose and Davis counties. In particular, a route began around Cincinnati in southwest Appanoose County near the Missouri border and ran toward Drakesville in northwestern Davis County. From there the routes branched either toward the Quaker settlements in Henry County (such as Salem) or northeast toward Washington County and then on to Burlington or Muscatine, where fugitives and their allies would cross the Mississippi River on their way to Chicago.

Like Salem, the town of Cincinnati soon developed the reputation of being a "hole of abolitionists" for Missourians and those in south-central Iowa who upheld the right to own human beings. This reputation was deserved, for Armstrong and his likeminded Lee County neighbors figured prominently in slave escape operations.[4] As early as 1839 Armstrong was one of forty members of a group of intermarried families—Adamson, Henkle, and Shepherd—from the Cincinnati, Ohio, vicinity who moved to western Lee County, Iowa, and who assisted runaways crossing the Des Moines River near Croton. Thirteen years later, members of these same families accompanied John H. B. Armstrong to southern Appanoose County, and there they continued to aid people escaping from slavery.

Like many settlers in Iowa and elsewhere, the families drew on personal connections in deciding where to settle. In this case, Luther R. Holbrook, a longtime Lee County neighbor of the Armstrong clan and a fellow underground railroad participant, had moved his family to this part of Appanoose County in 1850, building his sixteen-square-foot log house south of what would become Cincinnati. The next year his twenty-seven-year-old brother, Solomon Holbrook, arrived. Then, in 1852 the sight of people driving ox-drawn wagons and other livestock past Holbrook's place announced the arrival of John H. B. Armstrong and the associated Henkle, Shepherd, and Adamson families to their unplowed prairie claims. Others from western Lee County and elsewhere soon joined them. By 1855 Samuel Holbrook and Daniel and John McDonald were planning a new town to be called Cincinnati. Solidly antislavery in outlook, these Lee County transplants gravitated into Wesleyan Methodist, Congregationalist, and Free Presbyterian churches in their new Appanoose County home.

Family ties and religious communities here, as in so many underground railroad operations elsewhere, explained how the participants were able to organize their covert efforts and keep some very dangerous secrets. The strong ties of blood and belief that bound antislavery activists together made it extremely difficult for slavery's defenders to uncover and expose rescue operations unless they happened to spot runaways and their helpers on the road while an escape was in progress.

Kin and creed soon linked Cincinnati's antislavery activity to that of Drakesville, about thirty miles northeast. As soon as Cincinnati's Wesleyan Methodist church members began meeting in the twenty-by-twenty-four-foot hewed log schoolhouse just west of town, arch-antislavery man John Elliott of Drakesville came on foot every two weeks to lead services. John and his brother, George Elliott, and their blood relations, the Corner family, comprised the leading underground railroad operation in Drakesville.[5] Nearly all surviving stories of slaves escaping through Cincinnati indicate that runaways were guided northeast to the Drakesville area. (The exception was Seth B. Stanton, who in the course of his business dealings in Missouri would carry escapees to Ottumwa in Wapello County.)

## Flights and Rescues

We see these connections in the story of Davy Crockett, not the famous frontiersman, but a free black man living in Missouri. Frightened by his white neighbors' continuous demands that he prove he was not a slave, Crockett decided in 1861 to relocate to Iowa. After entering the state, he had not gone far before running into a suspicious proslavery resident who, after stopping him, then pointed him in the direction of John H. B. Armstrong's place. On his way there, Crockett happened to meet a Wesleyan Methodist man (his name lost to history) who advised the Missouri man to instead stop by his place for supper. Once darkness fell, he would guide Crockett to Armstrong's.

In the intervening time, the proslavery man gathered some forty men who showed up at Armstrong's house an hour before midnight, demanding to search the large barn. The small, thin Armstrong boldly replied that they would enter "at their peril," but after a protracted argument during which Armstrong insisted that he knew nothing of a fugitive, he relented, allowing the party to satisfy themselves that he harbored no runaway.[6] Soon after they left, Armstrong's brother-in-law, John Calvert, came by with Davy Crockett, but given the night's events it seemed unwise to shelter him there. They escorted their visitor to Daniel McDonald's farm, and from there McDonald took him two days later to their Drakesville colleagues.

But if Cincinnati and Drakesville were "a hole of abolitionists" in the sense of being home to conductors on the underground railroad, the south-central counties were also shot through with holes in the sense that relatively few people yet lived there. The nameless sixteen-year-old and Crockett were fortunate to find people to help them. Most people running from slavery through Missouri's unsettled northern frontier found the passage more difficult. In the 1850s northern Missouri and southern Iowa were still largely empty of farms and towns. The vast unfenced prairies, woods, streams, and marshlands offered the runaways little food or shelter, leaving many in a weakened, half-starved condition by the time they arrived at Cincinnati, Iowa.[7]

Two runaways, John and Archie, quickly encountered difficulties as their escape from central Missouri proved easier to plan than to accomplish. As they struck north toward the Iowa state line, they had to move more slowly than they had expected because John suffered from muscle and joint pains. Archie stayed with his friend even as the trip they thought would take only a few days stretched into three weeks. Finally they entered the woods near the Armstrongs' house. While John rested, Archie went and knocked on the door in hopes of finding help. His timing could not have been worse.[8]

Isabel Armstrong, John's wife, opened the door to see a black man in need, but at that very moment a neighbor unfriendly to the underground railroad sat in the next room. She quietly hurried Archie into the bedroom, where he waited until the visitor left. The relieved Armstrongs then gave him some food to eat and learned from him that his suffering companion lay in the nearby woods. John Armstrong had a dependable neighbor take the fugitive John some food while arranging for the two runaways to be taken that evening to the farm of John Shepherd, Isabel's brother. While feeding them supper, the Shepherds overheard Archie say to his buddy: "My good God, John! Who'd have ever thought we'd set down to a meal like this?" Rested for the night, the two traveled with Shepherd the next morning to their next stop at Drakesville.

The underground railroad crew living around this town did not just wait for deliveries from Cincinnati; they also acted on their own. In the 1890s old-timers especially remembered the complicated escape of an enslaved family through Davis County in 1860 that brought angry Missourians north into their community.[9] It began in March, when two white men showed up at the farm of George Elliott. Near the long, low log house he had built for his wife and six children, Elliott had established a nursery, and the visitors were interested in seeing what he had to offer. As they looked over the orchard stock, one mentioned they were from Lancaster,

Missouri, twenty-one miles south of Drakesville and just five miles from the Iowa state line. The man went on to say they knew a black family who urgently and repeatedly had asked them for aid in escaping north. Would he be willing to help?

A strongly religious man whose every meal began with a prayer for the powerless slave, George Elliott arranged with his visitors a specific night to bring the family across the border to a fork in the road about six miles south of Bloomfield, Iowa, where the northbound road from Lancaster, Missouri, joined one heading east. Elliott promised that help would be waiting for the fugitives there, but he would not be among the rescuers. George was already fifty-seven years old when he agreed to help, and, as in so many instances when Iowans aided people escaping from slavery, it fell to the young men of the community, excited by the prospect of adventure to further a great cause, to carry it off.

George consulted with his sons and his older brother, John Elliott, and together they devised a plan. To lead the venture they chose twenty-one-year-old George Elliott Jr. and Albert Corner, the twenty-eight-year-old son of John Elliott's brother-in-law, Arthur Corner. Accompanying them on the first leg of the rescue would be Dave Hardy, son of James Hardy, a Wesleyan Methodist church member and staunch abolitionist. According to the plan, once they picked up the fugitive family at the crossroads, they would go directly to John Elliott's house. Waiting there would be John's nephew, William E. Conner (age eighteen), whose father was also a Wesleyan Methodist minister, and his friend Adbell C. Truitt (age twenty-five). William Conner later recalled being notified after a church meeting to go to his Uncle John Elliott's house because word of fugitive slaves was "in the air," and, upon mentioning it to Truitt, learning that he was already in on the secret. The two were to accompany the runaways through the next several stops. As the plan matured, the ringleaders arranged for additional help along the projected journey eastward.

When evening came, George Elliott Jr. and Dave Hardy drove a shabby-looking covered wagon to the appointed junction, accompanied by Albert Corner on horseback. There they waited. Hours went by. Then about two o'clock in the morning, they heard what sounded like a runaway team of horses. Riding toward the sound, Corner suddenly met someone riding a mule—the pilot for the runaways. "We are a little late but all right," he gasped, as Corner took out a white handkerchief and blew his nose—the all-clear signal. A minute later the wagon pulled up with what the rescuers described as five "light colored mulattoes": a man driving the team with his wife and four children in the wagon box.

They had arrived late, explained the Missourian pilot, because the McQuitty family, who owned the fugitives, had gone off to church in the family wagon. Not until they returned and retired to bed could the runaways slip off to the barn, harness the team, load the wagon, and be on their way. During these preparations, the pilot's uncle watched from bushes nearby to give the alarm in case the escape activities had aroused the McQuittys' notice. Once all were aboard, the nervous father quietly drove the wagon to the main road, then pushed the horses hard for several miles. At last they arrived at the assigned meeting place, the team winded and soaked with sweat.

As the full wagon came to a stop, the Missouri man and Albert Corner unhitched the horses, removed the harness to toss it in the wagon, and took the animals down near a river to be set loose. Meanwhile, George Elliott Jr. and Dave Hardy pulled their own covered wagon alongside the other one. The fugitive family stepped across into the hay-filled wagon box, and then Elliott and Hardy grabbed the cover and dropped it over them. With the runaways ready to go on into Iowa, the Missourian pilot and his uncle left for home as the rest quickly turned onto the road north. Within two hours they drove into the farmyard of John Elliott, a mile and a half northeast of Drakesville. Awakened by one of Elliott's daughters, William Conner and Adbell Truitt hastily dressed and climbed aboard with the group. (Ten miles out, Conner noticed that he and Truitt, in the rush to dress in the darkness, had mistakenly put on the other's pants.) When the group reached James Hardy's farm a mile away, his son Dave changed the teams and replaced Albert Corner, who rode home.

Dave Hardy drove the wagon through the timber into Wapello County toward Blakesburg, a small hamlet reputed to be "a terrible proslavery neighborhood." Near there lived the father-in-law of William Clinger, John Elliott's neighbor, who had a fresh team of horses ready for the next leg of the journey. Hardy drove off with Clinger alongside on the seat. In the meantime, George Elliott Jr. and William Conner had lightened the wagon load by climbing out and saddling two small mules, on which they rode in advance of the procession moving toward Eddyville.

At Eddyville was the only bridge anywhere in the area over which a wagon could cross the Des Moines River, and the crossing was a toll bridge—meaning the rescue party would have to bear the tollhouse keeper's scrutiny. Elliott and Conner hurried their mules forward in the early morning light and crossed over to the tollhouse on the other side. When the two young men casually asked what he charged, the tollhouse keeper said ten cents. Just then the shabby-looking wagon began to cross the bridge, and the two said they would pay for the wagon as well. They handed the man a half dollar and got five cents in change. The satisfied tollhouse keeper paid no attention to the covered wagon as it rolled by, instead returning to his hut.

The party drove through Eddyville's quiet main street with no trouble, but no sooner had they left town than the going got tough on the eastbound road. The wagon's wheels sank into heavy yellow sand, and as they climbed up a ridge the passengers had to get out and walk, despite the danger of their being seen, until the team got beyond it. By eleven o'clock in the morning, they reached the next station. The drivers unhitched the weary horses, put them into the stables, and joined the rest of the party for dinner, William Conner recalling that the runaways until this time "had been as still as death all the way." After dinner, they hitched the wagon to a fresh team, with Clinger now taking the reins and Dave Hardy heading home.

Toward dusk, after going through the small hamlet of Kirkville, they pulled up at the farmhouse of Anfel and Margaret English in southeastern Mahaska County. When Margaret came to the door, she told them her husband was out working somewhere on the farm, but as soon as she learned about the wagon's passengers, she told Clinger to pull into the barn lot. By the time the horses were unhitched, Anfel English had returned. He told them Margaret would get supper for them all while he rushed to find his uncle, Alexander Pickens. When the two returned, the underground railroad crew had already sat down for their meal. Anfel then brought in the passengers, whom William Conner recalled looked "like scared quails, but they done justice to the supper."

As night settled in, English and Pickens hitched their own fresh team to the old covered wagon, and the weary fugitive family climbed into the back and started the next twelve-mile leg of their journey. They arrived early the next morning at the farm of a Mr. Durfus, who lived near what would become the town of Hedrick in southwestern Keokuk County. Durfus was just leaving to do his threshing, however, so the drivers went three miles farther to the house of an elderly preacher, who then took them to Washington County near the town of Washington. From there, others drove the family to Davenport and placed them on a train going to Chicago, and eventually to Canada.

The next day, as soon as English and Pickens came back with the old covered wagon, the Drakesville men left for home. William Conner and George Elliott Jr. traveled on their mules by way of Ottumwa, and William Clinger with the wagon and team went through Eddyville and Blakesburg. But while the fugitives were well on their way to freedom, the repercussions of the rescue were just beginning. The returnees found the Drakesville vicinity "overrun with Nigger hunters, as they were called," although William Conner remembered that "none ever suspected we had anything to do with the darkies." The Missourians, initially numbering some forty men, searched people's houses and passed out handbills offering $1,400 in gold (about $39,000 in 2011) to anyone with information leading to the recovery of the escaped slaves. Convinced the runaways were still hidden in the neighborhood, several slave-catchers kept an eye on the houses of reputed abolitionists for two weeks. Conner had fun with them, freely admitting that he had taken the enslaved family away, but they did not believe him.

The slavehunters' difficulty—one faced by many others crossing from familiar ground in Missouri to potentially hostile territory in Iowa—was how to track runaways when the locals refused to give them any information. Plenty of Davis County residents had no sympathy for blacks or abolitionists and would inform on them, but plenty of antislavery people knew how to get around their proslavery neighbors. In this case, two of the Missouri searchers knew perfectly well who the perpetrators were, for they were the same men from Lancaster who had first suggested the rescue to George Elliott.

From them the Drakesville men later learned that when the slaveowner, McQuitty, found out that his slaves were gone, he had men follow the trail. Where the wagon had been abandoned, they found his horses grazing fewer than a hundred feet away. Uncertain about the direction the escapees had taken from that point, the slavecatchers searched several Des Moines River crossings without luck. Not surprisingly, as William Conner summed it up, "when we were eating our dinner at or near Blakesburg, they were eating dinner at Bloomfield and that is as near as they ever got to the Darkies"—that is, about twenty-five miles. In the end, the fugitive family members all made it to freedom. George Elliott received a letter from the husband not long after his arrival in Canada, expressing his deepest thanks for their help.[10]

## Kidnappings

To their anger and dismay, antislavery people in southern Iowa would occasionally learn of neighbors who helped capture and return a fleeing slave to Missouri. Page County residents saw this happen in late October 1859 when an African American described as a "bright, intelligent looking" man about eighteen years old walked into Clarinda and inquired the way to Hawleyville, located a few miles farther northeast. No sooner had he walked beyond Clarinda's town limits than a local man caught up with him. Appearing friendly and good-willed, the local fellow invited the traveler to his house. As evening came on, three other white men drove up with a team and jumped the young black man. Ignoring his pleas for their sympathy, they tied him up, loaded him into the wagon, and drove south to find the man's Missouri owner. When word got around town, many condemned what happened and what it said about their community. "Those who were engaged in the affray," a county newspaper editor predicted, will find "that in their anxiety to serve the Slave interests, they have incurred a penalty for which they have been but poorly compensated"—the penalty of having earned the community's disrespect and disgrace.[11]

Even worse was the kidnapping of free African Americans so that they could be taken into Missouri and then "sold South" into states where bondage was more secure than it was in Missouri. Across southern Iowa ominous stories surfaced of such activities. In the summer of 1860 a short item in the Des Moines *Iowa State Register* reported: "Some two to three weeks since, a negro was arrested in Clark County, by slavehunters from Missouri. The negro . . . claims that he is free. Without any process of law he has been hurried away from the free State of Iowa into hopeless slavery." When no one came forward to claim him as property, the sheriff simply had him sold at auction.[12]

What attracted kidnappers to southern Iowa was in part the rapidly rising prices for slaves and in part the region's nearness to Missouri, where the victims could quickly be sold. All of the Northern border states saw this kind of crime, as many newspaper stories of the time attest. Iowa suffered its share of kidnapping attempts, and locals also foiled a few. Abductions were not limited to free states on the border, either, as Davy Crockett knew. Kidnappers in slave states would snatch free black residents in one part of the state and sell them into slavery in another. The constant danger of abduction kept free blacks in southern Iowa and Missouri wary and uncertain.

Schemes were not limited to simply grabbing someone unawares and driving off. Sometimes whites lured African Americans who trusted them into the hands of a slavetrader, often with confederates lying in wait to overwhelm the victim. In a more insidious variation, kidnappers employed a free black person as a decoy, arranging to ambush those who approached him or her.[13] In big cities like Chicago and St. Louis, gangs—some including policemen—exploited the unsettled nature of slavery along the border to fleece slaveholders, but such schemes also, of course, betrayed the suffering slaves. While some gang members helped enslaved people escape, their co-conspirators would bring them back to their owners and claim a reward.[14] In Indiana a group of men organized into a company that cashed in by recovering runaways they found traveling rail lines.[15]

Another common tactic was to capture a free black person and have bogus witnesses ready to swear in court that the victim was a runaway slave and that any legal papers demonstrating his or her freedom were forgeries. The nameless man accused of being the fugitive Dick was fortunate that the slaveowner called to testify to his identity was honest (see chapter 3).[16] Crafty kidnappers would also throw a black person into their hometown jail and then advertise for a slaveowner. If no master came forward, the captors and jail operator would sell the person into bondage and split the proceeds. There are also recorded instances of slavecatchers and lawyers working together. In this scheme a lawyer forged slave bills of sale so that an accomplice could sell abducted people into slavery without questions asked about their status. The attorney and his accomplice shared the profits.[17] In Ohio the increased activity among kidnappers in 1857 prompted the legislature to impose a sentence of hard labor for no fewer than three years or more than seven on those convicted of the offense.[18] Iowa had no such laws.

Certain kidnappings in the southern half of Iowa caused particular public excitement. "Deep indignation," wrote a Burlington, Iowa, newspaper editor, characterized talk on the street about the kidnapping of John Pembleton. Described as a "light-skinned mulatto" in his mid-twenties, Pembleton had escaped from slavery in Palmyra, Missouri, in 1856. In August 1858 he was a respected blacksmith with a shop on the upper end of Main Street when a man he had known in Missouri began stopping by to cultivate his friendship. A few days later this man asked the blacksmith to join him on a Sunday carriage ride to look at some possible mule pasturage. Once out of town, the man and some accomplices ensnared the former slave, handcuffed him, and headed off toward Missouri to collect a reward of $500 (about $14,000 in 2011) for delivering him to his former master. Rumors spread that one of Burlington's police officers had participated in Pembleton's capture. Indignant, the *Daily Hawk-Eye*'s editor declared that such a man should not "be allowed to run at large" for "he could be hired to cut his neighbor's throat for money."[19] Within less than two weeks, however, John Pembleton returned to Burlington. The person to whom he belonged had agreed to accept $400 from the blacksmith in return for his freedom.[20]

Kidnappers occasionally entangled themselves in their own schemes and got caught. John L. Curtis and James B. Little are good examples. Two young African American girls named Mary and Versa Old had been born into slavery in Tennessee. When Nancy R. Curtis married John Curtis in Missouri, she inherited the girls and took them with her to Iowa in 1856 when John established a large farm in southern Johnson County. Because they had moved from a slave to a free state, the girls now became free, but Curtis retained his control over them by obtaining guardianship. This the county court granted on the condition that he board, clothe, and educate the girls, who were now considered indentured servants. But the Curtises, having reared the girls as slaves, continued to treat them—now aged thirteen and fourteen—as property. At least this was the way it looked to some people in the township who became concerned about the girls' welfare and thought they ought to be removed from the Curtis family. When John failed to send the children to public school, his antislavery neighbors judged him to be holding them in ignorance, contrary to the requirements of his guardianship, and petitioned the county judge to do something about it.[21]

The county court served notice on Friday, January 27, 1860, for Curtis to appear the following Monday and show cause why the county judge should not appoint a different guardian. Curtis indicated he would be there to defend himself, but events soon demonstrated that he had made other plans. Early Sunday morning, some forty-four miles south of Iowa City, a two-horse carriage pulled up at an inn owned by a Mr. Allen. John L. Curtis and James B. Little stepped down with two young black girls to enter Allen's place for breakfast. Unaware that they had entered what Democrats described as "a rank and rabid abolition neighborhood," Curtis talked about keeping the children out of bad "abolitionist" hands by taking them to Missouri, where his relatives would keep the girls "in peace and in safe keeping." Three locals inside—Mr. Allen, Mr. Vincent, and Mr. McCoy—grew suspicious as they observed the visitors' manner. Their suspicions deepened as they listened to the guests talk about having traveled the entire night southward toward Missouri.[22]

After the party resumed its journey south, Allen, Vincent, and McCoy followed at a distance. Upon reaching Fairfield, thirty miles farther, the three pursuers sought out a justice of the peace to issue a warrant to stop the progress of the Missouri-bound party. Early the next morning in Iowaville (a small Des Moines River village some twenty miles from the Missouri border), Curtis opened his eyes in startled surprise to see Deputy Sheriff Cunningham standing before him. Accompanied by five men from nearby Brighton, the deputy held papers sworn out at Fairfield for the arrest of Curtis and Little. He duly arrested the two men, according to the editor of the *Page County Herald*, after "a scuffle and the handling of a loaded pistol." The deputy accompanied the carriage back to Fairfield and jailed Curtis briefly until a local man turned up to post bail. When Johnson County constable A. T. McElvaine arrived, he shackled Curtis, the man responsible for the children, and took him and Little to Iowa City on the charge of kidnapping.

Curtis posted bond, and the next day, February 3, Judge Miller heard his response to the kidnapping charge. Representing him were three attorneys led by J. D. Templin, an eloquent but windy local Democratic leader and onetime Methodist minister who by summer would become publisher of the Democratic Party's *Iowa State Reporter*.[23] Representing the state was William Penn Clarke, one of Iowa's most highly respected attorneys and an outspoken antislavery man who took the case without compensation. Joining him was Theodore M. Davis, who would soon afterward become Clarke's legal partner. When the trend of testimony increasingly showed that Curtis had no interest in the children's welfare, just as his neighbors had suspected, the defendant's lawyer stood up to propose that Mary and Versa Old be interrogated as witnesses.

Doubtless Curtis's lawyer soon wanted to swallow his words, for at the appearance of the two girls William Penn Clarke "broke out into one of those electrical bursts of eloquence—(thrilling the large audience that crowded the court room)," because he was "inspired by the sight of helpless beings exposed to nameless perils which mercenary men would drag them to through artless words spoken by their own mouths." His stirring appeal to consider the two girls as victims of ruthless men riveted the attention of those in attendance, as Clarke "for a while surpassed himself, and spoke with an eloquence befitting his great theme—human liberty."[24]

When Templin and local Democrats tried to depict the events as nothing more than excessive abolitionist zeal, their opponents immediately responded that they should "forego the pleasure of crying 'nigger,' and prating about 'abolitionism,'" and instead "stand up for justice before politics."[25] Curtis, seeing himself portrayed as exploiting Mary and Versa Old's value as slaves, understood that his efforts to defend his actions had come apart and his lawyers could do little about it. The next day, Judge Miller ruled that although Curtis could resume custody of the children, he would be required to post bail of $1,000 (about $28,000 in 2011) and await the action of a grand jury. Three days later the county judge returned Mary and Versa Old to Curtis, but with the proviso that he educate them and pay bail of $1,500 (about $42,000 in 2011).[26] (Whether one payment replaced the other or whether Curtis had to pay both is not clear.)

Democrats labeled the Iowa City kidnapping case "another instance of the mad and despicable policy of abolition interference with other people's business" and called the judge and jury "niggerworshipers" who were attempting to "strip John Curtis of his rights, his liberty and property, rob him of his wards and entail thousands of dollars expense upon Johnson County." The editor of the Democratic newspaper, the *Reporter*, added sarcastically that at least the verdict permitted Curtis "to enjoy the privacy of his own home, and to regulate his domestic institutions in his own way" and to "leave town without being dogged."[27] For those opposed to slavery, the case meant that Curtis's right to take his "Negro property" wherever he wanted had been defeated. Antislavery activists claimed that Democrats "are ready at any time to run a negro or mulatto into slavery; but, not only would not lift their finger to rescue a human being from a life-long bondage, but are ready to sneer at and denounce every effort to do the same."[28] The issue was property rights versus human rights: a central theme of the war to come a little more than a year after these events.

But this particular court case was not the end of the matter for those most intimately involved in it. Determined to maintain ownership of Mary and Versa Old, John and Nancy Curtis filed adoption papers for the girls on February 13, 1860. According to an 1883 recounting of the events, within a few months of the adoption, "Curtis again took the girls off south, being accompanied this time by David Lopp, of Fremont Township, and sold them in Memphis, Tennessee—one for $500 and the other for $800."[29] At last he had succeeded in exploiting the children's value as property.

Hardly had this Iowa City controversy faded when another kidnapping occurred close by, with even more tragic consequences. Jerry Boyd and his wife, Mary, whom Jerry had bought out of slavery from a St. Louis clothing merchant, had lived in Galena, Illinois, since 1840. He was known as "an honest, industrious and inoffensive colored drayman." In the late summer of 1860 two strangers visited Boyd in Galena and invited him and his family to move to Des Moines, Iowa, to live on a farm and work at a hotel in town. Persuaded it would be a good change, the hopeful couple prepared to leave. Accompanying the two were a twelve-year-old child and also a white child whom Mary took care of and whose mother had given them permission to take with them.[30]

They left Galena about September 27 in a covered wagon, guided by the two recruiters. Three days later people living north of Iowa City, in the Solon area, noticed four blacks and two whites staying overnight at a vacant house. A few days after that, locals discovered a dead black man three-fourths of a mile from the empty house where the travelers had stayed. An inquest showed the man's skull had been fractured. In his pocket was found a receipt for $20 (about $560 in 2011) paid by Jerry Boyd of Galena. When officials telegraphed an inquiry to Galena, they received a reply on October 14 stating that "Boyd & family, smallest girl white, others free, Kidnapped here, Five hundred (500) dollars reward for arrest of kidnappers and return of family."[31] Galena had already learned of the Boyd family's fate from another source. That source turned out to be a person in St. Joseph, Missouri, who had spoken to Mary Boyd and then contacted officials in Galena. Mary said that they all just had been sold as slaves, although money had yet to change hands. After they had been kidnapped, her husband had been killed and then the rest of them taken to St. Joseph for sale, along with the young white child, who was being presented as Mary Boyd's child. Whether the person who contacted Galena was an interested buyer looking to verify the status of his potential human property or simply a person reporting a crime is unknown.

The news set off intense public anger in Galena. Hastily, the townspeople collected $500 (about $14,000 in 2011) and sent two trusted Galena citizens to St. Joseph with the money: W. W. Weigley, a lawyer whose housekeeper was the mother of the white child being cared for by Mary Boyd, and the "fearless" Sam Hughlett, a Kentuckian.[32] From a circuit court judge they obtained a writ for the arrest of two men (a Mr. Goodwin, a Canadian, and a Mr. Bolton, a Caldwell County Missourian) who had apparently tried to sell the captives to a slavetrader. Authorities first arrested and jailed Bolton, charging him with kidnapping and murder. As he awaited trial or extradition to Iowa, they tracked down Goodwin in St. Joseph, Missouri.[33]

Under pressure, Bolton admitted to his part in the kidnapping scheme. His father-in-law and others, in exchange for a share of the take, had put up money for him and Goodwin to travel to Canada and seize some people who had escaped the family's ownership years back. Instead, Bolton and Goodwin got only as far as Galena before deciding to trick the Boyd family and then to steal an African American woman they knew to be living near Dubuque. Bolton's story was that the morning after the group's stopover at the vacant house near Solon, Jerry Boyd began loading his revolver in view of the others, causing Goodwin to reach for his shotgun and Bolton a revolver. Bolton's shot cut Boyd down in front of his wife and child. Mary Boyd's shriek of anguish caused the killers to throw a blanket over her head and threaten to kill her unless she stopped screaming. From there, the two kidnappers carted their four captives across Iowa to St. Joseph, Missouri, where, after they confided to their friends what had happened, one or more of them informed the authorities.[34]

After the sheriff in St. Joseph located Goodwin and loaded him on the train bound for Galena, he soon lost control of the situation. The numerous citizens who boarded the train along the way—some looking to lynch Goodwin and others trying to help him—distracted the sheriff's attention from the prisoner, who, as the train neared Hannibal going some thirteen miles an hour, slipped his shackles and leaped out the window, thus evading prosecution in Iowa. Despite the mixed outcome of efforts to bring the kidnappers to justice, with the help of the St. Joseph informants, Weigley and Hughlett succeeded in returning to freedom Mary Boyd and her child, along with the little white girl who lived with the Boyds and the woman kidnapped from Dubuque.[35]

The kidnapping trade, though lucrative, was also an unpredictable and dangerous one. As people poured westward into Kansas Territory during the 1850s and the struggle over slavery grew bloody there, a growing number of slaves seized the opportunity to escape from bondage. Some headed west into Kansas, along with many free African Americans seeking work. The members of this floating black population, often traveling in unfamiliar places among strangers, were especially vulnerable to kidnapping. The practice would not end until slavery itself was destroyed.

**⟩⟩⟨ 5 ⟩⟨⟨**

# The Kansas-Nebraska Act and
# Political Change in Iowa

## *James Grimes for Governor*

In May 1854 President Franklin Pierce, a Democrat, signed the Kansas-Nebraska Act. By superseding the Missouri Compromise of 1820, which had prohibited slavery in the Louisiana Purchase lands west and north of Missouri's southern border, the new law heightened the growing tensions over slavery. Now the question of whether human bondage would be legal in the newly opened western territories took center stage in national and local politics, transforming both in the process.[1] In Iowa, the Kansas-Nebraska Act seemed like good news to those who thought opening lands to the west would encourage railroad development. Others feared that the Democratic action might result in Nebraska Territory's becoming another slave state on Iowa's borders. One who quickly glimpsed the act's political implications was James Grimes, a prominent Burlington, Iowa, lawyer who had just entered the upcoming race for governor on the Whig ticket (see figure 13).

Odds for him at the time seemed poor. Democrats had always controlled Iowa's elected offices, and they dominated Congress and held the presidency. Nationally, the Whig Party was disintegrating because of the dispute over slavery: its Northern wing generally opposed it, while its Southern wing supported it. Antislavery Whigs were defecting to a variety of third parties, including the Free Soil Party, while proslavery Whigs drifted reluctantly toward the Democrats. Things did not look good for the Whigs in Iowa either. The Whig Party convention that nominated Grimes on February 22, 1854, was deeply divided and faction-ridden. It seemed unlikely that the Iowa Whigs would unite behind their candidate.

Although a forceful leader with many supporters in his party, Grimes had a direct manner that had gained him enemies and detractors as well. Two Northern conservative Whig factions—the "Silver Grays," who were fearful of losing control of the party to abolitionists, and the "Cotton Whigs," who were eager to avoid issues that might alienate party members who sympathized with the South—refused to support him. Although they admired his natural abilities, they detested his outspoken opposition to slavery. To Grimes's further consternation, within a month of the convention, three men selected as Whig candidates for other state offices declined to run.

Facing his party's virtual paralysis, Grimes sought an alliance with the Free Soil Party—just as other antislavery Whigs were doing throughout the Northern states. A meeting at Crawfordsville, Iowa, on March 28 produced an unstable coalition between the antislavery Whigs who supported Grimes and the Free Soilers, whose political agenda centered on opposing slavery's extension. Some leading regular Whigs denounced this partnership. And, of course, the Southern and border state settlers who likened antislavery sentiment to abolitionism remained a large proportion of Iowa's population. What Grimes had going for him was the great question of the day—the Nebraska Bill, which came to be called the Kansas-Nebraska Act after Congress passed it two months later.

Not one to play it safe, within two weeks of the pact between Grimes's faction of Whigs and the Free Soilers, Grimes presented an "Address to the People of Iowa" in which he tried to discredit the Democrats.[2] Selecting commentary and events from the national scene that reverberated among Iowans, he laid out two lines of attack. First, to erode the Democratic Party's past advantages, he blamed its leaders for plunging the country into renewed agitation over the expansion of slavery by proposing the Nebraska Bill, which would overturn the Missouri Compromise. If, as the Democrats claimed, no one expected that "slavery will take possession of

Nebraska," then, he asked, "why the strenuous effort to repeal the Missouri Compromise?" Iowa would reap vast benefits if it enjoyed a "free, enterprising population on the west," but, said Grimes, "with a slave state on our western border, I see nothing but trouble and darkness in the future. Bounded on two sides by slave states, we shall be intersected with underground railroads, and continually distracted by slave-hunts. Instead of having a population at the west who will sympathize with us, we shall find their sympathies and interests constantly antagonistic to ours."[3] The battles over fugitives and kidnapping victims in southern Iowa during the 1840s and 1850s demonstrated to many how right Grimes was.

Second, to rouse German American hostility toward Democrats, Grimes pointed out that the proslavery advocates of the Nebraska Bill had also wanted to deny German immigrants in Kansas the right to vote, while granting that right to the territory's native-born slaveholders.[4] And who had written this anti-German measure? Grimes fingered Missouri senator David Atchison. In doing so, he meant to associate this key border-state support of slavery with anti-immigrant sentiment, in the hope of prying German and German American voters away from the Democratic Party.[5]

In his address and through the summer campaign, Grimes put to good use the fact that Iowa's two Democratic senators, Augustus C. Dodge and George W. Jones, both favored the Nebraska Bill. The gubernatorial candidate pointed out that "on every question affecting the rights of free labor and free territory, the extreme South shall find its most willing and devoted supporters in the [Democratic] senators from this free state."[6] These points Grimes repeated over and over again in the thirty-one speeches he delivered during an extensive tour of towns across the state. And he was not alone in his fears about the effect of overturning the Missouri Compromise. Iowans held several "anti-Nebraska" mass meetings, adding to the worries of the hitherto dominant Democratic Party.[7]

## The Civil Bend and Tabor Stations

Even as tensions over slavery began to rise across the nation and throughout the state, Iowa's local communities continued to struggle with the issue, especially along the border. Southern Fremont County, which had been part of Missouri from 1837 until 1848, when the state boundaries were adjusted, was particularly vulnerable to conflict, even before the turmoil over the Kansas-Nebraska Act in 1854. For example, there is the story of Joseph Garner and his family, free blacks who moved to the small, isolated frontier hamlet called Civil Bend in the southwestern corner of the county, a few miles north of the Missouri line.[8]

Perhaps what drew Garner to this small cluster of settlers was the presence of two people he already knew, Ira Blanchard and his wife (see figure 14). Until moving to Civil Bend in 1848, the Blanchards had operated a Baptist Indian mission near present-day Bonner Springs in the as yet unorganized Kansas Territory. The tough-minded Blanchard cosigned paperwork enabling Garner to purchase twenty-five acres of land.[9] Lester and Elvira Platt, former missionaries to the Pawnee in Nebraska Territory (similarly not yet organized), also lived in Civil Bend, having moved there about a year before the Blanchards arrived.[10] In addition, settling in the hamlet for a time were members of an abolitionist Congregationalist group from Oberlin, Ohio—a town already famous for its racially integrated, coeducational college. Led by George Gaston (Elvira Platt's brother), they had arrived in late 1848 with the idea of creating a new community—an Oberlin in the West.

As Joseph Garner built his cabin near the banks of the Missouri River, Elvira Platt and another teacher from Oberlin opened a local subscription school. In the fall of 1850 the teacher invited Garner to send his school-age children for day school and Sunday school. Not everyone in Civil Bend was so open-minded, however—some 20 percent of the population had come from Southern states where slavery was legal. When news got around that black children were attending the school, opposition erupted in the neighborhood. On New Year's Eve, the schoolhouse burned down, and some blamed those who opposed allowing the Garner children to attend.[11] And this was far from the worst that the Garners would face (see chapters 6 and 8).

Perhaps because of such hostilities, but more likely because the area around Civil Bend sat in the Missouri River's floodplain (a fact made clear by the severe floods of 1851), the antislavery Congregationalists led by George Gaston moved to higher ground to build their "Oberlin" dream college community. After taking several lengthy rides beyond the bottomland sloughs and ponds in search of a suitable place, they found it twenty miles away in the county's northern reaches. There, on higher ground on the open prairie, they started to build their new town of Tabor. By summer's end they had two cabins up and by the next year added a few more for new family arrivals from the East. Early in 1854, just before the passage of the Kansas-Nebraska Act, the small group of residents decided to build a schoolhouse, passing the hat for subscribers to pay for building materials. With a half-dozen new families living in Tabor by late spring, their few carpenters were busy working on the schoolhouse as well as their own houses and barns.

Amid the bustle of a newly founded town, surely it was not surprising when three covered wagons drew up on the Fourth of July, 1854. Driving the first wagon was a white man with his wife and daughter. More surprisingly, the other wagons contained several black people—a man and wife about thirty years old with two young children, a young man about twenty-one, and an elderly woman. These newcomers did not intend to settle in Tabor. Residents soon learned that the leader, Mr. Dennis, was a Mormon elder from Mississippi who was on his way to Utah and meant to camp in town only overnight. As the Dennises set things up for the evening on the west side of what was marked out as Main Street, between Elm and Orange streets, Samuel H. Adams, the town's thirty-year-old lead carpenter, strolled up to chat with one of the black members of the party. Having confirmed his suspicions that they were enslaved, Adams whispered to them that, since they were in a free state, they could choose whether or not to continue their way to Salt Lake City. To this they replied that all but one would like to escape their bondage, the exception being the old woman, who also could not be trusted to help them or to keep quiet about their plans to escape.[12]

Adams took the news to the local minister, John Todd, telling him "the Lord had sent some of his colored children among us to see what we would do with them." Given that the Tabor residents held monthly antislavery prayer meetings, Adams believed that the Lord evidently "was trying us to see if we were willing to help answer some of our prayers," but Todd thought Adams's suggestion overzealous. There was nothing they could do, the minister advised, because the high proportion of proslavery men in this southwest corner of Iowa meant they would likely be betrayed in any effort to free the Dennis family's slaves. But Adams decided at least they ought to try, and he got together with five others in town to plan the escape. This first underground railroad rescue for Tabor's residents would set a pattern for their future efforts to help people escape from bondage (see chapter 6).

At nightfall, after Dennis and his wife and daughter retired to bed, five of the people they held in slavery slipped away to a nearby barn of George B. Gaston's, where Adams and his friends were waiting.[13] Then they walked east out of the village, trying all the while to cover their tracks through the easily trampled tallgrass prairie. They first cut south and then headed east across fields recently broken for farming.[14] Five miles out they came to the broad Silver Creek. Anticipating that they might have to haul each other across this unfordable tributary, they had brought a coil of rope along. It turned out to be unnecessary, however, because a large cottonwood tree had fallen across the water, allowing the fugitives to walk along its trunk.

After concealing the runaways in a grove of trees, Adams and his allies left to get back to Tabor before daylight. To transfer the group to another stop, they made two arrangements. First of all, George B. Gaston recruited a few ladies for a morning buggy ride north to the cabin of Charles W. Tolles on Silver Creek, near present-day Malvern, to alert Tolles of the fugitives' imminent arrival. Gaston knew of Tolles through Ira Blanchard, who had once employed the man and his wife at the Baptist Mission in Kansas. Tolles agreed to take care of the runaways until they could be moved to their next destination. The Tabor collaborators also recruited two local men, the young William Clark and the older Cephas Case (a relative of Tolles's wife, Sylvia), who lived not far from Tolles's place, and gave them an old horse to help carry those less able to walk.

Meanwhile, back in Tabor Mr. Dennis had awakened on July 5 to find his livestock untended, no fires burning, no breakfast being cooked, and all but his oldest slave gone. Evidently aware that many people in Tabor opposed slavery, he questioned no one in town, instead finding slavery sympathizers in a neighborhood a few miles south who were willing to help chase down his runaways. Soon they spread handbills announcing the "accursed deed" done at Tabor and offering $50 (roughly $1,400 in 2011) for the return of each slave and $200 (about $5,600) for information about the whites who had aided in the escape. Slavehunters started scouting the countryside, searching thickets and timbered areas along streams where the runaways might be hiding. Luckily, one of the slavehunters was sympathetic to the runaways and made sure he was the one who searched the most likely areas—including the one where they were actually hiding.

Within two days of the escape from the Dennis camp in Tabor, William Clark and Cephas Case had escorted the fugitives to the next stop. While moving east to a place where they might ford the West Nishnabotna River and now traveling in daylight, they came upon a man on horseback. Noticing that he watched their group closely, they asked him about the road to Quincy—a known antislavery town some thirty miles away in central Adams County—and about where to cross the East Nishnabotna. But as soon as he departed, they struck north up the East Nishnabotna Valley toward a small Mormon settlement called Indiantown in southwest Cass County, near which lived the Congregationalist minister George B. Hitchcock. Upon their arrival that evening, Hitchcock fed them supper, but fearing for their safety and his own, he directed them toward a Quaker neighborhood (probably in the Quaker settlements in Dallas County) near the Des Moines

River. With the escapees now out of immediate harm's way, Clark and Case returned to Tabor.

Knowledge of the runaways' journey beyond the Hitchcock place in Cass County would have been lost were it not for a reminiscence by a man named Felix Conner, recorded by his son William E. Conner. William remembered that a man had brought the runaways to his father's house, and then his father, an antislavery Methodist minister, took them southeast through Pella (Marion County) and into Mahaska County to the small hamlet of Fremont. Here he had old friends in the abolition movement: William Montgomery, Isaac Hockett, and Mathew McCormack. Montgomery took the runaways to Richland (Keokuk County), where others transported them to Washington and then Davenport to cross the Mississippi into Illinois.[15]

Two clues have survived about what subsequently happened in Illinois. Samuel H. Adams recalled that Todd's sister, who lived near Quincy, saw an advertisement for these runaways in a local newspaper. The ad included the editor's comment that a "party answering to that description was at our church last Sabbath and on Monday started for the Queen's dominion"—in other words, Canada. The second clue is a diary entry dated July 24, 1854, by Samuel G. Wright of Galesburg, Illinois, which noted that he had "received and carried on five fugitives who had escaped from their master as he was transporting them through Tabor."[16] Within twenty days, the escapees had made it all the way across frontier Iowa to the antislavery town of Galesburg in western Illinois.

In the meantime, the man on horseback who had met William Clark and Cephas Case on their journey learned of the Dennis family's missing slaves and rode to tell Mr. Dennis that he had spotted them on their way to Quincy. Dennis pursued this lead to no result, but along the way he posted more handbills, determined to retrieve what belonged to him. Putting off his journey to Utah, he stayed just north of Tabor throughout the fall and winter. He even made trips to Chicago and Detroit, where he rightly guessed his missing property had gone. While in Chicago, he placed an advertisement for the runaways in a newspaper there, which other papers reprinted—thus enabling Todd's sister to see it in Quincy. The luckless slaveholder again returned to Tabor, complaining that "people had abused him all the way."[17] At some point during this time, he learned that Cephas Case had been one of the people who had helped his slaves gain their freedom. One day, upon seeing Case, Dennis nearly beat him to death with a cane before others came to his rescue.

Events like the one in Tabor continually brought the slavery question home to Iowans, white and black, and connected their local struggles to state and national political turmoil. The escape of Dennis's five slaves occurred just fifteen days after James Grimes had made a campaign speech in Sidney, eleven miles south of Tabor.[18] Two weeks later newspapers reported that Burlington pastor William Salter had just faced down slave kidnappers in La Salle, Illinois, 150 miles east of Burlington. While waiting for a train at a depot of the Chicago and Rock Island Railroad on the night of July 13, 1854, he heard loud shouts on the platform. Walking out to investigate, Salter saw three white men grabbing two blacks who had purchased tickets for Chicago. Salter later reported that, among the threats and oaths in the air, he yelled out, "Are you officers?" The white men replied that they were not. "Have you served any papers?" Salter asked. Again they said no. The minister then said, "These men are not criminals, and they must go on." Salter "used a little force, and a pistol was presented," but in the end "the cars started and we with them" before a police officer arrived. Salter never knew whether the kidnappers ended up "secure of their prey" or whether the black travelers made it safely to Chicago.[19]

The spreading conflict over slavery had a powerful effect on Iowa politics. When the August 1854 election results came in, Grimes had won a narrow 52 percent victory over his opponent, Democrat Curtis Bates. The Democrats' complacent overconfidence dissolved in the face of Iowans' moral and political reaction against the Kansas-Nebraska Act, while it solidified the alliance between antislavery Whigs and Free Soilers.[20] "I am astonished at my own success in this State," Grimes wrote two months later to Sen. Salmon P. Chase of Ohio, a staunch opponent of slavery.[21]

Despite open opposition to him from certain old-line Whigs, he had received strong support from the more settled, populous areas. Additionally, enough Whig candidates got elected in the Iowa General Assembly to remove Sen. Augustus C. Dodge from office and replace him with an antislavery man, James Harlan. (At this time, U.S. senators were elected by state legislators, not by direct popular vote.) Grimes's weakest showing was in the southern half of the state and in the less settled western counties, the very areas to which more people would flee from slavery, thus exacerbating the divisions among free people as the troubles in Kansas intensified.

## The Battle for Kansas

With the passage of the Kansas-Nebraska Act in May 1854, "Kansas was opened to slavery, subject to 'squatter sovereignty,' that is, that the squatters had a right to pass on the subject—could have slavery if they wanted it."[22] The fact that Kansas settlers would determine whether the state was slave or free galvanized people on both sides of the issue. Antislavery advocates in the New England states began organizing emigration societies, and proslavery Missourians, to deal with what they judged to be distant meddlers, did the same.[23]

Missouri's Southern element, led by Sen. David R. Atchison and former state attorney general Benjamin R. Stringfellow, had established by midsummer 1854 a squatters' claim association to organize settlement in Kansas, as well as associated county self-defense groups along the border to force Free Soilers and abolitionists out of the newly opened territory. The proslavery people of western Missouri, while willing to let Nebraska become a free state, were convinced of "the fitness of Kansas for slave labor" and expected their institutions to be established there. After all, they "naturally . . . felt that they themselves should have the right to occupy the land in their neighborhood."[24]

Throughout 1854 and 1855 antislavery, proslavery, and other eager settlers raced to settle Kansas Territory. All wanted mainly to better their condition in life, but most were also aware of the significance of the fight ahead. Proponents of slavery, while calling for Southerners to settle Kansas, also tried to subvert the democratic process. Beginning with the election for Kansas's territorial delegate to Congress in 1854 and again during the elections for the territorial assembly in 1855, proslavery Missourians were urged to cross into Kansas and vote, even though they didn't live there. Senator Atchison told a crowd in Platt County, Missouri, on November 6, 1854, "When you reside in one day's journey of the territory, and when your peace, your quiet and your property depend upon your action, you can, with an exertion, send 500 of your young men who will vote in favor of your institutions." Crossing over to Kansas to vote would ensure that the question would "be decided quietly and peaceably at the ballot-box."[25]

By mid-1855 a combination of the intimidation of antislavery activists and ballot box fraud had given proslavery men control of Kansas's territorial legislature. The legislators consequently passed strong laws to protect slave property, one of which would punish by death or ten years imprisonment any person who would "entice, decoy, or carry away out of this Territory any slave belonging to another."[26] The outnumbered free-staters lived in fear of their neighbors. The *Squatter Sovereign*, a paper published in Atchison, Kansas, and owned by the Stringfellow brothers and Robert Kelley, warned that antislavery advocates "may exhaust an ocean of ink, their Emigrant Aid Societies spend their millions and billions, their representatives in Congress spout their heretical theories till doomsday, and his excellency [President] Franklin Pierce appoint abolitionist after free-soiler as governor, yet we will continue to tar and feather, drown, lynch and hang every white-livered abolitionist who dares to pollute our soil."[27]

Despite such threats, free-state settlers hung on and began to fight back. In response to the fraudulent elections and interference by Missourians that produced the aggressively proslavery territorial legislature, free-state leaders met at Big Springs in September 1855. There they established a Free State Party. Then, in a radical move, they assembled at Topeka in late October to draft a constitution, known as the Topeka Constitution, for a separate territorial government. To achieve consensus, the constitution banned slavery but also the migration of free blacks into the future state, and it allowed only white men and Indian men who had adopted white habits to vote. Voters ratified this constitution in a December election, setting the stage to seek congressional approval to make Kansas a free state.

Proslavery leaders decried the free-state men's actions in Topeka as an insurrection against the territory's established government. Even more troubling to them was the fact that the tide of immigration into Kansas seemed to favor those who opposed slavery. Recognizing this, the proslavery forces realized that the flow of settlers from the Northern states had to be choked off. The crucial year was to be 1856.

The free-state cause was in desperate straits by May of that year, reeling from the strong-arm measures meted out by bands of proslavery men. On the twenty-first the friends of slavery sacked Lawrence, Kansas, a stronghold of the antislavery community. The attackers destroyed two newspaper offices, razed homes and shops, and leveled the Free State Hotel with cannon fire. Still not satisfied, the militants then set about closing the Missouri River to the transport of supplies and reinforcements for the antislavery settlers. The proslavery men stopped steamboats, searched passengers' goods, and turned back groups of migrants from Northern states on the river, as well as those crossing Missouri into Kansas Territory by wagon.

Far from solidifying the proslavery forces' hold on the territory, the sack of Lawrence and the closing of the Missouri River moved many antislavery Kansans to decide that enough was enough. Their lives insecure and troubled in every direction, their hoped-for prosperity at risk because of the chronic violence, the flow of supplies endangered, and now the town of Lawrence ruined, they concluded that they had no choice but to fight. The more reckless young men began forming guerrilla bands to take the fight to their proslavery foes.[28] Kansas exploded with violence, and many Iowans threw themselves into the battle.

In Lawrence, the main early antislavery guerrilla leader was Charles "Charley" Lenhart, who had immigrated to Kansas from Iowa in the spring of 1855. The lean twenty-year-old had worked as a printer for a Davenport newspaper and found similar work at the free-state *Herald of Freedom* in Lawrence. By 1856, however, with Lawrence under siege and proslavery irregulars running amok, Lenhart began to spend less time at work and more time fighting. "If there was any wild adventure on foot," editor George W. Brown explained, "he was the leader and away!" Lenhart, a fearless daredevil, drew about him a band of some twenty equally bold young men—including John Cook, who later joined John Brown at Harpers Ferry—and they regularly ambushed and generally harassed proslavery partisans. Soon their efforts forced the freewheeling proslavery bands to be more cautious about when and where they went to raid and burn free-state cabins, take captives, and drive off livestock.[29]

Though Lenhart's wild and reckless guerrilla group helped convert proslavery bravado to hesitation, it also infuriated local free-state leaders who opposed such violent tactics. It was too unrestrained for the likes of conservatives such as Charles Robinson and editor Brown, who sought to keep the peace and avoid provoking the U.S. Army to move against them. They denounced Lenhart's outfit as a nuisance for which antislavery leaders refused to be held responsible. But Lenhart's band was not bothered by the criticism; it aligned itself with antislavery activists like John Brown and James H. Lane, who favored direct action. Lenhart's guerrillas continued to prowl the territory on the lookout for armed proslavery marauders and successfully evaded capture by them.

John Brown would soon become the most famous Kansas antislavery fighter in the nation. A one-time businessman who had owned and operated tanneries and raised sheep for wool, he had become increasingly opposed to slavery since the murder of antislavery newspaper editor Elijah Lovejoy in 1837. During the 1840s Brown lived in Springfield, Massachusetts, where he came to know many of the wealthiest antislavery advocates in the nation and worshipped at St. John's Free Church, which had been founded by African Americans and often hosted the leading abolitionists of the day. In 1850 Brown founded a militant antislavery group, and in 1855 he responded to calls for help from his sons, who had joined antislavery settlers in Kansas. Unlike many who opposed slavery, Brown believed that the institution could be overthrown only by violence, and he acted on that belief repeatedly between 1855 and 1859.

Three days after proslavery Missourians sacked Lawrence in May 1856, John Brown took the fight a chilling step further. He gathered together several men and rode through the night to the bottomlands of Pottawatomie Creek in Kansas, where a cluster of proslavery families had homes. There, Brown and his supporters executed five men by hacking them to death with broadswords. The massacre drove a shaft of terror through active proslavery communities, and in retaliation vigilantes sacked and burned the Brown family's cabins and captured two of the old man's sons, who were held in irons in the U.S. Cavalry camp nearby. Undeterred by the warrants issued for his arrest, Brown united his nine men with fifteen commanded by Capt. Samuel T. Shore, and the party successfully attacked Capt. Henry Clay Pate's Missouri militia on June 2 three miles away in the Black Jack area. In the skirmish the antislavery forces captured Pate and twenty-four of his men, holding them for three days until the U.S. Cavalry insisted upon their release. Although the cavalry officers ultimately ignored the signed agreement between Brown and Pate to exchange his Missourian captives for Brown's sons and an equal number of free-state prisoners, the abolitionist fighter and his allies counted this first regular battle between proslavery and free-state forces a victory. It showed that free-state settlers had fight in them and that proslavery raids would no longer go unchallenged. As a result, the once powerful proslavery militias began losing some of their former swagger.

## *The Overland Route to Kansas*

Nevertheless, the beleaguered free-state Kansans, crying out for provisions, guns, and more emigrants, needed to act quickly to improve their precarious situation. With Missouri and the Missouri River closed to them, the only feasible course for reaching Kansas was a northern overland route through Iowa, the closest free state. Urging antislavery supporters to use it was James H. Lane, a former Indiana congressman who had served in the Mexican War and was now an emerging free-state leader.[30] Making this route more attractive was the rapid extension of the railroad. The tracks running from Chicago first bridged the Mississippi River at Davenport, Iowa, in late April 1856, with Iowa City then the westernmost stop along the line. Within two months another rail line across southern Iowa reached from Burlington thirty miles west to Mount Pleasant, further shortening the distance that had to be traveled by wagon.

A National Kansas Committee with headquarters in Chicago hurriedly formed to coordinate relief efforts through Iowa. Even as various Kansas aid organizations met in Buffalo, New York, the Kansas Central Committee of Iowa was busy mapping out a three-hundred-mile overland route from Iowa City to the southwestern corner of the state, initially ending at Sidney, but the terminus was quickly changed to the antislavery town of Tabor.[31] Shortly afterward, a team from Topeka, Kansas, undertook to survey a drivable road from Iowa to their town. They graded slopes at stream crossings, blazed trees, and piled stones to mark the route.[32]

Meanwhile, free-state companies, including parties that had been stopped and turned back on their steamboat journeys up the Missouri River, began to gather at the rail end near Iowa City. Many of these passengers had returned to Alton or St. Louis and from there came up the Mississippi River to venture west across Iowa. The number of antislavery settlers passing through Iowa City for Kansas soon grew into the hundreds. Well-prepared for the violence they would face, they brought with them cannons and firearms supplied by contributions from Chicago and other places.[33] Emigrant companies small and large camped on the prairies surrounding Iowa City. They scoured the town for, as one put it, "teams, wagons, tents, cooking utensils, and all necessary appurtenances for the pioneer life we were about to lead." They competed for goods and equipment with the Mormon handcart companies that were encamped west of town preparing to depart for their long journey to Salt Lake City, Utah.[34]

The free-state response to the river closure spread alarm through northwestern Missouri and "greatly excited and exasperated" proslavery citizens in border counties. "A large body of armed emigrants are marching through Nebraska for Kansas," warned proslavery men. A writer to the *St. Louis Gazette* described Iowa City as "the central focus and hot bed of Kansas filibuster" and claimed to have seen as many as five hundred people "encamped in the grove east of the city." This writer believed them to be a military expedition led by James H. Lane, the Indiana congressman, in the writer's view a "fugitive traitor" who is "wild with excitement and exhibits a fury that strongly indicates insanity." They "take cannon and arms, *with munitions of war*," the writer insisted, "and are, in fact, organized into regular military squads of companies" paid for or "aided by contributions from Chicago and other places."[35]

Hoping to persuade the U.S. Army to halt the free-state migration, proslavery partisans painted the overland emigrant groups as highly organized paramilitaries "enlisting an army to exterminate" them. In contrast, a free-state organizer believed that his partisans were too few to "overawe" opposition and feared that "their provisions and money [were] nearly exhausted." The wagon parties, he wrote, were "designedly distorted by telegraphic dispatches and [Democratic] administration newspapers, into an organized army, under Gen. Lane, armed to the teeth with Sharp's rifles, Colt's revolvers and bowie knives!"[36]

In fact, the wagons of a caravan from Worcester, Massachusetts, carried fifteen hundred muskets taken from the Iowa state arsenal informally after a key was left on Governor Grimes's desk. This kind of under-the-table support for the free-state cause was not unique to Iowa; one of Ohio's emigrant groups, led by S. N. Wood, also took to Kansas twenty boxes of borrowed militia muskets. On the proslavery side, Missouri activists took armaments from the U.S. arsenal in Liberty in November 1855 and the state arsenal in Jefferson in early 1856. In November 1856 Iowa's governor secretly provided an additional two hundred arms to Robert Morrow, a member of the Kansas expedition led by Col. Shalor W. Eldridge, the route agent for the National Kansas Committee.[37]

Eldridge's was the first large emigrant train to depart, leaving Iowa City about July 4, 1856. It was composed of several smaller companies under his general direction. He had been the owner of the recently destroyed Free State Hotel in Lawrence, Kansas. A total of 396 people traveled in these initial caravans. Other parties that left separately later combined with each other along the way, all eventually congregating in western Iowa to enter Kansas in force.[38] The journey across Iowa, "three hundred miles of sparsely settled country, unprovided with coaches, hotels, or the ordinary facilities for travel," was far from easy, especially for individuals and families unaccustomed to crossing unsettled expanses of open prairie.[39]

One member of the caravan who had "traveled the whole breadth of the State of Iowa" found it a "tedious journey, partly through a country so sparsely inhabited that we had to sleep two nights in our wagon."[40] In dry weather, conditions were tough: there were no bridges over streams and no easy paths through swampy bottomlands, and what trails existed were badly rutted. When rains moved in, wagons bogged down, slowed to a crawl, or worse, got completely stuck. "Compelled to travel on foot in the heat of July over the broad Western prairies," the free-staters also suffered from the blazing summer temperatures. As one correspondent lamented, "the wild life which we are compelled to endure comes rather hard upon some of our party, who have been used to different fare."[41]

The overland route was tougher, more expensive, and more monotonous than traveling on a Missouri River steamboat. Forced to abandon the comparatively "easy and safe journey" by river through Missouri for the "long and harassing march through the uncultivated wilds of Iowa and Nebraska," many migrants were bereft of resources and facing starvation as they neared the end of their journey. A newspaper editor noted that "the slender purse of the emigrant is in many instances insufficient for the long overland journey through Iowa and Nebraska."[42] The weary settlers found the strongly antislavery village of Tabor a welcome way station where they could recuperate while waiting to safely enter Nebraska and Kansas. Some emigrant trains halted and camped in tents and wagons in the town square, while others proceeded over the ridge beyond the town onto the open prairie.[43]

From July through November 1856, as the free-state settlers streamed west toward Kansas and Nebraska, Tabor citizens did everything they could to help. Maria Cummings Gaston, wife of town founder George B. Gaston, later wrote:

> That summer and autumn our houses, before too full, were much overfilled and our comforts shared with those passing to and from Kansas to secure it for *Freedom*. When houses would hold no more, woodsheds were temporized for bedrooms, where the sick and dying were cared for. Barns also were fixed for sleeping rooms. Every place a bed could be put or a blanket thrown down was at once so occupied. There were comers and goers all times of the day or night—meals at all hours—many free hotels, perhaps entertaining angels unawares. *After* battles they were here for rest—*before* for preparation.[44]

The Kansas and Nebraska settlers remembered Tabor fondly. Massachusetts-based organizer Thomas Wentworth Higginson, who accompanied some of the wagon trains taking aid to Kansas and later became a confidant of John Brown, commented to the *New York Daily Tribune*: "The citizens of Tabor are entitled to everlasting gratitude for their unwearied kindness to our emigrants. The sick have been cared for, clothing has been made, and every house, stable, and melon-patch, has been common property. Let the Eastern States hold this thriving little village in grateful remembrance."[45] Similar credit to Tabor "for the sympathy and ready helpfulness of its people in supplying the needs of the forces marching to the relief of the besieged free-state men" came from Shalor Eldridge. "Kansas," he wrote, "will ever owe Tabor a debt of gratitude."[46]

By late July the first wagon trains had crossed into Nebraska Territory at Nebraska City and were encamped some twenty miles past that town. They had halted after hearing that Missourians were gathering in large groups to stop them. The wagon master of the largest caravan, Milton Dickey, wrote to Gen. Persifor E. Smith, the U.S. Army commander in Kansas, requesting a military escort for their travel into that territory. Free-state emigrants had exhausted their provisions and money waiting for protection from proslavery forces. If the army refused to help, as some predicted, several thought Smith might try to drive them back, but most expected to wait until other parties came up to create a larger "armed body of emigrants who can force their way in."[47]

Other wagon trains remained at Tabor, which had also become a safe haven for free-state fighters who were retaliating against proslavery bands. Maria Cummings Gaston recalled:

General Lane once stayed three weeks secretly while it was reported abroad that he was back in Indiana for recruits and supplies, where came ere long, consisting of all kinds of provisions, Sharps rifles, powder and lead. A cannon packed in corn made its way through the enemy's lines and ammunition of all kinds, in clothing and kitchen furniture, etc. etc. Our cellars contained barrels of powder, and boxes of rifles. Often our chairs, tables, beds, and such places were covered with what weapons everyone carried about him, so that if one *needed* and got time to rest a little in the day time, we had to remove the Kansas furniture, or rest with loaded revolvers, cartridge boxes, and bowie knives piled around them, and boxes of swords under the bed. Were not our houses overfilled?[48]

Word finally came in mid-September that the way was open and safe for all emigrants to pass into Kansas.[49] Particularly effective in quieting the turbulence was the forceful new territorial governor, John W. Geary. He arrived in Kansas on September 9, 1856, and soon directed all outside and unauthorized militias to disband—groups that his proslavery predecessor had earlier invited in to put down "open insurrection and rebellion." Geary's vigorous actions also prompted the force under free-state leader James Lane to pull out of Kansas, retreating to Nebraska and then Iowa.[50] On September 17, Rev. John Todd wrote his Congregationalist colleague, Rev. William Salter in Burlington, Iowa, to bring him up to date on happenings in Tabor:

> The wants of Kansas constitute the absorbing topic of interest here now. The Kansas forces had been congregating here for more than three weeks until yesterday. Our little village had been their headquarters on this side [of] the river ever since the arrival of Lane's company. You are right in saying that men are wanted. Such was the call for men that it was much feared that our friends in the territory would be reduced to a state of suffering before a sufficient force could be raised to conduct safely to them the provisions which were here waiting to be conveyed. The road is said to be now open. Several skirmishes have taken place, & Lane is in command of the territory. Messrs. [Samuel Gridley] Howe, [Thaddeus] Hyatt, [Thomas Wentworth] Higginson &c have been here, & anything which can be done here to forward the cause of Freedom will be done most cheerfully.[51]

While Geary worked to pacify Kansas, armed emigrants continued to arrive in Tabor in the fall of 1856. Preston B. Plumb's company went there from Iowa City in early September with three wagons, one containing relief supplies and travel provisions; another 250 Sharps rifles, revolvers, Bowie knives, and ammunition; and the third a brass cannon and its carriage, dismantled and boarded up so it could not be seen.[52] Their arrival in Tabor prompted a welcoming dinner by the community.

As General Lane and his company neared Tabor from Nebraska Territory, John Speer, who had joined the group, recalled that Lane stopped the company outside of town and "admonished the men that in regard for the moral and religious principles of Tabor people, the men of the company were to conduct themselves with utmost decorum." They camped on the public square, drilled daily, and engaged in various sports but avoided profanity and did not steal any chickens.[53] When they heard that the trouble had subsided, they moved to Archer, Nebraska, before reentering Kansas.

In late September Colonel Eldridge led a large expedition toward Tabor from Mount Pleasant. Some eighteen wagons loaded with small arms, edged weapons, munitions, tents, and provisions were accompanied by two hundred volunteers organized into artillery and rifle companies and equipped with a field gun. They met Lane's group at Quincy, Iowa, fifty miles east of Tabor, and marched into that town on October 1 to spend two days drilling and reorganizing.[54]

Tabor's public square accommodated both Eldridge's and Lane's militias. John Todd recalled that Eldridge's company

> proceeded directly to the southwest corner of the public square, where they proceeded to pitch their tents. It must be remembered that there was not a tree then on the public square, nor any fence around it. They camped in front of the parson's gate, placing the mounted cannon in the center, and hoisting on it the stars and stripes. The 18 covered wagons were arranged in a circle, around the national banner. Outside the wagons was pitched a circle of tents, and outside the tents campfires were built, and still outside of the fires were placed armed sentinels. . . . On the next day about 200 men drilled on the public square, a report of which was carried by the passengers in the stage coach to St. Joe [St. Joseph, Missouri], only the numbers were multiplied tenfold—the 200 had become 2,000.[55]

Todd also reported that General Lane and his men had some trouble. "There was not the best feeling" among the eastern free-state emigrants toward Lane because they had not received the Sharps rifles promised them first at Albany, then Cleveland, then Chicago, and finally at Tabor. Nevertheless, wrote Todd, General Lane "mounted the cannon carriage and, calling the men around him," was able to "pacify" and "prevail on them to go forward" into Kansas Territory on October 4.[56]

The Kansas antislavery fighter John Brown encountered the Eldridge company on its march into Kansas. Heading east, Brown led a party with two wagons, one pulled by a four-mule team and the second a one-horse covered wagon that carried inside the ailing Brown himself and a runaway slave. Acting as teamsters were three of his sons, John Brown Jr., Owen, and Jason; another son, Frederick, had been killed by proslavery vigilantes on August 30. With John Jr. and Jason now released from imprisonment and relative peace enforced by Governor Geary, Brown was returning east to raise additional funds. "The mule team," Jason recalled, "was full of arms and ammunition that father was taking out to Tabor." The Browns arrived there on October 10.[57]

"Here he stored arms he had brought with him," wrote biographer Oswald Garrison Villard, "and this place he chose as the coming headquarters of the band of one hundred 'volunteer-regulars' for whom he now planned to raise funds in the East." He would train them here "for war-service against forces of slavery." The men who supported John Brown in 1856 were mainly his relatives and a few free-state neighbors, working together on occasion with other groups. But as news of his exploits spread, antislavery fighters from Kansas Territory, Iowa, and elsewhere joined his militia. Though Kansas was momentarily at peace, Brown expected more conflict in the spring, and he wanted to be ready to fight. The sons continued on their way while John Brown—ill with dysentery—spent a week in Tabor recuperating among friends.[58]

When Brown got to Chicago on October 22 or 23, he learned that his sons Salmon and Watson had joined the wagon train led by Col. Milton C. Dickey and Dr. J. P. Root that was bearing freight and goods from Mount Pleasant, Iowa, to Tabor and thence to Kansas. His sons intended to avenge the death of their brother Frederick. John Brown turned back to Iowa to meet the train and sent word to his sons to wait at Tabor.[59] On October 30, Watson Brown wrote his family from St. Charles, Iowa, that they were well and "in the company of a train of Kansas teams loaded with Sharps rifles and canon [sic]. I heard a report that Father had gone east. The travel very slow. You can write to us at Tabor. On our way we saw Garret [Gerrit] Smith, F. Douglas [Frederick Douglass] and other old friends. We have each a Sharps rifle."[60] Upon reaching Tabor, Watson Brown stayed to wait for his father while Salmon went on to Kansas.[61]

Dickey and Root's train—the final such caravan of 1856—arrived in Tabor in early November. The freight included the much-desired Sharps rifles, but antislavery leaders were uncertain about whether they could get them through to Kansas at the time, so they decided to store the arms and supplies in Tabor. These two hundred rifles, donated by the Massachusetts State Kansas Committee to the National Kansas Committee, were added to other items being stored there along with the older arms just brought by John Brown from Kansas.[62] Thus by late fall 1856, arms, equipment, and other goods "overfilled," as Maria Gaston had written, every conceivable storage place in and around Tabor, including the Todd house. The presence of such military supplies in town was just one sign of the increasing effectiveness of the Iowa route opened that year, and of the impending storm.

Proslavery partisans now knew that the tide of Northern emigrants could not be quashed by simply closing Missouri River access. In fact, by shutting down the river, western Missouri proslavery men had angered St. Louis riverboat interests and lost the support of merchants in the other Missouri River towns. And notwithstanding proslavery efforts to gain the upper hand by pleading with Southern states to send more emigrants, the number of arriving Southerners failed to offset free-state settlers. These failures, joined with the emergence of free-state guerrillas willing to fight against proslavery militias, sharply deflated the Southerners' cause.

# 6

## Escapes and Rescues

*Escaping through Tabor*

When the last wagon train, led by Milton C. Dickey and J. P. Root, left Tabor for Topeka toward the end of 1856, things settled down in the village for about six weeks. Then on December 18 came three men from Jackson County, Missouri, looking for two runaway slaves. Knocking at George Gaston's door to ask what the family had seen, the slavecatchers learned nothing, but as they stepped away one made the parting remark that they had great fears for Tabor. Villagers expected to see them again, this time with warrants to search the town. If that happened and the men took a close look, they would discover the arms and ammunition being stored there for antislavery forces in Kansas.[1]

In addition to this danger, the community actually already knew about the two runaways the slavecatchers were seeking. Just that fall Dr. Ira Blanchard of Civil Bend had been to Topeka, where he met with a group to plan the use of the new emigrant trail north across Iowa for aiding runaways. Shortly thereafter, the two people who had escaped from Lexington, Missouri, were on their way toward freedom, the slavehunters hard on their trail.[2] But this first effort went awry. Although Civil Bend folks listened for and heard "the far-off whistle of a coming train [on the underground railroad]," one of the waiting recipients admitted, "the rails are newly laid, and there are no tried conductors, over the long, uninhabited prairie between us and the Kansas bondmen." Consequently, "days and nights were passed of anxious watching for the arrival of the passengers," but they never came.[3]

What had gone wrong? The two men escaping from Missouri had gone via Kansas City into Kansas and then moved northward into Nebraska. But as they journeyed toward Civil Bend, Iowa, they lost their way and the slavecatchers caught up with them. Fearing that the fugitives had been seized, some Kansans wintering in Civil Bend with Elvira and Lester Platt went on a night rescue ride, but when they reached the prearranged meeting site, they found they were too late. The slavecatchers had taken their quarry into northwestern Missouri. At Linden (twenty-five miles southeast of Civil Bend), the captors lodged the captives temporarily in the hamlet's small jail.[4]

Caged inside a log calaboose—part of which was underground— the runaways soon discovered that some of the lower logs were decayed. After one of the men complained of severe chills and fever, they received from their captors a kettle of coals, which they used to burn through the logs. Then they dug themselves out. Disregarding the slavehunters' warning that Civil Bend and Tabor "people got rich by selling slaves to New Orleans," the two continued north through the brush and icy marshes of the Missouri River bottom. They were within a few miles of Civil Bend when a snowstorm came on. One of the two stopped to build a fire while the other went on, perhaps scouting out shelter, and they got separated from one another.[5]

Meanwhile, the Kansas boys, unaware of what had happened to the runaways and fearing the two would perish in the harsh, driving snowstorm, went out again and searched until dark. Misfortune nearly claimed one of the searchers, who got lost and had to grope through the snow until he found a deserted cabin. Soon he was inside pulling up floorboards to make a fire. Without matches and having no luck striking sparks with his knife, he tried firing his revolver into a bit of combustible material without success. Cold and weakened, he finally pulled out some cotton filling from his coat and got it ignited. The next morning his companions were highly relieved to see him open the door at the Platts's home.[6] Presently they learned that one of the runaways had made his way not to Civil Bend, but to Tabor. There, while awaiting word of his companion's fate, he stayed at George Gaston's place and helped cut wood for the household in a nearby forest.[7]

The other fugitive, they later heard, had gotten turned around during the snowstorm and was headed back where he had come from. At length he came to a cabin whose occupants treated him well. He stayed several days doing work for the family, but one night, having drunk too much for caution, the family members revealed their plans to return him to jail for the reward money. The runaway immediately took flight and, although followed for some time by a woman in the family, was able to make his way to Civil Bend. In his rush to get away, however, he had lost a shoe and was forced to walk several miles barefoot in crusted snow. At Civil Bend residents attended to his condition, and by the next day, warmly clothed and with fresh shoes, he traveled with a townsman to Tabor to rejoin his companion. No sooner had the fugitive and his helper left for Tabor than Civil Bend folks "heard the bloodhounds on the track. We suffered them to scent and search and yell all they chose, well knowing they were not keen enough to find their prey."[8]

The next passenger on the underground railroad who came through Civil Bend arrived three months later in late winter. It went easier this time, with Kansas guide John Armstrong (not to be confused with abolitionist John H. B. Armstrong of Appanoose County) taking his passenger, Judy Clarke, all the way to Ira Blanchard's place.[9] During the previous year Judy had been enslaved to the notorious George W. Clarke, who shared ownership with the equally notorious proslavery guerrilla H. T. Titus, who lived nearby in the vicinity of Lecompton, Kansas. George Clarke, a stocky, loose-talking proslavery man of some influence and a violent temper who had killed a free-state man, Thomas W. Barber, in December 1855, was a federal agent for the Pottawattamie Indians.

Clarke came into full control of Judy in late 1856 when Titus left for Nicaragua after free-state men attacked and burned his stronghold. It was not long before Clarke, angered by something, beat the enslaved woman severely with a chair. When she ran away, he advertised a reward for her return. Judy escaped detection for about six weeks and when caught by slavecatchers feigned happiness to be returning to her master. On their way to deliver her to Clarke, her captors stopped at a hotel for the evening. They sent Judy to work in the kitchen, and she used that opportunity to escape out the back door. Helped by a physician making house calls, she reached John Armstrong's house south of Lawrence and spent a few weeks in hiding there until late February, when they could risk traveling north.

Like Tabor's residents, those in Civil Bend continued to aid runaway slaves whenever they could despite the danger from proslavery militias. Elvira Platt recalled how haste, chance, luck, and risk coincided during underground railroad episodes. On one occasion, she remembered: "We had retired for the night and were just sinking into the arms of sleep, when there was a knock at our door and without waiting for a response the question came, 'Are you going to Tabor to-morrow? I have a passenger for you, can you take him? He is a young mulatto [and] the last to escape'" his slaveholder. Elvira and her husband recognized the voice as that of Dr. Ira Blanchard and opened the door to discuss how best to move the runaway from his place to their wagon.[10]

Lester Platt had nearly completed manufacturing two wagon-loads of shingles for delivery to Tabor. He and Elvira decided that he would drive the fully loaded wagon and she the second, partially loaded one, which would have "packages of shingles on one side while on the other they placed a comfortable bed of straw—all being covered with a large wagon sheet." The next morning, once Lester had things ready, Elvira got onto the driver's seat and drove one-half mile north to Blanchard's house, where, as her husband waited on the road, she turned into Blanchard's drive and parked close to the door. The young runaway crept out of the house and climbed into the wagon bed. With a snap of the reins, she moved her team and wagon onto the main track and proceeded northward behind her husband's wagon. Two neighbors who were in on the secret "stood in the door of their house waving their dish-towels to cheer [her] on in [her] perilous undertaking."

As soon as they reached uninhabited grassland, the runaway took the chance to sit up in the wagon for a while. But no sooner had he done so, revealing what Elvira considered a "little and symmetrical form" with "great pathetic eyes," than Lester spotted "a man mounted on a mule" galloping behind them, "apparently bent on overtaking our teams." Elvira hastily signaled the fugitive to hide once again. The approaching rider caught up with the wagons and "slacked the speed of his mule and kept pace with our teams for sometime, eyeing us closely but saying nothing." After a while, he spurred his mule past the wagons, and the Platts continued on their way until reaching the small settlement of Plum Hollow. There at the lone store in town was the traveler's mule hitched in front.

Lester called out that he needed to stop at the store for something, and so Elvira moved past, driving along at a relatively slow pace so that Lester would be able to catch up with her. The Platts knew that most people in Plum Hollow were "of Southern proclivities and of course were never entrusted with a knowledge of the movements of the Underground trains," even though the store's owner was genial and friendly. Hardly had Lester gone into the store than Elvira looked back to see that the rider of the mule had walked out, "mounted, and rode after me." As Elvira worried:

> For sometime he kept behind the wagon—then rode up on one side, now and then casting furtive glances into my face but not even venturing a greeting. I had asked the young man who harnessed my team [that morning], to give me the black-snake whip, which was loaded,[11] as I might need it for protection, and while this stranger followed in this suspicious way, I was nerving myself for the expected contest, feeling so strong I was sure that with one blow from the end of my whip I could lay him senseless, should he endeavor to take my passenger from me.

But soon, "spurring his splendid great mule," the man "rode rapidly away, while I found my tense muscles so relaxed I could scarcely have killed a mosquito." Upon reaching Tabor, Elvira turned into the hay barn of J. L. Smith, where the runaway slipped out of the wagon and climbed the ladder into the loft. From Tabor, one of the townsmen took him to the next station at Lewis, in Cass County, some sixty miles away.

Although Elvira never learned whether the runaway ended up in Chicago or Canada, she did learn more about her "pursuer" on the journey to Tabor. She happened to be visiting two years later with the storekeeper at Plum Hollow when the subject turned to life on the frontier. She mentioned liking the "independence of choosing our work" and gave this example: "I often preferred to turn teamster that I might drink in the pure oxygen rather than the heat of the cooking stove." He replied, "Yes . . . and you sometimes travelled in the interest of the Underground Railway, did you not?" As Elvira looked at him for further explanation, the Plum Hollow merchant told her that "the man on the mule was a friend, secretly, to our cause—that he had in some way learned that the young mulatto was on the road, and in a kind of instinctive way, such as came to all of us in those days he knew the boy was in our train, had stopped to tell the merchant and for his own amusement had rode on before my husband to test my ability as a conductor."[12]

## *Dred Scott and the Founding of the Republican Party*

The Kansas-Nebraska Act and the resulting bloodshed in Kansas transformed national politics. The same divisions that James Grimes exploited to win the 1854 gubernatorial election in Iowa increasingly appeared on the national level. By the mid-1850s the Whig Party was largely destroyed by its partisans' disagreements over slavery. In 1854 two-thirds of the Northern Democrats who had voted in favor of the Kansas-Nebraska Act lost their seats when angry constituents turned against them. The Know Nothings, so-called because the party's sponsor was a secret society whose members were supposed to claim they "knew nothing" if asked about it, enjoyed a brief run of success in 1854–1855 by preying on anxieties about Catholic—mainly German and Irish—immigration to the United States. But the party faltered because it alienated newly naturalized voters and failed to address the burning issue of slavery. Indeed, when the battle for Kansas made the slavery issue seem like the main threat to the republic, the irreconcilable differences between proslavery and antislavery Know Nothings sank the party's national prospects even as a new party committed to preventing the spread of slavery grew.

More and more antislavery politicians, whether originally Whigs or Democrats, took the same path that Grimes had: they allied themselves with Free Soilers and anyone else who opposed human bondage. In 1854 several such tentative coalitions dubbed themselves "Republican," and the name stuck. Nevertheless, the new party's future did not seem especially bright, and it did not make much of a showing in the midterm elections of that year. But by 1856 the party had won important elections in Ohio and Massachusetts, and it held its first national convention.

For the 1856 presidential election, the Democrats nominated James Buchanan, a party stalwart who had conveniently been out of the country serving as ambassador to England during the struggle over the Kansas-Nebraska Act. The Know Nothings, amid their death throes, nominated former president Millard Fillmore. The Republicans put forth a cautious platform, saying nothing about slavery where it already existed but calling for Kansas to be a free state and for all territories acquired in the future to be free as well. The new party's candidate was the hero of the 1846 conquest of California, John C. Fremont.

Democrat Buchanan won the three-way race with a plurality, but the Republicans made a good showing, coming in second. More important, as observers noted fearfully, the nation had divided largely on sectional lines: most of the Northern states (including Iowa) went Republican, while all of the Southern ones (except Maryland, which voted Know Nothing) went Democratic. In fact, the Republicans were not even on the ballot in the slave states. In the few Northern states that voted for the Democrats, the party won just barely half the vote.

Once in office, Buchanan sought to shift the problem of slavery to the courts—specifically, to the Supreme Court, where the case *Dred Scott v. John F. A. Sandford* was pending. This case began in the 1840s when Dred Scott sued the man who owned him for his freedom. Born into slavery, Scott had lived in the free state of Illinois and the territory of Wisconsin (including near Davenport in the part that became the Iowa Territory in 1838) with his master, an army doctor. He argued that he should have gained his freedom by virtue of living in areas where slavery was illegal—indeed, areas where slavery was forbidden by the Missouri Compromise. A lower court agreed, but a state court reversed the decision and was sustained by the federal circuit court, and so the case arrived in Washington, D.C., in February 1856.[13]

The court, led by Chief Justice Roger B. Taney of Maryland, a supporter of slavery, could have decided the case in several different ways. Three of those ways would have minimized the case's implications for the current political unrest plaguing the country: upholding the lower court's ruling, ruling that Scott was a noncitizen who had no standing to sue in a U.S. court, or deciding the case on its merits without setting a precedent. The fourth option was to issue a bold opinion that would address the constitutionality of all federal and territorial laws concerning slavery. Buchanan, hoping to avoid a fight in Congress, urged the court to think big.

In March 1857 Chief Justice Taney and six of his colleagues heeded Buchanan's call for a broad decision. Their opinion denied that Scott had the right to bring suit because he, and all African Americans (slave and free), belonged to an inferior class of beings who were not citizens and had no political or civil rights. Moreover, Taney continued, the federal government had no right to restrict its citizens' property rights in any respect. This meant neither Congress nor any territorial government—for example, that of Kansas—could prevent slaveholders from bringing slaves to or keeping them on federal land or in the territories. This opinion not only nullified the Kansas-Nebraska Act but also the Compromise of 1850 and the Missouri Compromise of 1820. It threw out nearly four decades of efforts to resolve the slavery issue through political means.

President Buchanan cheered the decision, believing that it cleared the way for a resolution to the conflict in Kansas, but many people thought quite differently. Antislavery Kansans had already drawn up and passed the Topeka Constitution, which barred slavery, in December 1855. Following the Scott decision in September 1857, proslavery Kansans drafted the Lecompten Constitution, permitting slavery. The territorial governor correctly judged that the antislavery forces outnumbered their foes by then, and in the October 1857 elections, free-state candidates won control of the territorial legislature. Well-aware that a majority of Kansas voters opposed the proslavery Lecompten Constitution, its backers forwarded it directly to Congress for approval. When Buchanan supported it, Northern Democrats protested mightily, nearly breaking the party in two. The president's credibility was shredded, and the nation grew increasingly polarized.

By the end of 1857 Americans who opposed slavery began to feel much as those in Kansas had felt during the bloody summer of 1856: besieged by the supporters of slavery, who not only refused to accept any limit on their ability to own other human beings, but also had no respect for the democratic process. Political solutions to this impasse seemed ever more unlikely, and many gave up on them altogether.

*The Transformation of Iowa's*
*Political Landscape*

Antislavery advocates in Iowa benefited from but also struggled in the political crosscurrents of the mid- to late 1850s. Amos Bixby wrote to his brother from Grinnell in 1855: "the miserable 'Know Nothings' has arisen just at this time to distract and divide the anti-slavery sentiment of the county. The truth is, the old political parties are dead as a door nail, and from their decaying remains all sorts of new parties are springing up, like toadstools from a summer dung heap."[14]

In this time of political realignment, Iowa Democrats, divided after suffering heavy losses following the passage of the Kansas-Nebraska Act, still banked on denouncing abolitionists and "black Republicans" (as they labeled members of the antislavery party) as threats to the Union. During elections, both parties held mass meetings and sponsored torchlight processions, bonfires, and bands. They hung banners and sang songs, and of course they sent out the stalwarts to do plenty of stump speaking in county seat towns and at local festivals to arouse popular interest.

This electioneering style was clearly evident in the 1859 campaigns for governor. Iowans from around the state went to several southern towns to see and hear Samuel Kirkwood, a former Democrat who had recently joined the Republican Party, debate Augustus C. Dodge, a Democrat and former U.S. senator who had just returned from four years as ambassador to Spain. At Washington, Iowa, the candidates' differences became starkly evident. Amid a procession with a brass band, Dodge—a proper gentleman of the old school, dignified in bearing—came riding into the town square in the town's finest carriage pulled by four splendid white horses. Kirkwood's supporters, looking to portray Dodge as an aristocrat, brought their own candidate—common, plainspoken, with simple manners and careless in dress—into the public square riding atop a lumber wagon bearing a hayrack and hitched to a yoke of oxen. A grinning Kirkwood chuckled "clear to the square at the homespun humor of it."[15]

Fugitive slaves were a chief topic of the Kirkwood-Dodge debates, with both candidates thinking they could benefit from the issue.[16] Kirkwood was trying to establish his antislavery credentials and capitalize on growing public antislavery sentiment while offsetting his prior affiliation with the Democratic Party and his slaveholding father and brothers.[17] Dodge aimed to stir up voter anger against abolitionists' failure to admit that slavery was constitutional and legal. At the Oskaloosa debate, Dodge asked Kirkwood whether he would obey the Fugitive Slave Law, to which the Republican replied, "I would not resist the enforcement of that Law, but before I would aid in capturing a fugitive slave I would suffer the penalty of the law, but I would not aid into carrying it into execution." Then Kirkwood asked Dodge whether he would assist in capturing a runaway slave, to which the Democrat replied: "I would. I would do whatever the law requires me to do."[18]

Kirkwood sharpened these questions at their debate two days later in Bloomfield. Attorney James Baird Weaver attended the event and wrote of it:

> Kirkwood drew a picture of a slave mother with a babe in her arms fleeing from bondage with her eye on the North Star. In close pursuit was her cruel master with his bloodhounds hard after her, just as she crossed the Iowa line from Missouri. Clenching his fists and advancing toward Dodge he demanded to know if he under such circumstances would turn that fleeing mother and her infant back to her pursuing master. Before the breathless multitude Kirkwood shouted at the top of his voice "Answer my question!" Dodge replied, "I would obey the law." Kirkwood retorted, "So help me, God, I would suffer my right arm to be torn from its socket before I would do such a monstrous thing."[19]

All this resonated with those at the debates, for they had been reading plenty about "fugitive slave" happenings in their newspapers—and some of them no doubt had been directly involved in either aiding or catching such fugitives.

As the political pendulum swung against defenders of slavery, Iowa Democrats attempted to divert voter attention from the issue to Kirkwood's personal character. The Republican candidate, they claimed, "smells rank and strong of sweat and dirt" and "don't know enough to keep himself clean." His supposed habit of "dressing like a scare-crow, or smelling like a cod-fish," they said, showed disrespect for others. His politics, like his habits, were old-fashioned, according to the Democrats: "the time has gone by when the contemptible trick of wearing a coat out at the elbows, or pants with a hole in the seat, can produce the least effect upon the voters of this state."[20]

In addition to underscoring Kirkwood's personal idiosyncrasies, Iowa Democrats worked to excite racial fears, encouraging the entrenched prejudice against blacks. Their best chance came in May 1859 with news of an ostensible scheme to encourage black migration into Iowa. Democratic newspapers picked up the story from the Ohio papers, which reported that an Iowa man, the Reverend

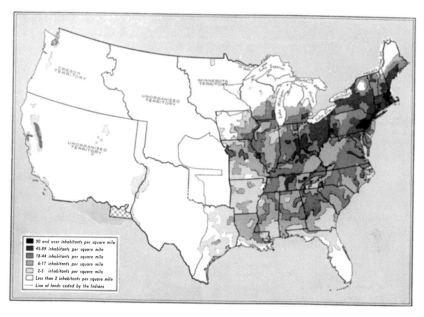

1. Density of U.S. population, 1850.

Source: G. O. Paulin, *Atlas of the Historical Geography of the United States* (Washington, DC: Carnegie Institution of Washington, 1932), plate 77a. Courtesy of the Carnegie Institution of Washington.

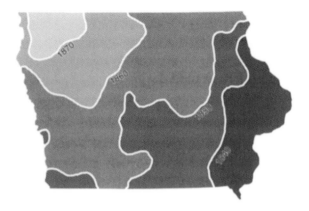

2. Settlement of Iowa, 1840–1870.

Source: Robert R. Dykstra, *Bright Radical Star: Black Freedom and White Supremacy on the Hawkeye Frontier* (Cambridge, MA: Harvard University Press, 1993), inset in map 1.1, xvi.

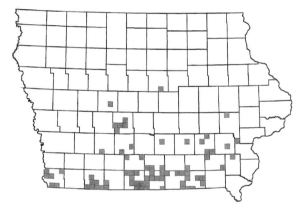

3. Iowa townships with 20 percent or more citizens born in the South, 1856. Created and © by Lowell J. Soike.

*facing page*

4. Routes and stations of the underground railroad in Iowa, with locations of related museums. The size of the arrows indicates the relative extent of underground railroad activity in the area.

Created and © by Lowell J. Soike.

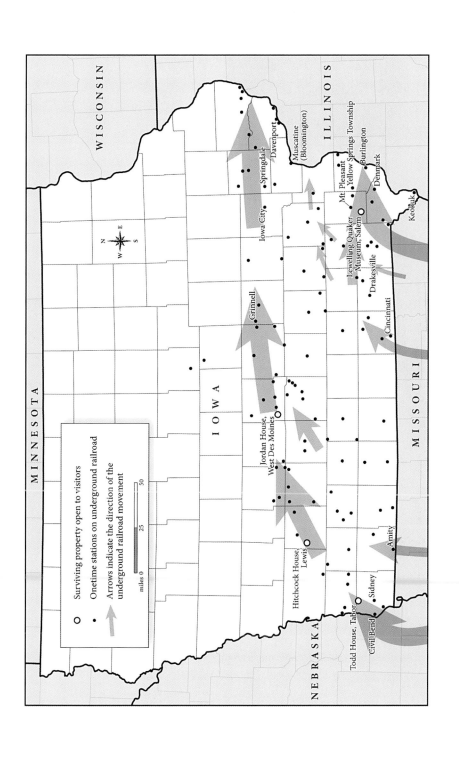

5. Reverend Asa Turner, a Congregationalist leader in Denmark, Iowa.

Courtesy of the State Historical Society of Iowa, Iowa City.

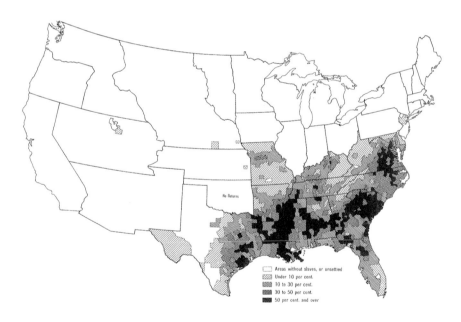

6. Percentage of slaves in U.S. population, 1860.

G. O. Paulin, *Atlas of the Historical Geography of the United States* (Washington, DC: Carnegie Institution of Washington, 1932), plate 68B. Courtesy of the Carnegie Institution of Washington.

7. Henderson and Elizabeth Lewelling's house, where Salem's justice of the peace began discussions with slavecatchers who were attempting to retrieve the Walker and Fulcher families for Missouri slaveholder Ruel Daggs. Courtesy of Lewelling Quaker Museum, Salem, Iowa.

8. Alexander Clark's house (on the right with stairs) at Third and Chestnut streets in Muscatine, Iowa. Clark hid Jim White from slavecatchers here during the fall of 1848, when the town was known as Bloomington.

Photograph by J. G. Evans, 1866–1867, from the collections of the Musser Public Library, Muscatine. All rights reserved.

9. Charlotta Gordon Pyles, who escaped from slavery in Kentucky along with her family and their former owner, Frances Gordon. They settled in Keokuk, Iowa.

Courtesy of Lee County Historical Society, Keokuk, Iowa.

10. Edwin James, a naturalist and abolitionist who lived near Burlington, Iowa.

Source: Johnson Brigham, *Iowa: Its History and Its Foremost Citizens*, vol. 1 (Chicago: S. J. Clarke, 1918), 215.

11. Edwin James's house, where runaway slaves often found help. The house is in ruins today, but this 1938 photograph, taken by the Federal Writers' Project (Iowa), shows what it originally looked like.

Source: Federal Writers' Project (Iowa), *A Guide to Burlington, Iowa* (Burlington, IA: Acres-Blackmar, 1938), 51.

12. Marion Hall (in the center of this 1866 photograph) once stood at North Fourth and Washington streets in Burlington, Iowa. The fugitive slave hearing in 1855 about the runaway named Dick took place here, as did the federal trial involving Ruel Daggs and the townsfolk of Salem.

Courtesy of the Burlington (Iowa) Public Library.

13. Iowa governor James W. Grimes.

Courtesy of the State Historical Society of Iowa, Iowa City.

14. Dr. Ira D. Blanchard operated a station of the underground railroad at Civil Bend on the Missouri River in southwestern Fremont County in Iowa.

Courtesy of the Kansas State Historical Society, Topeka.

15. Stephen F. Nuckolls, a founder of Nebraska City, Nebraska, was the owner of Eliza and Celia Grayson, who escaped to Chicago despite his determined efforts to get them back.

Courtesy of the Nebraska City Historical Society.

16. William Maxson provided room and board to John Brown's recruits while they trained for battle near Springdale, Iowa, during the winter of 1857–1858.

Courtesy of the State Historical Society of Iowa, Iowa City.

17. William and Hanna Maxson's house. Imagine how crowded this modest homestead would have been when it housed the seven Maxsons and eleven of John Brown's men.

Courtesy of the State Historical Society of Iowa, Iowa City.

18. The twelve people John Brown and his men liberated in December 1858 stayed in this Tabor schoolhouse for several days in early February 1859.

Courtesy of the Kansas State Historical Society, Topeka.

19. James Jordon, a farmer and Iowa state senator at the time that John Brown's men and twelve fugitives stayed at his house overnight on February 17, 1859.

Courtesy of Special Collections, State Historical Society of Iowa, Des Moines.

20. Josiah B. Grinnell, about 1889, an outspoken abolitionist who often gave sanctuary to runaway slaves, prompting the Democratic press to label him and the other residents of the Congregationalist town he founded and named after himself as fanatics.

Courtesy of the State Historical Society of Iowa, Iowa City.

21. Sam and Jane Harper were two of the twelve people whom John Brown and his men liberated from farms in Vernon County, Missouri, on December 20, 1858. In Springdale, Iowa, where the fugitives rested before heading for Canada, the Quaker justice of the peace, John Painter, conducted their marriage ceremony.

Courtesy of the Kansas State Historical Society, Topeka.

22. William Penn Clarke, a prominent lawyer, politician, and abolitionist, aided John Brown and runaway
slaves seeking help.

Courtesy of the State Historical Society of
Iowa, Iowa City.

23. Jesse Bowen, an abolitionist and active member of the
Kansas Central Committee of Iowa at Iowa City.

Courtesy of the State Historical Society of Iowa, Iowa City.

24. Jesse Bowen's house, where John Brown spent an evening in early 1859 and then was spirited out of Iowa City toward Springdale to evade men on the lookout for him.

Courtesy of the State Historical Society of Iowa, Iowa City.

25. Edwin (left) and Barclay (right) Coppoc of Springdale joined John Brown in the attack on Harpers Ferry. Edwin was captured and hanged, while Barclay escaped and returned to Iowa.

Courtesy of the State Historical Society of Iowa, Iowa City.

26. Gov. Samuel Kirkwood delayed Virginia's effort to extradite Barclay Coppoc for his role in the raid on Harpers Ferry while Iowa legislators warned the young man of his imminent arrest.

Courtesy of the State Historical Society of Iowa, Iowa City.

27. Jefferson Logan escaped from slavery in Missouri and moved to Des Moines, where he later achieved local prominence and respect within the community.

Courtesy of Special Collections, State Historical Society of Iowa, Des Moines.

28. The Reverend John Todd's house, one of the few surviving reminders of Congregationalist Tabor's involvement in the antislavery movement. It is now a museum run by the Tabor Historical Society.

Photograph by John Zeller, State Historical Society of Iowa, Des Moines.

29. The Reverend George B. Hitchcock's house in Lewis, Iowa, where the Congregationalist minister sheltered Missouri fugitives from slavery during the 1850s. Today the house is a National Historic Landmark and is open to the public.

Photograph by John Zeller, State Historical Society of Iowa, Des Moines.

30. The house of James Jordan, an active antislavery man, who offered sanctuary here to runaway slaves and to men like John Brown who helped them. Today a museum with an exhibit on the underground railroad, the house is run by the West Des Moines Historical Society.

Photograph by John Zeller, State Historical Society of Iowa, Des Moines.

John S. Prescott, was telling black Ohioans that they would have a better life if they settled with him in northwestern Iowa.[21] Prescott had arrived in Iowa at the Spirit Lake vicinity shortly after an Indian group had killed settlers there in March 1857. His aim was to buy land and lay out a town, with the proceeds from land sales helping him establish an academy and a college. He purchased some of the slain settlers' property and on May 11 conducted the first religious service in the county at the former Gardner family cabin.

Considered by his audience "a speaker of extraordinary ability and one to whom it was a pleasure to listen," Prescott was remembered by a fellow Methodist colleague in his earlier Wisconsin ministries as a skillful fundraiser and "a man of sharp, decisive movements, sometimes angular in his opinions and measures, but full of energy and not afraid of hard work."[22] Locally in Dickinson County, Prescott also came to be known as someone who "lacked discretion, was impatient and excitable, and while he was very enthusiastic in everything he undertook, he was, at the same time, visionary and often unpractical and impracticable." His outspoken support for the antislavery movement was well-known back in eastern Wisconsin, where he had "strenuously and vehemently opposed the repeal of the Missouri Compromise" and the "outrage in Kansas and Nebraska." In May 1859 people in Iowa learned just how radical his views were.[23]

In that month, many Democratic papers reprinted portions of articles from an Ohio Republican paper, the *Xenia Torchlight*, describing an evening meeting at an African American Baptist church in town. There, Dr. Prescott had detailed "the inducements that North Western Iowa offered for their [the congregants'] emigration." As he had done at similar meetings in Washington, Philadelphia, and Pittsburgh, he explained what he called "the liberal laws of Iowa with regard to colored residents." Prescott showed "how, in that new country, they could occupy whole counties, to the exclusion of the whites, becoming land owners and respectable farmers instead of mere day-laborers—hewers of wood and drawers of water."[24]

Another meeting followed four days later at which "the church was crowded by a large colored audience" to hear a committee report and resolutions. Those leading the meeting began by noting that "the colored people aspire to something more than the position of menials in Northern towns; that they wish to rise to the dignity of cultivators of the soil, and independent land-owners, but that the high price of land, and the unjust prejudices of the whites, render this impossible here," and so if "they can settle in a community by themselves, with the power to manage their own affairs, they would thus vastly improve their condition." They resolved to cooperate with brethren in the East and Cincinnati "to organize a system of Western emigration to the cheap and fertile lands."[25]

Prescott's politically incendiary action in Ohio handed Iowa Democrats a golden opportunity to stoke racial fears. "White Men of Iowa," asked the *Leon Pioneer* editor, "are you prepared for this? We know that many of you have voted the Republican ticket, but we have no knowledge that any of you ever voted it to your own degradation." The idea of black migration to Iowa had just begun, he warned, so "let the people look to it. If they are not willing to be put on a level with niggers, let them, like *white men*, set forth their rights, and stand to them." The editor's rambling diatribe was followed by another in the next issue, in which he asked, "Will they permit the free niggers of the Union to be dumped among us?" He then linked this dire possibility to the Republicans, for in Ohio Prescott "was joyfully received by the Republicans of Xenia, and all encouragement was given him." Why did the Ohio Republicans cheer Prescott? Not, in the editor's opinion, because of his efforts to help African Americans improve their lot, but because the blacks would, by going "to Iowa, burden and curse half a score of excellent counties with their filthy rabble."[26]

The Republican editor of the *Dubuque Weekly Times* defended Prescott. "The Negro race in the United States has at best a hard lot," the newspaperman wrote, being "shunned and proscribed in Nineteen of the Thirty-four States, and enslaved in the remainder." The mistreatment occurred even though "they are in the main an industrious, law-abiding and intelligent class," and he claimed that "if Iowa shall close its doors against them, it will commit an unjustifiable and un-Christian act." Noting that "the editor of the *Dubuque Times* has a strong *penchant* for niggers," the editor of the Davenport *Daily Iowa State Democrat* sourly countered that people of Iowa were not prepared to "embrace a colony of the off-scourings of the world." The editor of the *Cedar Rapids Cedar Democrat* joined in, writing, "If there are any negroes to colonize, send them to Africa, where God placed them"; and the editor of the *Anamosa Gazette* remarked: "we do not nor will not live among them. We want to live among white people. And when we cannot we will leave the state."[27]

The sly editor of the McGregor *North Iowa Times* saw in the imminent arrival of the African American settlers to Iowa hypocrisy on the part of Ohio abolitionists: "It may be that during the present summer and autumn the avenues of travel through northern Iowa will be enlivened by small armies of dark 'citizens' kindly furnished to our State by the excessively humane agitators of the east. These tender hearted fellows first agitate to get the negro to run away from a southern home and then they charitably beg money of the public to ship them out of their sight."[28]

Two of seven resolutions adopted by the Democratic Party state convention on June 23, 1859, opposed black immigration. These items charged that the Republican policy of inviting people of African descent into the state would bring "cheap negro labor into direct competition with the labor of the white man" and that Iowa would "become the great receptacle of the worthless population of the slaveholding States, to the exclusion of an equal number of free white laborers."[29] Samuel Kirkwood weathered the Democrats' attack, successfully pleading ignorance of Prescott's project and claiming it all to be "nothing but a Democratic trick to catch votes." No evidence ever appeared that Prescott's scheme succeeded in prompting any groups of black emigrants to enter Iowa.[30] Kirkwood went on to win the governorship in October 1860, putting Iowa firmly in the ranks of the Republican Party on the eve of disunion.

## The Otoe War

But even before Kirkwood's election, the battle lines had hardened along the borders between Iowa, Missouri, and Kansas. Every new conflict between supporters and opponents of slavery embittered both sides. Late in 1858 occurred the incident most remembered by southwest Iowa antislavery activists, one they called the "Otoe War" because of the Nebraska county where the man at the center of the conflict, slaveholder Stephen F. Nuckolls, lived (see figure 15).[31] Nuckolls held five people in slavery, three of them female house servants, at his home in Nebraska City. Doubtless, given the unsettled status of slavery in the territory in 1858, he was aware that other slaveholders in the area were selling off their enslaved blacks south, where they would have a harder time escaping.[32] But Nuckolls's own servants remained unsold, perhaps because he had not gotten around to it or because he thought they would not be inclined, or not dare, to run. A confident man who was prospering from the massive westward movement of settlers up the Missouri River and through Nebraska City, he did not foresee what was coming.

Nuckolls was an ambitious Virginian who had moved to Missouri in his early twenties and then founded Nebraska City in 1854. Being "wealthy, energetic and enterprising" and having "many friends and sympathizers," he was involved in a sawmill and construction, banking, freight operations, and mercantile stores. He also had political clout (in 1859 he would serve in Nebraska's territorial legislature) and owned the *Nebraska City News*. But in November 1858 the thirty-three-year-old developer experienced a setback in his go-getting operations.[33]

On Thanksgiving evening, two of the women he held as slaves, Eliza and Celia Grayson, escaped from the home that Nuckolls shared with his wife, Lucinda. Awakening to find them gone, the couple were doubtless in an uproar, for, as one newspaper editor put it, "The Nuckolls family are naturally excitable, and strongly prejudiced against Abolitionists."[34] Stephen quickly advertised a reward of $200 (about $5,600 in 2011) in a handbill dated November 26 and in the *Nebraska City News* on the twenty-seventh for the return "of [his] two negro women, who were enticed away from [his] house on the night of Nov. 25."[35]

On the morning of November 26, he and several other men rode down to his ferry, crossed the Missouri River to the Iowa side, and aimed for nearby Civil Bend, the place to which he suspected the Grayson women had been "enticed." Arriving at the door of Dr. Ira Blanchard's house, Nuckolls told him about the two runaways and asked that "if he saw anything of the fugitives, he would send them back to him." But the doctor "could not promise to send them back, as that might require force, but if he saw them, he would send him word."[36] With this less than satisfactory assurance, Nuckolls and his men rode to Tabor, the reputed next stop on the underground railroad. He probably contacted his two brothers who ran a store in Glenwood (the next stage stop, fourteen miles north of Tabor) and another brother in Pacific City. Almost at once he also sent men to watch river crossings at Silver Creek and the Nishnabotna River.[37]

At Tabor, the slaveowner inquired about his missing property while others in his group reconnoitered the town for clues. From what they learned, Nuckolls became "convinced that the girls could not have passed that way," and, as Elvira Platt wrote a few days later, "he returned to our place with the firm conviction that we had them concealed in our midst." Exasperated and believing that the runaways had not yet managed to escape the Missouri River bottom, he posted men "at different points to watch by day—and at night the prairie grass was lighted, so that no object could move without being visible."[38] A day and a night passed with nothing to show for it but some burned grassland and weary watchers. The slavehunters then started to suspect that free black residents of the Civil Bend neighborhood must somehow have had a hand in all this, an accusation Nuckolls leveled in an item in his newspaper.[39]

Stewing on these rumors, by Wednesday, December 1, Nuckolls and his Nebraska City friends decided to storm Civil Bend. About twenty to thirty Nebraska City horsemen, described by one anti-slavery man as "a mob of teamsters wintering in the city," ferried across the cold Missouri River to the Iowa landing and moved toward the Civil Bend neighborhood.[40] Alarm spread among locals that men armed with revolvers and clubs were descending on the town.

The first part of the mob headed for the residence of the late Joseph Garner, a free black man whose family continued to live there. The slavecatchers found two young men, the Garner brothers, Josiah (age twenty) and Henry (age nineteen). The pack of men pulled up the flooring and tore down adjacent outbuildings in search of Eliza and Celia Grayson. They then seized the two youths, and, under the pretense of taking them to jail in Sidney, the county seat, they took them to the nearby woods and assaulted them. Elvira Platt later wrote that Nuckolls's men, "with the hope of extorting something from them," grabbed hold of the Garner brothers and "commenced their tortures. One was stripped, tied to a tree and whipped with rods cut from the forest—while another was hung till he was nearly strangled, and a fire built near him, apparently with the intention of burning him, if he did not confess." Terrified, one of the prisoners, desperate to ease his suffering and save his and his brother's lives, gave the slavehunters the names of another young black man in Civil Bend, John Williamson (age twenty-three), and J. F. Merritt, a young white fellow, as those who had brought the runaways across the river.[41]

Leaving two men to guard the two prisoners along with threats "to return and kill them if they had not told the truth," the remaining men "mounted and rode furiously toward the house of R[euben] S. Williams," evidently thinking Williamson or the fugitives were to be found there.[42] Williams, at work in a nearby field, noticed a crowd at his house and walked into his yard to find men leaving his house after searching it. When Williams told the slavecatchers that theirs was a mean, lawless business, Stephen Nuckolls drew his pistol and one of his brothers swung his cane hard against Williams's head. The blow badly injured Williams and left him with lasting damage.

The Nebraska City men then rode to the home of Dr. Smith, an enfeebled elderly man, and forced their way in. Inside they "sought every nook and corner—then out-houses, sheds and hay stacks were examined, and in order that no Yankee trick should be played on them, they not only stamped on the hay, but thrust pitch forks into it." They did the same at the house of a man named Egbert Avery up the road. Elsewhere in Civil Bend, the invaders knocked down one person and fired at another while they went from one property to the next.[43]

Meanwhile, another group of slavecatchers was on the hunt for J. F. Merritt, the other man whom Nuckolls's prisoners had fingered as having helped Celia and Eliza Grayson escape. In a letter to his brother on the heels of these events, Merritt reported that Lester Platt had rushed into his house to warn him that the posse was on its way. He remembered, "I took my gear and ran about two miles to get to a place of security." In hot pursuit, Nuckolls's vigilantes "surrounded [him] three times." He was defenseless, he later told his brother: "I had no weapons and therefore [they] could do what they pleased; they were on horse and I on foot." At one point they nearly did Merritt in: "They smashed me with clubs and fists until I broke and ran, when S[tephen] Nuckols fired at me, the ball passed to the right of my head." Fortunately, it was nearly dark, and in the shadows Merritt got away.[44]

At day's end, the mob returned to Nebraska City by way of the Garner place, pausing to threaten all there that "if the whereabouts of the runaways was not discovered," they would come back tomorrow "to kill the boys and 'clean out the Bend.'"[45] The next day, despite ice now clogging the river, Stephen Nuckolls and some seventy men crossed into Iowa again for more illegal searches. Sturgis Williams (Reuben's nephew) of Tabor happened to be at the sawmill in Civil Bend when a man named Paul casually remarked that several men were riding up. A Nuckolls man immediately clubbed Paul over the head, "cutting a gash and causing the blood to flow freely" with a blow that "brought him to the ground."[46]

On this second day of the search for the Grayson women, Stephen Nuckolls again went to Dr. Blanchard's house, where the injured Garner brothers had been taken for safety and medical care during the previous night. Nuckolls, having heard that the doctor had harbored runaways in the past, demanded to search his place. Blanchard acquiesced:

> An underground room used for a kitchen, was most thoroughly examined—iron pointed cans sounded the floor for a hollow spot, and as there was no place in the wall unexposed, except where a dish-cupboard stood, the dishes were all taken out, and that removed, that they might examine the masonry behind it. No secret door, opening with a spring, as in days of old, being found, the men expressed themselves satisfied, and to prevent the necessity of such trouble thereafter, they wrote a notice stating that they had searched and were satisfied there was no passage into the Under-Ground Railway behind that dish-cupboard.[47]

In the meantime, the Civil Bend residents had not borne the invasion from Nebraska City idly. They sent word to their Tabor friends via Egbert Avery and another man, while J. F. Merritt started for Sidney to get the county sheriff and district attorney. Avery pulled into Tabor an hour before midnight, and within the hour some twenty-five men collected at the house of George Gaston. They opened boxes of guns intended for the antislavery forces in the battle for Kansas, and soon they were on their way to Civil Bend.

Hurrying toward Sidney on this deadly cold night, Merritt lost his way and did not get there until sunrise. Then, he later recalled, "I got the sheriff with two lawyers and hurried back. When we got to the school house, there were about 100 armed men of our party," the men from Tabor having arrived. Most of the Nebraskans had already left, but during the next two or three days the antislavery men rounded up some sixteen of Nuckolls's rabble and served them with warrants filed with J. C. Larimor, justice of the peace at Sidney. The warrants, one of which was against the men who had tortured the Garner brothers, were "served on about 15 or 16 of the company, who immediately gave themselves up and accompanied the constable to the magistrate's office." Several of the prisoners appealed for and were granted postponement of the court examination. Most were allowed to go home across the river for the night. Other warrants were also written and issued during the evening.[48]

When court convened the next day, December 3, however, many onlookers but few of the accused were present. The court granted the defense motion to subpoena John Williamson, but only on the condition that a guard would accompany the officer bearing the subpoena to make sure the slavecatchers were not using the legal maneuver simply to get hold of the young black man. During the afternoon several men were brought in, including Williamson. Some were placed under guard, and others, who "agreed to enter into bonds for their appearance at Court," were released. Stephen F. Nuckolls, claiming to be unable to cross the river, sent a letter requesting that a postponement be granted. Feelings ran high while people in Nebraska City and Civil Bend waited for the court to open, and a few who became primed with liquor "pitched into J. F. Merritt and gave him a beating."[49]

During the evening of December 4, Stephen Nuckolls crossed the river by laying boards on the ice, accompanied by two attorneys and about forty-five supporters. Confident as ever, the slaveowner filed a warrant under the Fugitive Slave Act for arrest of his runaway slaves. In compliance with the law, the authorities diligently but fruitlessly searched the Civil Bend neighborhood during the evening and next morning. When court convened on December 5, the parties agreed to waive any examinations and dismissed all the men charged except for Stephen Nuckolls, W. B. Hail, and G. Hail, the three involved "in arresting and whipping the negroes, [who] entered into bonds to assure their appearances at Court."[50] With that, court adjourned, and the Civil Bend invasion known as the Otoe War ended. The battles in court would continue long into 1859, however, as would Nuckolls's search for his property.

## The Aftermath

So where had Celia and Eliza Grayson gone after escaping from the Nuckolls's home? The Garner youth who had given his torturers the name of John Williamson while being beaten had told the truth. The Garner brothers' buddy, a shrewd small-time trader who traveled back and forth between Civil Bend and Nebraska City "buying butter, eggs, etc., of the farmers and selling cheap jewelry, trinkets, etc.," had gotten to know the Grayson women during his sales calls. He and Merritt had helped them cross the river Thanksgiving evening and had taken them to Blanchard's place. By next morning's light, Blanchard had taken the Graysons to Tabor and urged his friends to act with haste before hurrying home himself. Eliza and Celia stayed that day with a Mr. Ladd near Tabor, while Nuckolls and his men were searching the town for the first time. By evening the two women were on their way again, tucked in a covered wagon.[51]

Their escorts, Origen Cummings (a deacon in the Tabor Congregational Church) and a wagon driver whose name was not recorded, worked their way northeast, searching for places to cross the many streams and rivers. The going was slow, for it was a moonless, cloudy night and Cummings had to walk ahead of the team with a lantern in his hand so that the driver could see the road. Fortunately, Silver Creek was passable, as was the West Nishnabotna River at White Cloud, both of which they crossed before Nuckolls's scouts arrived. Once beyond these risky points, the party traveled through largely uninhabited land toward the Lewis settlement in Cass County, another Congregationalist outpost. Their destination was Oliver Mills's farm, located one-half mile north of Lewis.[52]

Believing themselves "closely pursued by Nuckolls and his men," the next conductors quickly headed east, along a route of the underground railroad that took fugitives across Cass and northwest Adair counties into southern Guthrie and Dallas counties before getting to the Des Moines vicinity, then on toward Grinnell in Poweshiek County and eventually across the Mississippi River into Illinois at Clinton or Davenport. The only other stop where the Graysons are known to have rested on their way to Chicago was in Clinton County, at the farm of Robert Lee Smith. Writing about his boyhood, Robert's son W. L. Smith recalled that his father was an independent-minded farmer-blacksmith living near DeWitt in Clinton County. "The first black persons I ever saw were two girls," he remembered, "whose names were Celia and Eliza." They "stayed in our house for weeks, waiting for the [Mississippi] river to freeze over at Camanche so it would be safe to cross on the ice."[53]

But the story of escape did not end here, for the court cases stemming from the invasion of Civil Bend remained to be heard. The trial of the men who had beaten and whipped Josiah and Henry Garner came first, in early June 1859, and was hotly disputed. Defending the arrested men, Nuckolls and W. B. and G. Hail, was a lawyer named Chapman, while the Garners were represented by Dr. Ira Blanchard, who had become guardian of the children after their father, Joseph Garner, had died. In short order Chapman and Blanchard were in "a warm dispute" that raised feelings "by no means friendly." After each man accused the other of lying, "Chapman struck Blanchard in the face, whereupon he was tried upon the charge of *Assault* and *Battery*,' and fined fifty dollars without appeal, which not being able to pay, he was committed to jail."[54] When the trial resumed in the September term of the Fremont County District Court, the jury delivered to the three defendants a verdict of guilty for carrying out "an assault with intent to commit great bodily injury" and imposed fines: in addition to court costs, Stephen Nuckolls was required to pay $100 (roughly $2,800 in 2011) and the Hails $50 (about $1,400) each.[55]

Then there was the case of *Williams v. Nuckolls* concerning compensation for the Nebraska City slaveholder's illegal, forcible search of Reuben S. Williams's property and the permanent head injuries Williams received. Eventually in mid-1860 a jury found Nuckolls guilty and awarded Williams $8,000 (about $223,000 in 2011), but in the end the slaveholder paid his victim just $2,500 (roughly $69,800), plus jury fees. (Several years later when Nuckolls happened to be at Nebraska City visiting friends, the barn that Williams built with the money obtained from the verdict mysteriously burned down.) The *Garner v. Nuckolls* case ended in a settlement, with the slaveholder paying the Garners $6,000 (about $167,000).[56]

The final court case stemming from the Otoe War began in December 1859, one year after Eliza and Celia Grayson had escaped, when Stephen Nuckolls brought suit in the Second Judicial Court of Nebraska Territory against sixteen people, including Reuben S. Williams, George B. Gaston, and Lester W. Platt. He demanded $10,000 (about $279,000 in 2011) in compensation for the value of two slaves who, he alleged, had been abducted by these men. The defendants sought to quash the suit, objecting that Nuckolls did not have enough evidence to prove their involvement. But the judge overruled this petition, finding that the Nebraska man had enough information to file the charges. Ultimately, however, the case seems to have come to nothing.[57]

Even as the Graysons succeeded in reaching Illinois and Nuckolls and his allies faced legal action, the slaveholder continued to search for his human property. His luck seemed to brighten in November 1860, when he received a letter stating that Eliza Grayson was in Chicago and the letter-writer knew where to find her.[58] At that time some 955 blacks lived in Chicago, making up less than 1 percent of the city's 109,260 residents. Eliza, described as a "stout and sharp girl," had found work as a housekeeper with Mary Beebe, who operated a "house of ill fame" at 315 South Clark Street. The brothel was in a mainly residential neighborhood made up of single-story houses, several blocks south of Lake and Water streets (then the principal commercial roads). Here lived about three-fourths of the black population, interspersed among the white inhabitants.[59]

To one of the white prostitutes there, Eliza had told in confidence "her story of escape and former condition." Unfortunately, the woman let the tale slip to a man who saw in it a chance to make some money. He coerced Eliza into revealing the name of the man who had owned her and where she had come from. Then he and a confederate wrote to Nuckolls, asking $200 (about $5,600 in 2011) for Eliza's return, which he agreed to. The plan hatched by the Chicago men "was to go to the house in the night time, knock her down and render her senseless and then put her in the box of a peddler's wagon and carry her out of the State in this manner." But Nuckolls, uneasy about the idea, "determined to come here and obtain her."[60]

Given his unhappy experience acting without a warrant at Civil

Bend, he decided this time to stop in Springfield, Illinois, to procure one from Stephen A. Corneau, U.S. commissioner under the Fugitive Slave Act. Despite taking a legal course, however, Nuckolls had miscalculated again. Although people in most of Illinois were helpful to masters recovering their runaways, those living in northern Illinois were far less so. Slavecatchers entered Chicago at their own risk. In this region, "successful returns were accomplished without legal action" and only if the slaveowner went about it "quietly and without being discovered."[61]

Nuckolls, warrant in hand, went to Chicago ignorant of the strength of antislavery feeling there and handed the document to U.S. Commissioner Philip A. Hoyne, whose job included appointing a deputy marshal to assist in apprehending Eliza for her owner. But try as he might, Hoyne found no deputy marshal willing to serve the warrant. Finally, he turned to a muscular local political hack, Jake Newsome—a large man in weight and height who was affiliated with the Democratic Party. In the early evening on November 13, Newsome and Nuckolls drove an open two-wheeled carriage down South Clark Street to Mary Beebe's house. They found no one at home except "a girl named Mattie and the colored girl, Eliza."[62]

Seeing Nuckolls, Eliza immediately "begged of him that he would not carry her away," and Mattie also pleaded on her behalf until one of the men drew a pistol on her. Eliza resisted stubbornly, but to no avail, for "in spite of her cries and implorings, she was dragged into a hack, stationed outside." Holding Eliza between them, Nuckolls and Newsome drove toward the jail, intending to keep her there overnight. But it was not to be.[63] Whether Mattie ran for help or people nearby heard Eliza's cries is not known, but somehow the neighborhood's black residents fast awakened to what was going on and gathered to pursue the carriage. Quickly changing plans "for their own safety," Nuckolls and Newsome headed instead to the jail at the nearby armory. But despite their efforts, the carriage "came to a stand still in a literally 'dark and angry sea,' dark much, and getting angry very fast." Over the surging crowd Newsome bellowed out "*Police, Police*," and to his surprise some officers "actually came" and agreed to put Eliza "into the City Lockup, at the Armory. . . , quartered for the night with an inebriated Biddy." Newsome and Nuckolls meanwhile quickly walked away.[64] But the excited crowd continued to swarm about the armory. "You would have thought their 'queen bee' was shut up," wrote the *Tribune* reporter, "but it wasn't anybody's queen, only a young colored woman named Eliza."[65] The *Tribune* was an antislavery paper, and its reporter clearly enjoyed the missteps of Nuckolls and his allies, while admiring the determination of Eliza's black neighbors to rescue her.

Nuckolls's luck then went from bad to worse. Perhaps thinking the crowd would melt away by the time he returned, he went about getting a warrant from "Justice DeWolf against the girl, Eliza, for disorderly conduct, and Deputy Sheriff George Anderson, attempted to remove her from the lock-up to the jail." But the crowd had not given up. Anderson "had hardly got out of the door with his charge, however, before she was wrenched from his grasp and with the rapidity of lightning hurried down Adams street by the agents of the U. G. R. R. [underground railroad], and removed to a place of safety." The sheriff "was left sprawling in the mud, his new election hat battered out of shape, and an infuriated crowd of negroes with clubs, threatening his life. He at last managed to make his escape."[66] The crowd, still agitated, next headed up South Clark Street. Some had a mind to tear down Beebe's brothel, while others wanted to rough up a man whom they believed to be implicated in Eliza's seizure. Stephen Nuckolls "was only saved from violence by placing a policeman's badge upon him and marching him under escort of a strong police force to the Briggs House [a hotel]."[67] At last, about midnight, the crowd broke up and people went home.

The next day Stephen Nuckolls blamed Deputy Sheriff George Anderson for the loss of Eliza and demanded that the officer pay him the value of his slave. But others identified a more serious matter: Jake Newsome "never was sworn [in as a deputy] at all and served the writ without authority." As a result, he would probably be investigated by the grand jury of the U.S. Court currently in session. On November 20 the grand jury brought in indictments against Justice DeWolf, who had issued the warrant for Eliza's arrest; Deputy Anderson, who had executed it; and seven others—three of them black—for violating the Fugitive Slave Act by preventing Nuckolls from taking Eliza back into slavery.[68] Nuckolls, however, was in no mood to accept anything less than the recovery of his lost property or reimbursement for her full value. He told a reporter he would "spend $20,000 'in following the thing up,' if necessary." The reporter continued: "He avers that he has got plenty of money and is willing to spend it in this way. He has two or three other fugitives formerly belonging to him now in this city, and says there are several more here who belong to his brother."[69]

Others shared his anger. A newspaper editor in McGregor, Iowa, viewed Eliza's escape as the unlawful act of a mob, when "at 10 o'clock at night the negro was got out amid the hurrahs of the crowd and is now in Canada without doubt. This we suppose is giving to the South her 'rights under the Constitution!'" But that was tame compared with the *Chicago Tribune* reporter's coverage. He mocked his paper's competitor, the *Times and Herald*, for its exaggerated "daily moanings":

> In the presence of thousands assembled, a mob of drunken and infuriated negroes forcibly overrides the constituted authority of the constitution of the United States, and rescues a fugitive from the custody of the law, amid general rejoicings and midnight howls! Who can doubt henceforth the strength of the federal government? Who can question our loyalty to the constitution? Let the south dare to talk of seceding, with this glorious evidence of our fidelity to our obligations to the law? Grand government! Magnificent civilization! Down with the lawless southern barbarians! Stocks rising! Illinois banks sound! Niggers going up! The jubilee of freedom actually come!
>
> Go it darkies! Hurrah for free speech, free homes, free mobs, and free negroes. The day of jubilee has come![70]

Even as he had multiple lawsuits pending in Chicago, Stephen Nuckolls still had plenty to worry about back in Nebraska City. He had scrambled to avoid the collapse of his Platte Valley Bank during the Panic of 1857, a severe recession. And just six months before he went to Chicago in search of his fugitive slaves, he suffered severe losses from a fire that swept through thirty-eight buildings in Nebraska City's commercial area. These troubles, along with the Graysons' escape, occurred just as he and his wife were moving to Denver, Colorado, to expand a freight and outfitting business and undertake some mining.[71] Despite these troubles, Nuckolls lived to manage several other business enterprises and serve a term in Congress before dying in 1879. The ultimate fate of Eliza and Celia Grayson is unknown.

## *The Rescuers from Amity*

Fugitive slaves often yearned for and attempted to rescue family members still in bondage. In the summer of 1859 one such man arrived in Amity, Iowa, a strongly antislavery settlement in western Iowa's Page County, about three miles from the Missouri line. He persuaded several young men of the town to undertake a daring raid into Missouri to free his entire family.[72] Clark Smith, a son of Ammi Smith, the local Wesleyan Methodist minister and ardent abolitionist, described later what happened.[73]

What the runaway asked was far more dangerous than simply aiding someone who had already escaped from a slave state. Freeing his family would involve going sixty miles into Missouri to somehow liberate several people and bring them safely back to Iowa, in the face of concerted efforts by slaveholders and their allies to prevent the rescue. Several of Amity's young men, including Clark Smith, discussed the man's plea and decided that five of them, one driving a wagon and four on horseback, would "undertake the precarious task," guided by the fugitive. The raiders—Smith, George Gibbs, Martin Bisbee, Isaac Feltch, and Stover Hilton—started on their way in the afternoon, planning to stop for the night after about twenty miles and by evening of the next day arrive at the farm where the fugitive's family worked. Clark remembered the trip having both danger and "its frolicsome side." Fortunately for the young men, much of northern Missouri was still uninhabited. But in their inexperience and hasty planning they also made a serious miscalculation; by noon the second day they had used up all their provisions. The rest of the way to their destination plus all the way back had to be done without food for men or horses.

When the five young men of Amity and their guide reached the farm where the man's family lived, Clark stayed with the weary team while the rest went to smuggle out the family. He spent an hour or so in the "midst of heavy timber" where the "inky black" darkness exuded a "creepy loneliness," before he saw "something white" approaching down the road. It turned out to be "the first installment of contraband [runaways] 'toting' its earthly [goods] all tied up in a white bundle. Soon another white bundle appeared; then another, and another." As people came up, "their bundles were tossed into the wagon, and the children on top of them." While Clark was helping one of the women, a heavy older one lost her balance and fell into the wagon bed, to the muffled snorts and waving legs of occupants, but without a word being spoken. Then, turning the team about, the rescuers "headed for Iowa and liberty as fast as their jaded strength would allow."

As soon as the sun rose, the Amity men saw that the wagon contained some fifteen occupants, many of them small children. Most troubling to Clark was the young man carrying his "very pretty" sweetheart atop "a milk white steed whose flowing silken mane fell below his knees and whose heavy tail almost touched the ground." The horse, the young men from Amity learned, had been brought "from France by way of New Orleans and [it] had cost one thousand dollars" (about $28,000 in 2011). The weighty load and the conspicuous, expensive, stolen white horse gave serious pause to the rescuers, who worried that they had bitten off too much and began to fear for everyone's safety. Consequently, they laid plans to protect themselves and the fugitives. They selected George Gibbs, "upon whose judgment, courage and ability [they] could absolutely rely," as leader. He rode a quarter of a mile ahead of the wagon along with the young man on the white horse. Isaac Feltch, accompanied by the man who had instigated the raid, took charge of the horses and wagon. The others (Martin Bisbee, Stover Hilton, and Clark Smith) rode as a rear guard a quarter of a mile behind.

But the horses were hungry and tired, and the load they were pulling was heavy even when some of the runaways took the risk of walking, so the party traveled very slowly. Then the rescuers also became aware of another miscalculation on their part: they had failed to bring along extra relief horses for the wagon team, and their lighter saddle horses could not do the job. Their hasty preparations and ignorance of the number to be liberated undermined their efforts. These flaws in planning were offset only by good weather, decent roads, and the sparse settlement in this part of Missouri. By midafternoon, they knew they could not reach Amity before nightfall, but they were relieved to see no sign of pursuit. Clark Smith, whose own horse was exhausted, proposed that he ride the white horse back to Amity ahead of the others to get food and fresh horses. All immediately agreed, and Clark got home by dusk, greatly surprising his father by riding in on such a magnificent white steed. His father notified neighbors of the incoming party, told them to spread the news to others, and asked them to bring to his place "plenty of eatables." That ended Clark's part. Feeling "all used up," he headed in to get some rest.

Once the party of runaways arrived in Amity, the residents divided them among themselves and took them to several dwellings to eat and rest. The next day, everyone gathered at one house to find "the dining room table opened full length" and "piled with edibles, which were ravenously devoured by the hungry slaves." As soon as they finished, "two men each with a team and wagon came up and dividing the cargo 'shipped it' to the next 'station' for relay eastward." This daring rescue, like the Otoe War, demonstrated that Americans on both sides of the slavery issue had grown more convinced of their beliefs and bolder in acting upon them, regardless of the law. But nothing before the onset of civil war underscored Iowans' growing disregard for the Fugitive Slave Act more than the aid they gave to the militant abolitionist John Brown.

# 7

# Iowa and the Martyrdom of John Brown

## *The History of John Brown in Iowa*

John Brown, perhaps the most famous white opponent of slavery, was closely connected with Iowa's antislavery communities, as his stay in Tabor in 1856 revealed (see chapter 5). He relied heavily on these connections between 1857 and 1859, as he planned an ambitious national assault on the institution of slavery. Probably the first Iowa antislavery guerrilla to get to know Brown was Charles Lenhart, since they met briefly after the Black Jack fight in 1856. But the first Iowans to join Brown's militia in 1857–1858 were Charles W. Moffett (a Montour, Iowa, man who had captained a Topeka detachment of James Lane's militia in 1856), George B. Gill, and Stewart Taylor. Of the three, Gill is better known to history because in his later years he wrote about his association with Brown. Back in 1856 he was a twenty-four-year-old freethinker from West Liberty, Iowa, who traveled with a wagon train crossing the state on the overland trail to Kansas. There he joined a free-state militia and participated in the August 30, 1856, battle at Osawatomie that Brown helped to lead. This experience is probably why Brown recognized Gill when in March 1858 he and Stewart Taylor approached the Old Captain, as Brown was known, in Springdale about joining his forces.

After the fight at Osawatomie, Gill had returned to West Liberty, where he met Taylor, who had lived there since 1853 and was working as a wagonmaker in a blacksmith shop. By early October 1856 the Old Captain, sick with the ague (malarial fever and dysentery), had retreated north to Tabor in two wagons driven by his three sons—John Jr., Jason, and Owen—and carrying a runaway and some weapons. After storing the arms in town, John Jr. and Jason continued east, while Owen and the fugitive stayed to work among Tabor's antislavery activists. After spending eight days recuperating, John Brown departed by stage for Chicago and the East to raise money for the war in Kansas.

Brown Sr. and Owen returned to Tabor nine months later, in August 1857, to pick up a shipment of two hundred revolvers sent by the Massachusetts State Kansas Committee. In December of that year, the Old Captain also took two hundred Sharps rifles that had been provided by a Kansas aid organization and delivered to Tabor by the Dickey and Root wagon train in the fall of 1856. While in Tabor during the summer of 1857 the Browns lived at Jonas Jones's house, awaiting the arrival of Hugh Forbes, who drifted in on August 9. John Brown had hired this English adventurer and author of the *Manual for the Patriotic Volunteer*—a textbook on guerrilla warfare—to instruct the recruits he expected to join him in armed action in Kansas. Although the constantly needy, vainly arrogant Forbes grated on Brown's nerves, the three men cleaned up the Sharps rifles and practiced shooting them in fields outside the village. The abolitionist leader grew ever more mistrustful of Forbes, though, and they came to disagree about everything, including Brown's latest plan: an attack on the federal armory at Harpers Ferry, Virginia, with the aim of raising the area's enslaved population in rebellion and founding a black-run republic. By November 2, Forbes left Brown's company.[1]

Despite his continual ill heath, Brown quietly went back to Kansas in search of volunteers for his upcoming ventures. After touching base in Lawrence, he rode to Topeka and visited with John E. Cook, a sharpshooting friend of Charles Lenhart whom Brown had met after the Black Jack fight. Brown spoke in general terms about his plan to gather a group for military training to curb proslavery aggression along the Missouri line or elsewhere. Cook showed interest and put him in touch with three others who might also be willing to participate, and they in turn connected him to still more men. By December, from long personal talks with some of them and the word-of-mouth invitations of friends to friends, Brown brought together in Tabor nine men in addition to his son Owen. The nine recruits, unmarried men nearly all in their twenties, were impressed by Brown's quiet but persuasive opposition to slavery, which he expressed in a low-key manner. What he proposed also appealed to their adventurous leanings. The men included former soldier and 1856 fighter Aaron D. Stevens; talkative, genial John E. Cook, who had training in the law; well-read John Kagi, who kept up a vigorous correspondence with the newspapers; literary figure and journalist Richard Realf; short-tempered, impassioned Charles P. Tidd; ingenious but rather wild young William H. Leeman; Charles W. Moffett, an Iowan who had fought for the antislavery forces in Kansas the previous year; an Illinois man named Luke F. Parsons, who had been a clerk at the Free State Hotel in Lawrence before proslavery forces razed it in 1856; and Richard Richardson, who had escaped from slavery in Lexington, Missouri.[2]

By the time these men gathered in Tabor in early December 1857, John Brown feared that sentiment in Kansas Territory was turning toward peace and that the free-state leaders there seemed to be willing to make the best of the situation, so he turned his focus from the West to Virginia. But when he told his new recruits about the plan, they were startled. Cook, Realf, and Parsons balked, arguing that they had come to Tabor to train for Kansas border warfare and that they heartily disagreed with Brown's proposed new field of battle. Since they had no money to return to Topeka and their newfound comrades pleaded with them to stay with the group, the three finally relented. Within a few days Brown's group had two wagons ready, the weight of Sharps rifles distributed between them, with additional arms packed in one and travel supplies in the other. By December 4 they were on their way.

Apart from the wagon drivers, the rest walked across the bleak, snow-crusted hills toward the Quaker village of Springdale, some 280 miles away in east-central Iowa. The party avoided main roads and camped off the trail at the end of each day to avoid notice.

Their evening's chores, gathering feed for the mules and putting up a lean-to with a fire at the front to warm themselves and cook a meal, would frequently be followed by political discussions and singing. Three and a half weeks later, the weary crew finally arrived in Springdale.

Here, Brown had intended to sell the wagons and teams to pay for his men's travel to Trumbull County, Ohio, for winter training, but this was not to be. The financial panic of 1857 was setting in, and no one had ready cash to buy the horses and wagons. Brown was finally able to make an arrangement with nearby antislavery farmer William Maxson. In exchange for the wagon teams, Maxson agreed to put the men up in his house for three months at the rate of a dollar and a half for each man per week (see figures 16 and 17). With that done, Brown arranged with another local man, John Painter, to ship the boxes of Sharps rifles, labeled carpenter's tools, to Ohio for storage.

Then, as he had the previous winter, Brown went east and north to raise funds, and he also met with possible supporters for his Virginia idea among black communities in Chatham, Canada, about fifty miles from Detroit, Michigan. Back in Springdale, the men, under the leadership of Aaron Stevens, trained three hours daily and occasionally hired themselves out to chop wood and husk corn for local families. On a few winter evenings they held mock legislatures and led public discussions at the schoolhouse, and John Cook, John Kagi, and Richard Realf gave lectures in the vicinity. By the time Brown returned to Springdale on April 26, 1858, he found his winter-weary bunch, now tired of their closely stuffed quarters, ready to leave, which they did two days later. With them were two new recruits from West Liberty, just south of Springdale: George Gill and his friend Stewart Taylor. The company's destination was Chatham, Canada, where Brown had visited earlier.

Intending to convene a black constitutional convention under the guise of creating an African American Masonic lodge, Brown had invited numerous antislavery notables and black citizens to Chatham in late May. Few attended, however, and none of them was influential, so the resulting constitution, despite the worthy ideals stated in its preamble, did not succeed in building black support for an incursion into Virginia. Nor was Brown able to recruit any additional men for his band of fighters. To make things worse, the Old Captain discovered that Forbes, the English guerrilla trainer, had leaked information about the Harpers Ferry plan to some congressmen. As a result, Brown's financial backers persuaded him to postpone the raid on Virginia. Three weeks after his visit to Chatham, Brown and two of his men, Tidd and Kagi, returned to Kansas to throw Forbes off the track. Meanwhile, the rest of his men had scattered to find jobs to support themselves until Brown summoned them again. Gill and Stevens would rejoin Brown in early July.

After an initial stop at Lawrence, Brown's small group traveled to southeastern Kansas, which was still in turmoil because of the massacre of some antislavery settlers a few weeks earlier. Missourian Charles Hamelton and his proslavery fighters had herded five free-state men together in a ravine, shot them down, and returned to Missouri. Brown's group camped near the massacre site and went to see free-state guerrilla chief James Montgomery, thinking they might join forces. Although Brown found Montgomery too independent-minded to be a willing lieutenant, two of Montgomery's men would eventually join Brown at Harpers Ferry: one an Iowa man, Jeremiah Anderson, and the other a Pennsylvania emigrant, Albert Hazlett.

The "heaven-sent" opportunity Brown had been looking for to make a visible strike against slavery and to refute Forbes's allegations that they were about to strike at Harpers Ferry came on December 19, 1858. George Gill, scouting the Missouri-Kansas Territory line, met a man (whom he described as "a fine-looking Mulatto") who identified himself as Jim Daniels and claimed to be selling brooms. Daniels soon told Gill that he and his family were about to be sold in an estate sale, and he requested help in freeing them before that happened. When Gill brought the news to "Old Brown," they set about planning how the rescue of the Daniels family might be carried out.[3]

They settled on a two-pronged raid the next night and recruited men from both Brown's and Montgomery's bands. At twilight they crossed into Missouri. One group of a dozen, led by Brown, stayed north of the Osage River and headed for James Lawrence's place, then occupied by Lawrence's son-in-law, Harvey Hicklin, with his family and the enslaved Daniels family. The second group of rescuers, eight men led by Aaron Stevens, split off to go south, crossing the Osage River and heading for David Cruise's farm, the home of a friend of the Daniels who also wished to escape. By night's end, Brown's half of the raiding party had liberated eight adults (Jim and Narcissa Daniels, Sam Harper from Hicklin's farm, and five more people from the nearby farm owned by John Larue) and the two Daniels children. They also took with them an ox-drawn Conestoga wagon and some provisions. Stevens's part of the band made it back from the Cruise farm with the Daniels's friend Jane, along with a wagon, provisions, oxen, and several mules, but the plunder came at a high price. In the dim light, Stevens thought he saw David Cruise grab for a revolver, so he shot and killed the Missouri man.

For the next month the raiders lay low, while Brown and Gill shifted their liberated companions from place to place. On January 25, 1859, they began their trek from the Lawrence vicinity back to Iowa, first driving two wagons west toward Topeka, then turning north. On the third day, they encountered trouble just beyond Holton. At Fuller's Crossing, Straight Creek was overflowing from runoff from the recent mild weather, making it impossible to ford. The party stayed in two nearby empty cabins for two days, waiting for the creek to recede. During that time, a sizable proslavery posse made up of men from Lecompton and Atchison and led by John T. Wood gathered around them. Though besieged, Brown's men could see that Wood's men were reluctant to engage them and kept well out of Sharps rifle range. One of Brown's men persuaded a local antislavery man named Wasson to race to Topeka for help.

Shortly after Wasson located John Richie at the Congregational church in Topeka, he and fifteen others marched north with arms and provisions—some riding and others walking—to aid Brown's party. The Topeka antislavery men had apparently already been stirred up by the recapture of ten fugitive slaves and their return to Missouri when Wasson arrived with the news of Brown's plight.

Within two days the *St. Louis Democrat* carried an account head-lined "Old John Brown under Siege," reporting that although "the assailants are afraid to attack him," they had him outnumbered and intended to remain until reinforcements arrived.[4]

The Topeka rescuers arrived at Fuller's Crossing the next morning, and after they rested briefly, Brown placed them in a double line in front of the wagons and told them to cross the creek and charge straight at the proslavery posse because they would "be sure to run." Scarcely had they crossed Straight Creek when the Atchison and Lecompton men could be seen scurrying for their horses to get away. The mounted free-state men chased them, eventually capturing four men and five horses in an encounter that came to be known as the Battle of the Spurs.[5]

### Across Iowa in Winter

Using long ropes, Brown's raiders and their Topeka allies got the wagons across the swollen stream and then moved north. The next morning they released their four captives to find their way home on foot and gave the five horses to the Topeka men in thanks for their help. Several of them now turned back toward home, while others accompanied the original band of rescuers. In four days they crossed the Missouri River at Nebraska City into Iowa, staying the night at Civil Bend. The next morning the small caravan crossed the half-thawed Missouri River bottoms and arrived at Tabor on February 4. Townspeople, curious and helpful, put up the fugitives at a small schoolhouse that they equipped with a cooking stove (see figure 18). The refugees' main escorts—Brown, Gill, Kagi, Stevens, and Tidd—found shelter in the homes of antislavery townspeople.[6]

The Old Captain had fully expected a proud welcome and a stay of a couple of weeks in Tabor. His overworked animals needed rest, as did the newly freed families. Also, he hoped to shake another bout of ague before continuing the trek eastward. Instead, however, he found a marked chill toward his party within the community.[7] Not a little of this ill feeling arose from events of which Brown was unaware: the escape of Celia and Eliza Grayson the previous

November, Stephen Nuckolls's invasion of Tabor in search of them, and the subsequent legal actions. Now Brown's arrival alarmed the already rattled townspeople and made them worry that another proslavery storm might be coming their way. Furthermore, although Tabor's antislavery residents had willingly assisted fugitive slaves in reaching safer free states, this time they thought Brown had gone too far. Journeying into Missouri to free slaves instead of aiding those who had already fled, killing a man, and stealing horses, wagons, oxen, and provisions looked a lot less like a morally defensible breach of an immoral law than like robbery and murder.

On Sunday, February 6, the morning after his arrival, Brown entered church for morning service and handed the minister, John Todd, a note that read in part: "John Brown respectfully requests the church at Tabor to offer public thanksgiving to Allmighty God in behalf of him self & company & *of their rescued captives, in particular* for his gracious preservation of their lives, & health; & his signal deliverance of all out of the land of the wicked, hitherto."[8] The pastor, like his congregation, was already aware of Brown's Missouri exploits and was unsure how to respond to the note, so he turned to a visiting Congregationalist minister from western Iowa, H. D. King, for advice. Counseled not to bring Brown's petition forward at the service, Todd acknowledged to parishioners his receipt of the note and announced that a public meeting on the subject would be held the next evening.[9]

Citizens crowding into the meeting on the following night witnessed a remarkable exchange. As John Brown and his companion John Kagi looked on, a deacon thought previously to be an abolitionist urged his "fellow-Christians to declare that the forcible rescue of slaves was robbery and might lead to murder, and that the citizens of Tabor had no sympathy with John Brown in his late acts." When Brown was called upon to respond, he stood and began to speak but then noticed the arrival of a Dr. Brown, known to him as a physician and slaveholder in St. Joseph, Missouri. Lowering his voice, John Brown stated that "one had just entered whom he preferred not to have hear what he had to say and [Brown] would therefore respectfully request him to withdraw." But a locally prominent man jumped up to exclaim that he "hoped nothing would be heard that all might not hear." With that, the Old Captain replied that he had nothing more to say and sat down.[10]

What to do now? John Kagi scribbled out a substitute motion to test the group's seriousness. He handed it to town resident James Vincent, who offered it before the meeting. It reportedly included words to this effect:

> *Whereas*, John Brown and his associates have been guilty of robbery and murder in the State of Missouri,
> *Resolved*, That we, the citizens of Tabor, repudiate his conduct and theirs, and will hereupon take them into custody, and hold them to await the action of the Missouri authorities.

If Brown's raid into Missouri had been too much for Tabor's antislavery residents, nevertheless they could not stomach arresting him and handing him over to slaveholders. Those at the meeting evaded taking action on this acerbic motion, instead continuing to make their points about Brown's unlawful acts. The abolitionist listened for a time and then rose in silence and walked out the door. Ultimately, Tabor citizens passed the following measure: "*Resolved*, That while we sympathize with the oppressed, and will do all that we conscientiously can to help them in their efforts for freedom, nevertheless we have no sympathy with those who go to slave States to entice away slaves and take property or life when necessary to attain that end." The vote, according to townsman Samuel Adams, was not unanimous. Tabor's founder, George Gaston—even though he was hosting Brown and some of the liberated people at his house—urged adoption of the resolution because he had always opposed intervention in the slave states. All others in the room voted for it except four. "Three had the courage to vote 'No,'" wrote Adams, "while I was too big a coward to vote, but kept looking out the window, expecting any minute to see a detachment of Missouri cavalry surround the school house. I was too scared to let my voice be heard."[11]

Brown, wounded by this condemnation of his actions, had returned to George Gaston's house. As Maria Gaston recalled, he was suffering from the ague again and was so upset at "not finding the same sympathy as formerly, it almost broke his heart." She continued: "I never shall forget his disappointment and vanquish accompanied by many tears, when his men returned from a meeting expressing disapproval of his course. He said he must trust in the Lord alone and not rely on earthly friends."[12]

Four days after Tabor's resolution disapproving of the raid, the disenchanted abolitionist rode north with his wagon train into Mills County. He and his party made it fifteen miles to the cabin of Charles and Sylvia Case Tolles, friends of Ira Blanchard's who regularly aided fugitives. There they stayed overnight. In early morning, despite a snowstorm, they moved off in a northeasterly direction to their next destination, which lay a long fifty miles away over largely unbroken prairie. George Gill's list of the stops they made on the journey does not mention an overnight stay between the Tolles place and Lewis, Iowa, but they likely stopped midway between the two. In southeast Pottawatomie County lived a farmer named Calvin Bradway, a man known to shelter runaways. During this time George Shinn was living at Bradway's farm, and he recalled that Brown stayed there on his way from Kansas in 1859.[13]

On February 13 the caravan reached Oliver Mills's farm on the East Nishnabotna River, about one-half mile north of Lewis in Cass County. The thirty-eight-year-old Mills, a cousin of John Brown, was active in Republican political affairs and supported himself raising livestock. His farm was a frequent underground railroad stop, and he worked closely with the Congregational minister George B. Hitchcock, who lived two miles southwest of his place on the west side of the Nishnabotna.[14] John Brown's party rested overnight with Mills before heading northeast for ten miles, stopping at the Grove City Hotel owned by David A. Barnett. The since vanished town of Grove City, situated on high tableland above Turkey Creek, was at that time undergoing a brief boom as residents hoped it would become the Cass County seat. Barnett, who also owned a large farm one mile north of Grove City and was a local real estate promoter, often worked in underground railroad operations.[15]

On February 15 Brown's party traveled some thirty miles to the hamlet of Dalmanutha, situated on the stage line running from Des Moines to Council Bluffs. On this high divide between Beaver and Bear creeks and the Middle River was Porter's Tavern, owned by long-time abolitionist John J. Porter, a fifty-nine-year-old farmer with a family of seven. Porter put them up for the night, and in the morning they reloaded the wagons and continued eastward.[16] About twenty miles out, they crossed the Raccoon River and arrived at the farm of Jonathan Murray, a fifty-year-old Methodist farmer with a wife and three children. Here, perhaps in Murray's barn, Brown's raiders found comfort for one more night.[17]

From Murray's the wagon party went yet another thirty miles toward the western edge of Des Moines. James C. Jordan's farm lay in Walnut Township of Polk County, about six miles west of Des Moines, which was then a small city of about thirty seven hundred residents. The forty-six-year-old Methodist farmer and stock dealer hailed from Virginia but had since become a dedicated antislavery man and had sheltered Brown in the past (see figure 19). When the Kansas-Nebraska Act stirred antislavery sentiments in Iowa during 1854, voters elected Jordan to the Iowa state senate, where he was still serving. Upon Brown's arrival at his place, the gruff and helpful Jordan directed the travelers to a sheltered timber lot in back of his residence where they would be hidden from passersby on the road.[18]

A mutual friend of the two was John Teesdale, a radical antislavery man and owner/editor of the *Des Moines Citizen* (renamed the *Iowa State Register* in January 1860). John Brown had attended the same Akron, Ohio, Congregational church as Teesdale, had visited him in Iowa City when Teesdale was an editor there, and had seen him once previously in Des Moines. Now the Old Captain sent Kagi to find him. Teesdale vividly remembered what then happened:

> [Brown] sent me word that he had camped out near Mr. Jordan's west of Des Moines, and would be through the city at a stated hour. He would see me at the bridge on Court Avenue, but desired to avoid observation as much as possible for fear his train should be inter-

cepted. He stopped his train near the bridge. None of the slaves were in sight, the covers of the wagons being closed. He said to me that that was probably his last trip. He was on his way to Virginia, where he meant to begin a conflict for freedom that would fire the whole country. I deprecated the struggle as madness that would probably cost him his life without benefiting the poor blacks. His soul was on fire. He seemed to be imbued with a conviction that the hour, big with the fate of the country, was about to strike, and there could be no failure.

Teesdale, accustomed to seeing Brown clean-shaven, now looked upon a man resembling an old prophet, his face "covered with a long snowy beard." The newspaper editor bid him farewell and paid the wagons' toll to cross the bridge.[19]

From the bridge the teams pulled their loads up the wintery spine of the Des Moines River valley. They reached its eastern bluffs and by evening had made it to Brian Hawley's place southeast of Des Moines. Hawley, a forty-nine-year-old New Yorker with a lumber operation and a sawmill, had been an early convert to the Republican Party.[20] Brown's group rested at Hawley's overnight and then crossed the partly thawed Skunk River marsh bottoms and the river to reach the farm of Cornwall Dickinson in Jasper County, just west of Grinnell. Dickinson, a forty-five-year-old farmer, had originally come from strongly antislavery Ashtabula County in northeastern Ohio. Brown's party stopped for a period of needed rest and food and then, still favored by mild winter weather, proceeded to the five-year-old settlement of Grinnell.[21]

A cluster of some ninety houses occupied by five hundred residents made up the village of Grinnell in 1859. Located on level but high prairie land, it had very wide streets that the unusually mild winter had turned to mud and that were unavoidable, since the roads were "guiltless of anything like side-walks or crossings."[22] Apart from its soggy streets, Grinnell was an inviting abolitionist stronghold for the weary travelers. Founded by Congregationalist Josiah B. Grinnell of Vermont (see figure 20), the community had since its 1854 beginnings gained a reputation as a safe haven for runaways from slavery.[23] The leading antislavery townsmen included New Englanders (Grinnell himself and lawyer Amos Bixby of Maine) and an Oberlin, Ohio, contingent (head teacher Leonard F. Parker and newspaper editor Samuel F. Cooper). Together, they did much to fan sentiment against the evils of slavery.

And yet, though Brown knew of the community's antislavery leanings, he had not been there before, so he left the wagons in a grove at the edge of the village and rode in alone to see about staying the night. He knocked on the door of Josiah B. Grinnell's house, and the town's founder recorded the exchange that followed: "'Good evening sir. I am a stranger here—pardon me—is this Mr. Grinnell?' 'That is my name.' 'I have heard of you and do not feel like a stranger, for you married a daughter, I am told, of my old friend, Deacon Chauncey Chapin, of Springfield, Mass., where I once resided.'" After a few such pleasantries, Brown explained:

> My company is just back here in the grove, and I am only a scout. Don't put yourself and family in jeopardy—I came for advice. I was in the "wool business" [meaning the underground railroad], and am still, they say derisively, and I hear you are [doing so] openly. We are sixteen persons, with horses, and man and beast must be fed, and stop with friends if we can, and not spies. Then, it is Saturday and we want rest. I make it a rule not to travel on Sunday if it can be avoided, and to save expense we can cook our own food; and we need a rendezvous to stack our arms. What do you advise?

Grinnell then "opened the door into the parlor" and said "'this is at your service, and you can occupy the stalls at the barn not taken. Our hotel will be as safe as any place for a part of your company, and there is no occasion to wait until night, for you have too much of an outfit for concealment.'"[24]

Wearing "a plain, well-worn suit" and "a wide-rimmed hat and half-concealed pistol," Brown then walked across "to Mrs. Reid's hotel and engaged stalls for the horses, and supper for the women" before returning to his party in the grove. Word spread quickly through Grinnell, and many turned out to watch the arrival of the "canvas-covered wagons followed by horsemen"—an unusual sight in these pre–Civil War years. The men brought their arms into

Grinnell's parlor and stacked them in the corner. Into this room some of the fugitives were brought to sleep, while Brown was given a room upstairs and the remainder bunked at the hotel.[25]

Josiah Grinnell's bold welcome of Brown's party fit his character as an energetic town founder and politically active man who was then serving as the state senator representing a four-county district. His open support of the notorious John Brown was widely shared among the townspeople, who soon decided a reception for the new arrivals was in order.[26] The reception took place on Sunday at a large room being used for church services. Before a large gathering—including "many from the groves [outlying townships], brought, not by sympathy, but by curiosity"—Brown, "calm in manner, but full of emotion," defended his violent actions in the Kansas struggle. "But," asked one in the audience, "are not your black people from Missouri?" "Yes," he answered, they "were to be sold; we saw them in jeopardy. . . . They called to me and I rescued them. I have never counseled violence, nor would I stir to insurrection which would involve the innocent and helpless. Twelve was the number rescued, and led out from Missouri, a kind and grateful but ignorant company."[27]

As for the horses and oxen the raiders had taken, Brown said, "we don't steal horses. [The fugitives] take those raised by their care, and sell them to get what is 'kept back by fraud.' Now on Monday there will be shown some of our surplus horses for sale." But, asked another, "Was not that stealing?" Brown replied, "Every man has a right to a reward for labor, and I have made them men, and they want the fruits of their industry for clothes and food." After Brown sat down, John Kagi stood and, taking a different tack without Brown's somberness, told the gathered crowd that "the half of border warfare had never been told" and that "from my leader who has struck terror on the border, you will hear again."[28]

At a Sunday evening meeting, Brown spoke again, after which three clergymen offered their prayers for the wagon train's safety. A hat was passed to collect money for the party's traveling expenses, even as rumors circulated of trouble ahead. Reportedly an Iowa City marshal named Workman had written to Josiah Grinnell warning him to "get the old Devil away to save trouble, for he will be taken, dead or alive."[29] When Grinnell told Brown about it, he responded that he and his men were well-prepared for trouble in case it should happen. Loading their canvas-covered wagons with the fugitives and baggage the next morning, the party moved eastward across the spongy prairie roads.

Amos Bixby, writing to his brother the day after Brown's departure, noted that the weather was as warm as in April. Then this local attorney remarked:

> I may as well say that last Saturday old Capt. John Brown of Kansas arrived here with 12 slaves on the way to Canada. The old hero & his company created quite an excitement in our little town. They stayed over Sunday. We gave them $25 [almost $700 in 2011] & provisions enough to last them several days. I mean *we* the people of Grinnell gave it. You have doubtless read the account of 'old Brown's invasion of Missouri' something like two months ago; & of his being besieged near Paris in two log houses, and of the attempt to take him by Marshall Woods.
>
> He thinks of returning to Kansas, but if he does I very much fear he will be taken.
>
> The *colored* people with him are the slaves he liberated by the invasion mentioned. He is a quiet, resolute, keen eyed old man of about sixty years; nothing of the ruffian in appearance, but seems to actuate by high moral and religious principles.[30]

Brown's stop at Grinnell enthused that town's local citizens, but it roused anger elsewhere. When word got out, the Democratic editor of the *Des Moines Statesman* exposed it as "Hell Let Loose!—Fanaticism in Grinnell, &c." Denouncing Grinnell citizens for "applauding Brown and his confederates upon the Sabbath day—of endorsing murder, robbery and arson, together with a number of other hideous offences," the *Statesman*'s editor alleged that Brown had "boasted of having stolen 12 negroes they were speeding to Canada, and taking with them all the property they could lay hands on, shooting one of the masters, tying and carrying off others, burning barns, houses, &c." Opposing Republican papers responded, declaring such condemnation "the grossest, rankest falsehood; never uttered or warranted by anything said by Brown," and they accused the *Statesman* of having "maligned" the people of Grinnell and being "mean, slanderous and devilish from beginning to end."[31]

Meanwhile, although roads soft with snow melt and prairie mud slowed the horses and mule teams to a walk, Brown's sluggish caravan made steady progress throughout the long day of February 22, and by the next day, a little more than forty miles from Grinnell, it stopped one-half mile south of Marengo at the farm of fifty-four-year-old Draper B. Reynolds, who had lived in Iowa four years. The Pennsylvania-born Reynolds received the party at dusk as he and his daughter were milking cows in the barn and agreed to shelter them for the night. The wagons departed in the early morning of February 24 and, upon crossing the bridge over the Iowa River near Marengo, made good time. Thirty-five miles later they passed through Iowa City during the forenoon, Gill noting "no effort having been made to conceal our movements."[32]

The prairie village of Springdale lay fifteen miles ahead. By sunset the travel-worn company of people and horses trudged into the loose grouping of newly built cabins and houses. The Quaker hamlet offered them a breathing spell in which to rest their feet and weary limbs; they stayed there for the next twelve days. During that time, two of the former slaves, Sam and Jane Harper (see figure 21), were married by the Quaker justice of the peace, John Painter. With an attempt to capture Brown and the fugitives widely rumored, the latter stayed in a building where watchful community members kept an eye to their safety.

With some time to catch up on his correspondence, Brown could not resist writing to Tabor's citizens to tell them about his reception in Grinnell. He mailed them a six-point summary of his welcome there and reported that he and his party were "loudly cheered, and fully indorsed." He asked that "friend Gaston, or some other friend, give publicity" in Tabor to the events that occurred in Grinnell. Meanwhile, though still troubled by "something of the ague yet hanging about" him, Brown contacted people to help arrange rail travel to Chicago and Detroit, and he tried to raise money by selling off a wagon and some horses.[33]

William Penn Clarke (see figure 22), the forty-two-year-old Iowa City lawyer who would take on the case of Mary and Versa Old in 1860, took the lead in organizing travel after Josiah B. Grinnell laid the groundwork. Hardly had Brown's caravan left Grinnell when its founder went to Chicago on the Old Captain's behalf. Traveling there as a "wool-shipper," he met John F. Tracy, general superintendent of the Chicago and Rock Island Railroad, to request that a boxcar be forwarded to West Liberty, Iowa, to ship some unspecified freight. The suspicious Tracy wanted no details and refused to take the $50 (roughly $1,400 in 2011) Grinnell offered as payment, because, as the railroad man said later, he was afraid that the company "might be held for the value of every one of the niggers" if the railroad could be shown to have participated in the transportation of escaped slaves. Nevertheless, the superintendent did issue a draft for $50 in the name of Brown. Grinnell then gave the draft to William Penn Clarke, who joined it with a supportive letter from Davenport's Hiram Price, a member of the board of directors for the railroad line that ran through West Liberty. With these two documents Clarke was able to persuade the local depot agent at West Liberty that railroad officials already knew about and approved of the boxcar arrangements.[34]

Clarke completed his preparations with help from editors of the *Iowa City Republican*. Using their telegraph connection, he requested a permit from Davenport officials of the Chicago and Rock Island to have the boxcar delivered to West Liberty. William P. Wolf, then a law student who lived northwest of Springdale, had walked into the *Republican* newspaper office while the editors were waiting for an answer from Davenport about the boxcar permit. They asked him to wait until it arrived and then deliver it to Brown on his way home. In late afternoon came approval on the understanding that the boxcar "was to be loaded at night, without being billed, and pulled out under the direction of the officers at headquarters." With the permit in hand, the editors told Wolf to inform Brown that he could stay the night in their building if he came to Iowa City. William Wolf got on his horse and rode out of town toward Springdale.[35]

A chilly March rain had begun to fall. About two miles out he saw a horseman on a side track coming toward him, and he pulled up to visit with him. The man's evasiveness suggested he might be involved with Brown, so Wolf told him he "had an important communication that [he] must deliver that night." The rider replied: "I guess you are all right. I am a friend of John Brown's. My name is Kagi, and John Brown has just passed by us." Turning about, Wolf and Kagi overtook Brown, finding the Old Captain sitting beside "a rag peddler in his wagon," with "a blanket over his head and shoulders, concealing his face." Wolf handed him the boxcar permit, warned him of plans afoot to capture him, and mentioned "the room prepared for him where he could overlook" the scheming saloon crowd—the room was above the offices of the *Iowa City Republican* newspaper. Brown "simply smiled and said 'Ah!'" and "replied that he and Kagi would occupy it and observe any further proceedings." That evening Brown and Kagi quietly met with the Iowa City abolitionists Dr. Jesse Bowen (see figure 23) and William Penn Clarke about final preparations to take them east. Word somehow got out about Brown being in town, however, and soon others were on the lookout for the so-called antislavery fanatic. Dr. Bowen kept Brown at his house in eastern Iowa City (see figure 24) until, during the early hours of the morning, S. C. Trowbridge guided them via back roads out of town.[36]

Springdale residents took care of one of Brown's final tasks before leaving: selling one of the wagons and a team of horses. The wagon went to Moses Butler, who not long after sold it to Gilbert P. Smith for $75 (roughly $2,000 in 2011).[37] The second wagon and team, loaned to Brown by Samuel Tappan back in Lawrence, was somehow returned to him. Tappan reported in April 1859: "My team just returned from a trip to Iowa City via Nebraska they came back through Missouri, pretty well used in the service."[38] With business taken care of and the boxcar scheme ready, Brown, his men, and the runaways waited in Springdale until it was time to leave for West Liberty, some seven miles south.

This small railroad village, platted in early 1856, had grown to some eighty houses by 1859. Down near the tracks stood Keith's

Mill, a modest grist operation with a steam engine turning two stones for grinding wheat and corn. Albert F. Keith, a thirty-five-year-old Ohioan, had been a dedicated antislavery man since arriving in Iowa in 1852. Most other early West Liberty settlers evidently shared his sentiments. George Gill remembered the mainly Presbyterian settlement to be "a very hotbed of abolitionists and in full sympathy with Brown's ideas." To Keith's Mill friends delivered Brown, his four men, and the twelve fugitives on the evening of March 9. There they remained for the night.[39]

Early the next morning an engineer running the first eastbound train from Iowa City dropped off an empty boxcar at a siding close by the mill. Before long, as friendly residents looked on, Brown's men ushered the liberated families and other material into the freight car so they would be ready for the next Chicago-bound train, due in late morning. Once they had boarded, Brown, Stevens, and Tidd joined them in the boxcar. George Gill described the scene: "As Kagi closed and locked the door upon them he did so with this remark, 'Now if there is any one who wants a through ticket to hell just let them come on.' He stood sentinel on the platform of the car, Stevens on the inside." The car now needed to be moved from its siding to be ready for connection to the scheduled train. An old Democrat, the only one in the place—Mr. Alger, postmaster—helped to push it forward, eliciting such a grand booing from the citizens that he immediately excused himself, saying that "he had stumbled and only put his hand against the car to keep him from falling down." The Chicago-bound train at last arrived and left West Liberty with the boxcar placed between the engine and the express car, containing its mixed shipment of parcels and mail sacks.[40]

West Liberty resident George B. Gill was able to write about this departure because he did not join his companions on the train. After he had joined Brown in Kansas a year earlier, his health had suffered during the harsh two months of travel, his joints now aching with inflammatory rheumatism. He watched as his friends got onboard, comrades he had gotten to know so well since the spring of 1858 when had had given away all his books and joined Brown's group.[41]

Brown stalwart John Kagi boarded the passenger car along with William Penn Clarke, who had been so instrumental in making the party's railroad arrangements. Since arriving in Iowa in 1844, the staunch abolitionist had been a rising figure in the Whig Party until 1848, when he joined the Free Soil ranks and then spent some time in the Know Nothing Party before shifting finally to the Republicans. In 1860 he would become chairman of the Iowa Republican State Convention and lead the Lincoln delegation to the party's national convention in Chicago. He had learned of John Brown while working with Dr. Jesse Bowen as an active member of the Kansas National Committee in Iowa and admired his actions.[42]

Now, on March 10, 1859, Clarke and Kagi had stepped "into a passenger coach to keep an eye on a man" who had threatened to reveal to U.S. officers in Davenport the character of the freight in the boxcar. The two Brown supporters kept this man quiet during the train's short stay in Davenport with the help of the conductor, an Englishman named Jones who sympathized with their actions and "knew how anxious [Clarke] was to get the fugitives safely out of Iowa." From the depot the Iowa City attorney walked to the nearby hotel, where, "from a window of the old Burtis House I watched the train crossing the bridge over the Mississippi and felt greatly relieved when the train started on its journey to Chicago, where the negroes were safely landed the next morning."[43]

His feelings of relief were warranted, for U.S. Marshal Laurel Summers in Davenport had been warned that Brown was coming his way. Within a week of Brown's arrival in Springdale, a man had written to Summers to inform him that "'Old Osawattumi Brown' is at Springdale P. O. Cedar Co. with 12 Negroes & lots of property stolen from their masters in Missouri if you let me know what time you will meet me at Davenport I will go there at once. They will not stay long where they are hurry up." Accounts differ on what the Democratic marshal did on March 10, when the twelve fugitives and John Brown and his men passed through. One source states that Laurel Summers had several men "watching the wagon road and ferry for the party," while another indicates that the marshal and his deputies "searched the passenger cars, but did not examine the freight car" immediately behind the engine. Whichever is true, the result was the same—John Brown's party crossed the Mississippi undetected.[44]

Late in the night the Chicago and Rock Island train pulled into the company's rail yards in Chicago. By 4:30 a.m. the group made their way to the Adams Street house of the private detective Allan Pinkerton, who quickly invited them in. Leaving some at his house, he moved Brown and others to the home of a black friend, John Jones. But Jones's worried wife resisted hosting the notorious abolitionists. Mary Richardson Jones, interviewed some years later, recalled: "I said to my husband: 'I do not want John Brown's fighters. I am willing to take care of him, but not his fighters,' and told him that he would lay himself liable, but he said: 'They are here, and I am going to let them in.'" When he did so, she recalled, "I don't know how many, but four or five of the roughest looking men I ever saw" stood in her house. Despite her reluctance, she fed them and they "behaved very nicely." Pinkerton, known to be an "indefatigable" friend of slaves and runaways, was able to raise $500 (about $14,000 in 2011) and arrange for a rail car stocked with water and provisions from the superintendent of the Michigan Central Railroad before the group departed on the next leg of their journey.[45]

During late Friday afternoon of March 11, the fugitives left Chicago for Detroit under Kagi's guidance (Brown had taken an earlier train). At the ferry landing in Detroit, the eleven-hundred-mile journey finally ended for the rescuers. There, the Old Captain and his men saw their twelve jubilant former slaves off across the narrows separating Detroit from Windsor, Canada.[46] In addition to freeing twelve people, this long and much-publicized journey through Iowa from Kansas Territory and on to the Canadian border had nicely achieved Brown's other goal: discrediting Hugh Forbes's allegations that Brown's company was about to invade Virginia. But, in fact, after this journey was accomplished, John Brown's thoughts returned to Virginia.

*The Raid on Harpers Ferry*

Beginning in May 1859, while Brown went east to see his bene-factors and others about money, John Kagi began lining up men for their fall plans. At the moment the only ones ready to go were Aaron Stevens, Charles Tidd, and John Cook, the last of whom was at Harpers Ferry working as a teacher and lock-keeper while do-ing reconnaissance. Kagi sent many letters to his former comrades from Kansas and Iowa and also wrote several to John Brown Jr. urging him to find and send men. The Old Captain's son had little luck, though.

Kagi's recruitment troubles stemmed partly from the break in time between the previous winter's training and the delayed launch of the Virginia mission. Of the men who trained at Springdale, Charles Moffett now had new commitments, the runaway Richard Richardson had moved to Canada, Richard Realf's whereabouts were unknown, and Luke Parsons was no longer willing to come back. Parsons remained miffed that he had not been among the men whom Brown took back to Kansas after the Chatham, Can-ada, convention. Brown's explanation that Parsons "had a good trade and could take care of himself, anywhere" but others "had to be taken care of" did not satisfy him. The disgruntled man decided to go to the Colorado goldfields, heeding the advice of his mother, who had written: "You have fooled away time and money enough with Brown, keep on to Pike's Peak. Brown will come to some bad end, and then you and I will be glad you are out of it."[47] Of the other Iowa men who received letters from Kagi, George Gill also bowed out, writing: "Captain, I fear I have not moral courage enough to go with you. It seems to me that we should do no good and that it will be only useless suicide." Ultimately, the long delay since the winter in Springdale and the Chatham convention cost Kagi and Brown five of their twelve winter trainees.[48]

Gill's friend Stewart Taylor of West Liberty did gladly rejoin, however, and Brown also gained three new Iowa recruits. The first new man to step up was Jeremiah Anderson, a lieutenant in James Montgomery's guerrilla force in Kansas. Anderson had grown up at Round Prairie near Kossuth, in Des Moines County, Iowa, the youngest of eight children in a Wesleyan Methodist family. Though reserved by nature, his resolve to play a part in the Kansas struggle showed first when he had moved to the Little Osage River in Bourbon County in 1856 and joined free-state actions. Twice imprisoned for his involvement, he had ridden with Brown's group into Missouri on December 20, 1858, to liberate the Daniels family and their friends. By late April he was traveling with Brown from Ohio to New York and elsewhere in search of material support.

The other two from Iowa were the Coppoc brothers, Edwin and Barclay, young Quakers from Springdale who had watched while Brown's group trained for three months in their town the previous winter (see figure 25). They had also seen the Old Captain and his men bring twelve liberated blacks out of Missouri on their way to Canada. George Gill later described Edwin as a popular man with many friends, in contrast to his more cautious and asthmatic brother, whom Gill disliked. He admitted, though, that Barclay radiated a "restless" and "adventurous" inclination.[49]

By July 1859 Brown had leased the small Kennedy farm a mile downstream from Harpers Ferry on the Maryland side of the Potomac River. To cook and keep house, Brown brought in his daughter Annie, age sixteen, and his daughter-in-law Martha (Oliver Brown's wife), age seventeen. John Kagi arranged to have the Sharps rifles and revolvers they had stored elsewhere freighted in, plus, in September, some pikes that Brown had ordered. During August, Kagi and Brown's twenty willing recruits drifted in, half of them fighters from Brown's battles in Kansas and Iowa in 1857–1858. The remainder included three of his sons and two of their former neighbors, five black men he had met during his eastern travels, and finally an erratic but devoted man named Francis Meriam, who also contributed several hundred dollars.[50] By day the men stayed inside the one-and-a-half story farmhouse, where they ate meals in shifts in the tiny dining room with too few dishes. To offset monotony, they read magazines, played cards, carried on occasional religious or political debates, and listened to John Brown read the Bible each morning. Their greatest fear was early detection. Some especially feared what their talkative comrade in town, John Cook, might say accidentally.

Unknown to them, another risk to the scheme had emerged back in Iowa. Before Brown left Springdale in March, he listened to but dismissed the arguments of friends and confidants that he should abandon his plans for such an impossible action in Virginia. Leading Springdale residents, fearing for their own loved ones who accompanied Brown, persisted in their efforts to abort the raid even after the abolitionist fighter left town. On a Sunday in August, one Springdale man, Moses Varney, received a visit from his old friend A. L. Smith and his cousin David Gue, both of whom lived in Scott County. Soon the subject of Brown and his men came up, for the topic constantly stirred up feelings within the hamlet. Later that evening Varney pulled Smith to one side and divulged more of what he knew about Brown's operation. "Something must be done," said Varney, "to save Brown, his followers, and the young men from Springdale" from a violent death. While he could not betray what had been told him in confidence, he urged Smith and his cousin to do what they could.[51]

"On their long ride home," Benjamin F. Gue, a relative of David's, would write, the two "tried to think of some plan by which the tragedy could be averted without harm to the stern old emancipator." Reaching the cabin that David Gue and A. L. Smith shared with Benjamin, the two men who had visited Varney reported his urgent appeal to their housemate, and talking into the night, the three devised a plan. They decided to send two letters from different places to President Buchanan's secretary of war, John B. Floyd, in hopes he would reinforce the guard at the Harpers Ferry armory. They predicted that John Cook would notice the reinforcements and give the alarm, forcing John Brown to abandon his plan. Putting each letter into two envelopes—the inner one addressed to the secretary of war and the outer one directed to postmasters in Philadelphia and Cincinnati—the Gues and Smith sought to avert the raid without betraying their own identities.[52]

The letter that actually reached Secretary Floyd went through Cincinnati, and it said the following:

Cincinnati, August 20.

Hon. Mr. Floyd, Secretary of War, Washington, D.C.:

Sir: I have lately received information of a movement of so great importance that I feel it my duty to impart it to you without delay. I have discovered the existence of a secret organization having for its object the liberation of the slaves at the south by a general insurrection. The leader of the movement is "Old John Brown," late of Kansas. He has been in Canada during the winter drilling the negroes there, and they are only waiting his word to start for the south to assist the slaves. They have one of their leading men (a white man) in an armory in Maryland—where it is situated I have not been able to learn. As soon as everything is ready those of their number who are in the northern states and Canada are to come in small companies to their rendezvous, which is in the mountains of Virginia. They will pass down through Pennsylvania and Maryland, and enter Virginia at Harpers Ferry. Brown left the north about three or four weeks ago, and will arm the negroes and strike the blow in a few weeks, so that whatever is done must be done at once. They have a large quantity of arms at their rendezvous, and are probably distributing them already. As I am not fully in their confidence, this is all the information I can give you. I dare not sign my name to this, but trust that you will not disregard the warning on that account.

Unfortunately for Brown and his men, Secretary Floyd did in fact disregard the letter. Believing it to be a fabrication, he treated it like the many other anonymous letters he received: other than showing it to his wife, he ignored it. For weeks the Iowa letter-writers scoured the *New York Tribune* looking for mention of Harpers Ferry. Then, just when they had convinced themselves that their plan might have succeeded, on "Monday, October 24, the weekly mail brought our *Tribune*, and there we read the fatal news."[53]

Instead of abandoning his plan, Brown had advanced it by eight days because he had heard that a local sheriff had issued a warrant to search the farmhouse. Kagi rushed off a note and a map to Charles Moffett, at home in Montour, Iowa, urging that he hurry to join them, but the rush put the plan at risk. Also endangering the effort was the fact that Brown had not been completely honest with his men. Their understanding was that they would only carry out a surprise raid on the federal armory in Harpers Ferry and then quickly retreat, so when Brown told them he intended to occupy it while they waited until mutinous slaves in the area had time to join them, they burst into argument. Four men supported Brown—Cook, Stevens, Anderson, and Leeman—and four strongly resisted—Brown's sons Owen, Oliver, and Watson and also Charles Tidd. Brown's three sons argued that their father's natural caution would entrap them all. Only after John Brown told the men that if they didn't like his plan, they should select someone else to lead did the objectors yield. Their judgment of the plan to attack and hold Harpers Ferry had not changed, though. Rather, as one son said, "We must not let our father die alone."[54]

On Sunday night, October 16, all but three of Brown's band marched on Harpers Ferry, and by morning they had control of the armory. But they were deep in enemy territory; antislavery militias could not reach them there, and the enslaved people living in the area did not rise up. Soon, local militia and residents had them under fire, and by afternoon Col. Robert E. Lee had been ordered to Harpers Ferry with a force of marines. Despite their desperate plight, Brown refused to heed Kagi's pleas to evacuate, and he rejected Lt. J. E. B. Stuart's offer to preserve their lives if they would surrender. On Tuesday, October 18, the disastrous raid came to an end. It cost the lives of ten men: Jeremiah Anderson, Oliver Brown, Watson Brown, John Kagi, Lewis S. Leary, William H. Leeman, Dangerfield Newby, Stewart Taylor, Dauphin Thompson, and William Thompson. Five were captured immediately: John Copeland, Edwin Coppoc, Shields Green, Aaron D. Stevens, and John Brown himself. Two more, Albert Hazlett and John Cook, were captured later.

The next day, the five prisoners taken from Harpers Ferry were transferred by train to Charlestown (then in Virginia, now in West Virginia) for trial. To reach the train, authorities had transported the two wounded men, John Brown and Aaron Stevens, by wagon. Walking behind the wagon, flanked by files of local militia men and followed by an angry crowd, were the three other captives, including Iowan Edwin Coppoc. Put on trial for murder, inciting slaves to rebel, and treason, Brown was found guilty on all three counts and condemned to hang. Refusing one ally's offer to help him escape, he died on the gallows on December 2, 1859. Six of his men were also hanged: John Cook, John Copeland, Edwin Coppoc, Shields Green, Albert Hazlett, and Aaron Stevens.

Brown's trial and especially his execution had been covered at great length by all of the nation's many newspapers, and at the instant of his death he became an abolitionist martyr. On that Friday morning when he climbed the scaffold to his death, sympathy meetings occurred across the free states. In Chicago, a writer observed: "I find the popular sympathy in favor of this unfortunate man wherever I go. In the streets, on the cars, the general topic of conversation is the execution of Brown, and one sentiment—that of Sympathy—is almost universal." At a sermon on his death at a Baptist church in Lafayette, Illinois, "more than a thousand persons were compressed within the walls of the church." An observer of these sympathy meetings pointed out that "clergymen were prominent in conducting them" and that "they were attended principally by the abolitionists, the colored people, many ladies, and some of the extreme Republicans." Some meetings "gave entire approval to John Brown's course, but as a general fact they stopped at sympathy with him and his family and with the hostility to slavery which prompted his rash effort."[55]

Public sympathy was far from universal, however. The meeting in Philadelphia grew stormy, and in Manchester, New Hampshire, the mayor climbed up to a church's belfry to stop sympathizers from tolling the bell for Brown. At the Cooper Institute in New York City, speeches by Wendell Phillips and other antislavery advocates were constantly interrupted with hisses, boos, shouts of treason, and whistles, with three cheers given for Virginia's governor Henry A. Wise and three groans for John Brown. The rowdiness forced police officers to remove many of the attendees from the hall.[56]

In Davenport, Iowa, the editor of the local *Democrat and News* snidely described the sympathy meeting of "colored persons" at a Mrs. Johnson's house as a way for the nonattending white Republicans "to hide in the actions of their sable friends, the *darker* sentiments of their own hearts." But the editor reserved his deepest disgust for what local German residents had written in a black-rimmed article in *Der Democrat*. It portrayed Brown as "victim to the preservation of slavery in this 'land of liberty,'" one who had suffered "the obstinacy of a handful of aristocrats." Then the editor of the *Democrat and News* described a visit to Davenport's German section:

> Yesterday morning we took a stroll through the lower part of town to satisfy ourselves as to the truth of a rumor we had heard, that several Germans were to drape their premises and persons in mourning for that "noble" assassin, old Brown. We found that what we had heard was true, several of the prominent business houses having crape hanging on their door handles. On top of the German Theater building the stars and stripes were hanging at half mast with crape flying above them. Some *very* Black Republicans had heavy bands of crape tied around their hats which they displayed with disgusting satisfaction. We noticed several private dwellings were also draped in mourning—And who, pray, is all this mourning for? Is it for a patriot and Union loving man? It is mourning for a man who has committed more crime and caused more trouble than any other being in America.[57]

Worse, in the editor's view, even "intelligent *native born* Americans, who move in good society were foolish enough to allow their incendiary principles to get the upper hand of them and they, too, hung crape on their store doors." As for the American flag being hung at half-mast in Davenport, Chicago, and elsewhere, he agreed with the *Rock Island Argus* that it was done "generally by German abolitionists," many of whom were "yet aliens," occupying positions "they could never have found at home," and yet they were now offering "the most gross and outrageous insults to the flag and the government which protects them." All this for a man "arrested, tried, fairly and impartially tried, convicted and sentenced to suffer death for the triple crime of insurrection, murder and treason!"[58]

Both sympathy and hostility extended beyond the cities, too. In

Sweetland Township of Muscatine County, according to a Democratic newspaper, a rural school teacher eulogized Brown on the day of his hanging, but his students recoiled when the teacher wanted "the school bell to be rung at 11 o'clock as a token of their respect to the memory of John Brown who was crucified and died to save the negro." Instead, in the words of the editor, the boys informed the teacher "that if he didn't want to raise an insurrection suddenly he had better desist—if he did not they would stand him outside to cool." So the teacher contented himself with "giving the school a short lecture for their want of discipline."[59]

## The Harpers Ferry Fugitives

Of the rest of Brown's twenty-one men, seven escaped in the confusion of the hopeless debacle. Two of them, Osborn Perry Anderson and Albert Hazlett, paddled across the Potomac and made their way toward Pennsylvania, but Hazlett soon got caught and was extradited to Virginia by Pennsylvania authorities. The other five—Barclay Coppoc, John Cook, Charles Tidd, Francis Meriam, and Owen Brown—managed to reach the Kennedy farmhouse, where they quickly gathered up some food, blankets, a pair of rifles, and some revolvers and ammunition for each before they ran into the mountains.[60]

Led by Owen Brown, an experienced woodsman, they initially traveled only at night, avoided roads, stayed to the edges of clearings, and built no fires. But as their food ran out and they grew weak, the men risked getting caught by stealing a chicken here and there and picking up some dry apples, hard corn, or a few potatoes in the winter fields—much as fugitive slaves had to do. During their month-long struggle west toward Ohio amid bouts of freezing rain and snow, the five men were reduced to three. John Cook was captured while searching for food, and Owen Brown helped the exhausted Francis Meriam get close enough to a train to go home that way. Finally, when the remaining three men reached northwestern Pennsylvania, Owen Brown and Charles Tidd continued northwest to find work. Barclay Coppoc, along with a box of arms and a few other items, rode a stagecoach to a railroad station and then took the train to the home of Quaker relations at Salem, Ohio.[61]

Although naturally slight and now exhausted, Coppoc had proved his ability to endure suffering and hardship. He remained briefly at Salem before moving on toward Iowa. Reaching Davenport, Iowa, forty-five miles from his home in Springdale, he rested a couple of days above Eli Adams's bookstore. Then, escorted safely out of town by two young Quaker men, one of them his cousin, he took a train to within seven miles of Springdale (either Atalissa or West Liberty). At this station on December 17, twenty-three days after saying goodbye to his two comrades in Pennsylvania and one day after his brother died on the scaffold, Barclay got off the train. There, as he described it, "I met several hundred persons who were anxiously awaiting my arrival."[62]

Coppoc's hard weeks on the move were not yet done. Within a week, on December 22, the *Muscatine Daily Journal* noted that he was among those welcoming Thomas Winn, Springdale's postmaster, back from his trip to Virginia to plead for Edwin's life and then to Ohio to see the young man buried in Salem. The next day a Muscatine reader, William McCormick, no Brown sympathizer, wrote to Virginia's Governor Wise to alert him that Barclay Coppoc was "with his mother in Springdale and was in Muscatine yesterday." In McCormick's opinion, the fugitive could "be arrested without much trouble" because "he is in the country away from any town of any note, but [I] am told that he has many friends among his neighbors." The Muscatine man was right; a number of men had come together for Barclay's protection.[63]

Within two weeks the Virginia governor had an agent on a steamboat headed for Iowa to call on Gov. Samuel Kirkwood to arrest Barclay Coppoc and deliver him to Virginia for trial, just as had been done in Pennsylvania when that state's governor had handed over Albert Hazlett and John Cook. The agent, Courtland Camp, disembarked at the Mississippi River town of Muscatine on January 9 and stayed overnight under an assumed name at the Mason House Hotel. Thirteen days later, on January 23, 1860, after traveling via stage from Iowa City, he sat down with Governor Kirkwood in Des Moines and asked him to follow Pennsylvania's example by extraditing Coppoc (see figure 26).[64]

He soon learned he could expect nothing of the sort, for he found himself in a western border state more radicalized than coastal Pennsylvania—Iowa's Republican Party having been born, bathed, and constantly engaged in turbulence over the Kansas-Nebraska Act. Governor Kirkwood's inaugural address, given just twelve days before on January 11, 1860, contains clues as to why he refused to extradite Coppoc. The speech dealt extensively with the slavery issue and the Kansas struggle. "The free state men of that Territory," the new governor had declared, "were treated by their pro-slavery brethren in the Territory and in the States, and by the General Government, as if they had not any rights, legal or natural, which either were bound to respect." And Kirkwood held that "while the great mass of our northern people utterly condemn the act of John Brown, they feel and they express admiration and sympathy for the disinterestedness of purpose by which they believe he was governed and for the unflinching courage and calm cheerfulness with which he met the consequences of his failure."[65]

Camp's meeting with Kirkwood did not go well, for the governor identified four flaws in the Virginian's paperwork that would prevent Iowa from fulfilling its legal responsibility to extradite Coppoc.[66] Two antislavery members of the Iowa General Assembly who happened to come by the governor's office overheard a heated discussion in progress. One of them, Benjamin F. Gue (the same man who had tried to derail the Harpers Ferry raid), recalled, in writing of that day, that Camp was "a pompous-looking man, who seemed to be greatly excited." He continued:

> Governor Kirkwood was calmly listening to the violent language of this individual, who was swinging his arms wildly in his wrath. The governor quietly suggested to the stranger, that "he had supposed that he did not want his business made public."
> The rude reply was: "I don't care a d—n who knows it now, since you have refused to honor the requisition."
> The pompous man then proceeded to argue the case with the

Governor, and we soon learned that he was an agent from Virginia bearing a requisition from Governor Letcher for the surrender of Barclay Coppoc.

In reply to a remark by the agent that Coppoc might escape before he could get the defect in the requisition cured, the Governor, looking significantly at us, replied: "There is a law under which you can arrest Coppoc and hold him until the requisition is granted," and the Governor reached for the code. We waited to hear no more, but, saying to the Governor that we would call again when he was not engaged and giving him a look that was a response to his own, we walked out.

While Kirkwood listened to Courtland Camp's complaints, the two antislavery men immediately got together with leading legislators, including J. W. Cattell, Josiah B. Grinnell, David Hunt, and Amos Hoag. A messenger must be sent to warn Coppoc, they decided, before Camp could correct his paperwork and catch a stage for Springdale. This meant that the legislators had to find someone who could successfully reach Springdale by the next evening, before the stage was scheduled to arrive the following morning. They turned to Isaac Brandt, a Des Moines underground railroad operator, for help in finding a hardy person able to endure the 125-mile journey on horseback in the dead of winter.[67]

Brandt found a lean, experienced young horseman named Williams (his first name is lost to history), whom they prepared with credentials to show each time he stopped to change horses. Wearing a large buffalo overcoat, fur cap, and fur-lined boots and breeches, he mounted a fast horse with a leather saddlebag that contained food and letters, along with a message to John H. Painter in Springdale. It read: "There is an application for young Coppoc from the Governor of Virginia and the governor here will be compelled to surrender him. If he is in your neighborhood, tell him to make his escape from the United States." It was signed "Your Friend."[68]

In the darkness Williams rode out of Des Moines over the frozen old stage road and on to Four Mile Ridge. By the time he reached the half-way point in Grinnell, some sixty miles out, Williams was on his fourth horse. There, residents warmly received him and provided quarters where he got four hours of sleep. At 9:00 a.m. he was again in the saddle. With frequent changes of horses he made it to Marengo, but by then the fatigued rider could hardly stay on his mount. Receiving food and a brief rest, he nevertheless went on with a fresh horse that got him to Oxford, where he climbed onto yet another horse that would take him to Iowa City. When he got within five miles, he dismounted at a final stop to rest, while a son of the household there rode into Iowa City to let the proper people know that a messenger would be soon arriving.[69]

When Williams arrived in Iowa City, he was greeted by antislavery activists William Penn Clarke, Samuel C. Trowbridge, Dr. S. M. Ballard, and Dr. Jesse Bowen. Over the previous twenty-four hours, Williams explained, he had come from Des Moines as fast as relays of horses could take him, and he wanted to continue the last dozen miles to Springdale. But the Iowa City men could see the young rider's great exhaustion, and as they thawed him out and fed him a warm supper, they persuaded him to wait until the next day, because Camp could not reach Iowa City on the Des Moines stage until noon anyway. Meanwhile, as a precaution they sent a man to inform John Painter of the situation. Early the next morning Williams arrived at Painter's home in Springdale.[70]

Unknown to those alerting Coppoc to the danger he was in, it turned out that Governor Kirkwood had refused to issue the arrest order until Courtland Camp resubmitted a new affidavit. As a result, Camp had to take the stage through Iowa City all the way back to Muscatine to await the delivery of a revised official requisition traveling by steamboat from Virginia. When on February 10, 1860, Camp received Virginia's revised extradition request, Kirkwood signed it, ordering Barclay's arrest. Sheriff Jesse Bradshaw of Cedar County was directed to execute the order. He rode to Springdale, asked a few questions about Barclay's whereabouts, and poked around in a few sheds before returning from his token examination to report that he had "made diligent search and the party could not be found." A more careful search would have yielded the same results; Barclay Coppoc had already taken flight well before Sheriff Bradshaw received the arrest order.[71]

The Harpers Ferry survivor, though still in a weakened condition, rode north with his friend Thaddeus Maxson (son of William Maxson) in a sleigh driven by John Painter the day after receiving Williams's warning. They crossed the Cedar River at Gray's Ford and moved toward Mechanicsville, twenty-three miles away. At this station on the Chicago and North Western Railway line, Coppoc and Maxson caught a night train toward Chicago, but then for reasons unknown they got off that train before reaching Clinton and made their way to Davenport. There they boarded another train for Chicago, where the two stayed with black friends before eventually going on toward Detroit, intending to enter Canada. But before crossing the border they received word from John Brown Jr. asking that they come instead to his place at Jefferson, Ohio. After a brief reunion with their fellow escapees from Harpers Ferry, Owen Brown and Francis Meriam, Coppoc and Maxson traveled seven miles southeast to the rural hamlet of Dorset, Ohio, where they were protected for the next thirty days before returning to Iowa.[72]

Iowa newspapers naturally weighed in on the Coppoc matter. While friendly papers printed Governor Kirkwood's letter refusing to act on the initial requisition, the *Davenport Democrat* charged that Kirkwood's "real motive" was his "evident desire to screen Coppic [*sic*]." Iowa Republican papers, claimed the *Democrat* editor, take "their cue from the great fugleman of their party, the *New York Tribune*," which approves "resistance to law" by "the [John] Brown Republicans out in Cedar County," if authorities attempted young Coppoc's arrest. To this possibility the editor of the *Tipton Cedar Democrat* chimed in, stating, "Things are coming to a pretty pass when criminals cannot be arrested on account of an armed mob of the citizens defending them."[73]

Letters by the Coppoc boys' mother, Ann L. Raley, also received press attention. To the *Davenport Gazette* she wrote about her three sons: "one was 'offered up as a willing sacrifice,' in Virginia, on Friday last; the second is now safe in Canada; and the third, the youngest, is going to school at Springdale." Although she did not believe "in the principles of war or the taking of human life," she wrote, "my Bible tells me to do unto others as I would have them do unto me, and to undo the heavy burdens and let the oppressed go free, &c." To Gov. John Letcher of Virginia (with a copy to the *Chicago Press and Tribune*) she wrote that the "most disgraceful part" of Virginia's actions was "hunting all through the land a poor fatherless boy, whom somebody has said that somebody imagined, had had some connection with Brown." Though Barclay had not been in Virginia, she claimed, "you are chasing him with biped bloodhounds and big bloated marshals, secret patrols and spies, and most inhuman of all, the thousand dollar reward for him dead or alive." Indeed, she charged, "You hang men for murder while at the same time you are encouraging it by your rewards," which only creates "radical abolitionists faster than scores of Northern lecturers could do it."[74]

Ann Raley was right. John Brown's execution and those of his men (three of them Iowans—Jeremiah Anderson, Edwin Coppoc, and Stewart Taylor) only worsened the polarization across the United States. Americans regarded Brown as either a martyr or a traitor, a soldier who sacrificed himself in a just cause or a rebel seeking to destroy the Union. Though his raid on Harpers Ferry failed to achieve what he hoped it would, its failure moved the nation much closer to a war over slavery.

# 8

# Fearless Defiance

## *Rush and Excitement*

Going into 1860, the Northern and Southern sections of the nation were increasingly at odds, including in Iowa, which was trending steadily Republican. The state's antislavery activists continued to help as many fugitives from slavery as they could even as national tensions tightened to a breaking point. By this time, runaways had less fear of getting caught, for slavehunters had become reluctant to venture into this more and more unfriendly state. Nonetheless, Iowans still helped when they could, sometimes giving such hurried assistance that "all was rush and excitement," as Elvira Platt put it at the turn of the twentieth century.[1]

On February 3, 1860, four black men in their early twenties walked into Tabor after escaping from slavery on the Choctaw Indian lands in Kansas Territory.[2] The names of three are known: brothers William and John Thompson and John Martin; the other has been lost to history.[3] By early evening, two townsmen with a two-horse covered wagon carried their four passengers northeast over the snow-covered ground toward Lewis, Iowa. Sixteen miles out they approached Mud Creek, a tributary of the West Nishnabotna River. There, two young Democrats from a nearby settlement spotted them. Suspecting that the travelers were helping runaways, the two rushed to a local justice of the peace at the next farm. They got a warrant and sped back to take the travelers into custody, which they did with a show of arms.[4]

They forced the two white men to drive to the justice of the peace's house, where the drivers were detained, and then they took the black fugitives to the jail in Glenwood, the county seat, several miles west. Once they arrived, however, they learned that the sheriff was out of town. Unsure of what to do, they listened as a Glenwood man named Joe Foster and a couple of his friends began pushing a scheme to "run [the escaped slaves] to Missouri," but the two slavecatchers thought that was "more than they had bargained for."[5]

Joe Foster then took charge, converting the idea of jailing the prisoners and waiting for a legal resolution of their status into a kidnapping scheme. The two original captors helped Foster take the fugitives to his place eight miles away on Silver Creek, and then bowed out. So Foster recruited five men to help him make the run for Missouri.[6] Another local man got wind of the plan, however, and informed a neighborhood Congregationalist who brought word to Tabor, thirteen miles south, that the wagon party had been caught. George Gaston quickly brought together several people at his house to figure out what to do. About midnight, they showed up at the Mills County jail in Glenwood, but the fugitives had already been taken to Foster's house. Thinking the kidnappers were already transporting the runaways to Missouri, the Tabor men rode toward the anticipated route. Finding no one, they returned to Tabor and waited for news.[7]

Two days later, when the justice of the peace convened the court to determine whether the two men who had tried to help the fugitives were guilty of violating the Fugitive Slave Act or perhaps of stealing slaves, fourteen Tabor men were present. A Glenwood resident came up to two of them and whispered that the fugitives were at Joe Foster's place. The two hurried down the snowy road and concealed themselves near his house. As soon as they noticed five men loading a four-horse wagon, they ran back to the court to announce that the kidnappers had started out for Missouri. It was 9:00 p.m. and the hearing was just ending. The two Tabor men who had driven the wagon carrying the runaways had been released.

Grabbing clubs of fresh-cut hickory stakes from a nearby farm, the Taborites climbed into two sleds and soon found the kidnappers' trail heading southeast. In the light of a full moon, the track was easy to follow because one wagon wheel continuously cut into the unbroken snow. A hot chase ensued in the crisp chill of the night. Ten miles east of Tabor and twenty miles north of the Missouri line, the rescuers' horse-drawn sleds overtook the kidnappers' tired four-horse team, which was dragging a wagon containing five white men and four black men through the deep snow. The Tabor residents got ahead of the wagon and, swinging their own team about, entangled them with their adversaries' horses.

The kidnappers, surrounded and outnumbered, gave in, even though they outmatched their pursuers in guns and knives. According to one account, "not a shot was fired on either side, except by the blacks, who for joy, discharged two up in the air." The four-hour chase now over, the rescuers gathered up the weapons and escorted the kidnappers to Tabor.[8] At daylight they pulled up before Jesse West's hotel, where all could warm up and get some breakfast. When the proslavery party refused to eat with the fugitives, Tabor folks took the chance to spirit the four off again toward freedom. The kidnappers never saw them again.[9] By morning the next day, the rescued men were eating breakfast at Oliver Mills's place just north of Lewis and resting up to continue their eastward flight.[10]

They were next heard of when they arrived at Grinnell, 150 miles from Lewis, in a wagon driven by a Quaker. Here their story took another turn. While boarding with local families, they mentioned an interest in learning to read and received encouragement from leading townspeople.[11] After all, a female runaway in town, sixteen-year-old Frances Overton, had already been enrolled in the school. But when some community members learned that four runaway men were about to enroll, they balked. Resistance swelled; talk was in the air that "the niggers must go" and that "their daughters should not sit with the niggers." Even in antislavery Grinnell, prejudice was common.

The opposing sides gathered at the schoolhouse for the annual school meeting on March 12, 1860. A motion to exclude the Thompson brothers, Martin, and their companion brought a torrent of heated debate, and abolitionists and their opponents flung insults at each other. In the end, the motion to keep the blacks out fell short by five of the fifty votes cast.[12] The losing side, more than disgruntled, determined to overturn the election, by force if necessary. The next morning, when the four men were slated to begin school, people on both sides, now armed, again carried their convictions to the schoolhouse door.

The opposition leader, an old sea captain named Nathaniel Winslow Clark, approached the building first. To him, blacks were nothing more than property without rights, and he had a history of trying to stir opposition to the harboring of runaways in Grinnell. As Clark and a friend entered the school, Superintendent Parker ran downstairs to confront them, insisting that they take up their concerns with the directors, who had already decided which pupils could attend the school. Unsatisfied, but seeing that Martin, the Thompsons, and the fourth man had not yet arrived, the two "withdrew to intercept them before reaching the school grounds." Word swiftly spread through the village, and a crowd surrounded the four black students in the church lot. Although they stood their ground, and a majority stood with them, insisting that they be permitted to attend school, the four men shortly consented to "return to their boarding places." The school's directors, fearing more outbursts, ended the school term ten days early.[13]

### An Ill-Fated Rescue Attempt

Days later the Thompson brothers, Martin, and their companion left Grinnell for Springdale, where they stayed for a few months. In August they met four young Quaker men—Charles Ball (cousin to Edwin and Barclay Coppoc), Ed Morrison and his cousin Albert Southwick, and Joseph Coppoc (the youngest of the Coppoc brothers)—who had just returned from Kansas, where they had been with the antislavery men John Stewart, Charles Leonhardt (no relation to the guerrilla fighter Charley Lenhart), and others escorting a sizable group of runaways and free blacks from Topeka. Joseph Coppoc remained at Springdale, but after a brief stay the three other Quakers left to return the wagon teams to Topeka and stay at their parents' new homes in northeastern Kansas Territory just south of Pardee, in Atchison County. There lay the new rural Quaker neighborhood where Charles Ball's and Ed Morrison's parents and several related families from Springdale had set down new roots.

No sooner were the young men settled in after returning from Iowa when three of the four runaways whom they had met in Springdale showed up. They wanted their new friends' help to free family members left back in Choctaw lands, and they quickly persuaded Ball, Morrison, Southwick, and a recent companion in Pardee, Chalkley Lipsey, to join in this new rescue effort. First they all headed for Lawrence to recruit others, finding three more men to join them. John Dean, who became the leader, was originally from Allamakee County, Iowa, and had a wagon shop in Lawrence. An outspoken antislavery radical, he also had a reputation as a cowardly blowhard. He brought along a friend, William Clarke Quantrill, then going by the name Charley Hart. The Quaker men did not know that Quantrill was an unprincipled drifter who hung around abolitionists, pretending to share their views in order to find out their plans. His main interest was selling information to slaveholders about runaways' whereabouts or getting his share of reward money when joining efforts to return runaways to their owners.[14] Nothing is known about the third man, John S. Jones.[15]

After the assembled group left Lawrence for Osawatomie, the rescue plan began to collapse. There were too few men in the group, winter was about to set in, and the three black men grew to distrust Quantrill. At this point the unscrupulous man began talking up another idea he had been nurturing, namely, to raid Morgan Walker's farm in Missouri and free the enslaved people there, along with Walker's stock. At Osawatomie, Eli Snyder, a man with his own antislavery band and a price on his head in Missouri, warned the would-be rescuers of trouble ahead if they followed Quantrill. He knew and strongly distrusted him as a man of bad repute. Once they heard Snyder's opinion of Quantrill, the three black men, more alarmed than ever, withdrew from the rescue attempt but remained in Osawatomie. But the young men from Springdale, likely seeing an opportunity to emulate John Brown's daring raid of two years earlier, agreed to go with him.[16] For their early December raid, the party, now reduced from ten to six, assembled blankets, cookware, revolvers, and knives. To avoid attracting the notice of anyone they met on the way, they decided not to take rifles. Within two days of leaving Atchison County, Kansas, they approached Morgan Walker's farm in Jackson County, Missouri, and hid in the nearby woods during the afternoon. Walker was a longtime settler with eighteen hundred acres of land just southeast of what today is Independence. He had a large log house plus cabin quarters for his slaves, along with various outbuildings for his stock operation.[17]

At about 1:00 p.m., Quantrill told the others he was going to scout out the farmstead. He went instead to the home of one of Morgan Walker's sons, Andrew J. Walker, a quarter-mile away, and informed him of the upcoming nighttime raid. The two agreed that Quantrill would receive a horse and gun in return for the particulars of the plans and for helping to foil the raid. The double agent then went back to the men he had just betrayed. Andrew contacted four proslavery neighbors and persuaded them to arrive armed at his father's place. After Morgan Walker returned from a day in Independence, his son filled him in on what was about to occur. Morgan wanted to kill all the raiders, but his wife and Andrew persuaded him to accept the deal with Quantrill.[18]

After the two-horse wagon driven by Albert Southwick and John Dean reached Morgan Walker's house, Ball, Morrison, Lipsey, and Quantrill walked through the moonless night toward the large log house about a quarter-mile from the road. Concealed in a small tack room at the north end of the fifty-foot-long porch were three men, all with shotguns. Andrew Walker and another man crouched on the porch behind his mother's loom.[19]

Walker's bloodhounds immediately announced the raiders' arrival as their representative, Ed Morrison, their spokesman, stepped to the door. Morgan let him in, along with Lipsey and

Quantrill, and listened while Morrison explained that he and his companions were going to liberate the Walkers' thirty-two slaves. While Quantrill remained inside as a guard, Charles Ball turned to gather Walker's slaves, and Ed Morrison and Chalkley Lipsey stepped outside. At that moment, Andrew Walker's companion rose up and fired a premature shot that prompted a volley from the others. "Morrison fell dead. Lipsey fell from the porch with a charge of balls in his thigh." Ball, unhurt and firing his revolver in the general direction of Walker's men, had to run for cover as they fired another volley. Lipsey's cries for help immediately brought Ball running back, and he managed to carry Lipsey into the brush. They expected the wagon to be there to help them escape, but Southwick and Dean had driven off, the latter having been hit in the foot, evidently by a stray shot.[20]

Ball and the wounded Lipsey succeeded in hiding in the brush near the Walkers' house for two days, when a local enslaved man found them beside a small campfire with a horse nearby. The two men tried to persuade the slave to escape with them if only he could bring a wagon and team. He agreed, but then he went directly to his master, who informed the Walkers about the discovery. Morgan Walker, two of his sons, and Quantrill got their guns, walked to the campsite, and killed both of the antislavery men. The Walkers then had slaves dig graves for them, interring Ball and Lipsey without coffins. Not more than a day later, local physicians dug the bodies up and took them to be dissected.[21] Ed Morrison, who had died on the Walkers' porch, had been buried earlier in a crude coffin out by the road and did not suffer this fate, which was common at the time in order to advance medical understanding.[22]

All the dangers that faced would-be rescuers were revealed in this ill-fated raid. In this instance, three young Springdale Quakers, with all their enthusiasm and strongly felt antislavery ideals, died because they followed a companion who betrayed them and because they trusted in friends who deserted them when the scheme went awry. The three young fugitives who had stayed behind in Osawatomie, William and John Thompson and John Martin, eventually served as teamsters for the Union Army during the Civil War. The fourth member of their original group, who had not gone with the others back to Kansas, reportedly returned briefly to Grinnell in 1861. Riding a cream horse, he visited for a while with the Homer Hamlin family, who had previously sheltered him.[23]

## Grinnell and Alexander Majors's Human Property

In Nebraska City during 1860, while Stephen F. Nuckolls nursed his grievances about losing Eliza and Celia Grayson to Iowa abolitionists at Civil Bend and Tabor, a fellow townsman and influential businessman also lost his slaves. Alexander Majors, a forty-six-year-old self-made man, was a partner in the largest wagon freighting business in the prairie and mountain region. Along with William H. Russell and William B. Waddell, both from Lexington, Missouri, he operated the firm Russell, Majors, and Waddell. From 1854 until the firm's collapse in 1862, they held a near monopoly on shipping, thanks in large part to government contracts to carry supplies and army stores from Fort Leavenworth to other western posts and forts. Majors was the field man who oversaw the road business, the huge scale of which "required the employment of more than four thousand men, forty thousand oxen, and one thousand mules."[24]

Kentucky-born, Missouri-raised, and strongly religious, Majors held his teamsters to uncommonly high standards of personal conduct. Each man was required to make the following pledge: "While I am in the employ of A. Majors, I agree not to use profane language, not to get drunk, not to gamble, not to treat animals cruelly, and not to do anything else that is incompatible with the conduct of a gentleman."[25] Nevertheless, Majors was a slaveholder, as were his two partners, and had little sympathy for abolitionists.[26]

In 1858 Majors had moved his family and six slaves from his mansion in Kansas City, Missouri, to a large residence in Nebraska City, Nebraska Territory, to better oversee the firm's greatly increasing number of shipments of government military supplies from Nebraska City up the Platte River Valley to Fort Kearney and then to Utah. By 1860 the firm, staggering under debts, was struggling to maintain its main Nebraska City depot. Majors and his trail leaders were busy "buying wagons, outfits, and oxen and hiring teamsters" for their 1860 contract to haul military supplies. While also running his own separate transportation line to Pike's Peak in Colorado, Majors "assembled 500 wagons, 2,140 head of oxen, and 100 mules" for the army, in addition to handling large amounts of Missouri River freight unloaded at his Nebraska City wharf. The firm had also recently started a daily stagecoach line from Fort Leavenworth to Denver, and in April they initiated their famed Pony Express.[27]

With so many business ventures to manage, Majors must have relied heavily on the people he owned to manage the household when he was away. Majors's wife had died in 1856, leaving him with eight children aged twenty and younger. The 1860 census identifies no one but children and servants living in the Majors home. At the end of June, however, five of his six house slaves had escaped, throwing his household into chaos. The runaways included three women (described in the census as one black and one mulatto, both age forty, and another mulatto, age twenty), and two mixed-race boys ages twelve and fourteen. Only one slave, a girl of fourteen, remained in Majors's household.[28] As soon as news of the escape got out, the excited editor of the *Nebraska City News* blamed the neighbors across the border in Iowa: "We can hardly think that our city is infested with such misguided philanthropists as nigger thieves and abolitionists. This dirty work is doubtless left for the nasty abolitionists of Civil Bend and Tabor." Majors offered a $1,000 reward (about $28,000 in 2011) for the slaves' return.[29]

Information is scant on what happened to the runaways after their escape. Two weeks later the five were at Grinnell, at which time Josiah B. Grinnell scrawled a note about them to William Penn Clarke, who was to receive them after they left the village of Brooklyn for Iowa City.

Grinnell, July 14, 1860

Hon. W. [Penn] Clark [*sic*]:

Dear Sir—

I sent forward 5 chattels—3 women and 2 children—boys this morning as far as Brooklyn.

I have just learned that there is a reward of $1,000 for them offered at Nebraska City.

I wish that all [three indecipherable words] and that they may [indecipherable] be got once by [indecipherable] north as soon as possible.

Yours Truly J. B. Grinnell

By July 25 a local man alerted the Democratic editor of the Des Moines *Iowa State Journal* that "J. B. Grinnell & Co. have recently received another consignment of negroes from Missouri" (though they were actually from Nebraska Territory). The five runaways remained in Grinnell for a few days before a brother of Josiah B. Grinnell reportedly passed them along to the next place east. It is unknown whether Majors ever recovered his human property.[30]

### Rescuers and Kidnappers

Amid all the unrest in the region, kidnapping gangs remained active during 1858 and 1859, preying on both free and fugitive blacks living in Lawrence, Kansas. The first major community effort to help them had occurred in 1859. On January 25 Dr. John Doy and his son volunteered to take thirteen African Americans—most of them free—from Lawrence, Kansas, to Iowa in two wagons. Unfortunately, a few miles outside Lawrence, a kidnapping band led by the locally notorious Jake Hurd captured the party and took the free black people to Missouri to be sold into slavery.

With Doy's failed attempt to bring free people from Kansas to Iowa in mind, the Reverend John Stewart joined with Charles Leonhardt and others in June 1860 to organize a well-armed escort for another group of African Americans fleeing to the relative safety of Iowa. They got three wagons and, with teams and supplies readied, moved north with a full complement of equipment and armed men. Despite some bad weather and occasional hostility, the caravan party successfully reached the state, was warmly received at Tabor and Grinnell, and finally arrived in Springdale on August 17, 1860.[31]

On September 20 gang leader Hurd and two other men, N. H. Beck and Joel Wildey, were in western Iowa on a road south of Council Bluffs. It is unknown whether they were hiding from Kansas problems or were just on the lookout for easy money. In any case, they saw going north on the road three black people—two young men and a woman—along with a horse. Near the Willow Slough bridge, Hurd's group pulled the three travelers into the brush, bound them, and headed south to sell them into slavery. The next day the horse arrived at the home of the farmer who had loaned it to the young travelers, and he knew something had gone wrong.

The three turned out to be members of the Garner family, the free blacks who had long lived at Civil Bend and who had suffered greatly at the hands of Stephen Nuckolls and his men (see chapter 6). In 1859 John Williamson had married Betsy Ellen Garner, and they had moved to Council Bluffs, where he worked as a laborer. When Betsy became ill, John went to Civil Bend to get her sister Maria (age seventeen) and brother Henry (age twenty-three). They were on their way back to Council Bluffs when they were waylaid by Hurd and his friends. When their horse returned without them, Ira Blanchard, who had cosigned for the Garners' land and later became guardian of the Garner children, and George Gaston of Tabor immediately rode out looking for them.

Meanwhile, John Williamson had escaped from Hurd's men and, after being arrested for vagrancy and spending a night in the Rock Port jail, some twenty miles into Missouri, had returned to Council Bluffs. Scouring northeastern Missouri, Blanchard and Gaston learned that the Garners had likely been taken to St. Joseph and on to St. Louis. Gaston then returned to Tabor as Blanchard took the steamboat to St. Louis. At the slave pens there, according to an account by John Todd, the auctioneer tested Blanchard's claim that he was the Garners' guardian and that they were free by seeing how two of his recent arrivals reacted when Blanchard entered the room. Although Henry, having suffered a blow, did not even raise his head to look, "Maria no sooner looked up than she jumped up and ran and threw her arms around him, exclaiming, 'Oh! Dr. Blanchard! Where did you come from?' The testimony was indisputable."[32]

The kidnappers were taken into custody, and three policemen, along with Blanchard, accompanied the prisoners on their return trip overland to be tried for abduction. It was not easily accomplished, for Hurd regularly became violent at stagecoach and steamboat stops. Ultimately, he and his men were deposited in the jail in St. Joseph, Missouri. After receiving a letter from Iowa's governor that contained the Missouri governor's approval to extradite Hurd, St. Joseph officers delivered the kidnapper to Council Bluffs. While he awaited trial, some friends helped him escape, but two years later he was reportedly hanged for stealing horses.[33]

# 9

# War and Rebirth

## Secession and War

Six of what would eventually be eleven Southern states had seceded from the Union by the end of January 1861, following the election of Illinois Republican Abraham Lincoln to the presidency. Everyone in Iowa and throughout the country was talking about secession and wondering what it meant for the nation. A traveler on the train from Elkader to Dubuque, writing of his trip, quietly listened to conversations among the passengers. "One may go where he will at the present time," he observed, and "will hear nothing talked of except Disunionism, and the masses take such an interest in it that they become excited and even angry if any one apparently differs with them in their opinion of the best mode of settling our national difficulties." The Republican *Dubuque Times*, in the traveler's view, was nicely holding its own against those in this "stronghold of Democracy in Iowa," where people hotly charged Republicans with being the cause of the troubles.[1]

Missouri, Iowa's closest slave state neighbor, quickly split in two over whether to stay with the Union or join the Southern Confederacy. Union elements soon proved too powerful for the secessionist-minded Gov. Claiborne Fox Jackson. By midyear his pro-Confederate government had taken flight from the capital in Jefferson City and set up operations in Springfield until they were pushed even farther, into Arkansas.

Slavery was not about to end, however, in Missouri or anywhere else. The state's Union government, under Gov. Hamilton R. Gamble, took the politically expedient position that "if we would preserve slavery, we must preserve the Union."[2] Gamble issued a proclamation that "no countenance will be afforded to any scheme or to any conduct calculated in any degree to interfere with the institution of slavery existing in the State" for "that institution will be protected." A few days later Sterling Price, one of the deposed Confederate governor's men, also issued an order guaranteeing the protection of Missourians' slave property. Both the Union and secessionist forces in Missouri were proslavery during the early years of the war. Both meant to reassure slaveholders about their property and to guarantee continued white supremacy in the state.[3]

Almost immediately after war began in April 1861, Iowa and Missouri felt their nearness to the battlefield. Fourteen days after the first battle of Bull Run in Virginia on July 21, 1861, armed forces clashed on southeastern Iowa's border at Athens, Missouri. Though the Iowa militia, based just across the river at the supply depot in Croton, did not enter the fight, the violence was close enough to make everyone nervous, and rumors spread that other actions were imminent. In Page County on the western border, two hundred citizens fortified the antislavery town of Amity against an attack expected from forces six miles to the south. And when a messenger to Bedford in Taylor County warned of Union men about to be attacked thirty miles south in Maryville, Missouri, "in half an hour forty or fifty armed men were on their way in wagons and on horseback," successfully deterring the enemy's attempt to take the town. And then there was the mistaken claim in the *Burlington Daily Hawk-Eye* in July 1861 that three hundred rebel cavalry were invading Appanoose County, heading for the county seat town of Centerville after having burned Milan, Missouri, and Unionville, Iowa.[4]

Though Iowa soil was never stained by formal battle, many thought it imminent during that first year of war. Nerves were on edge, especially in southwestern Iowa's isolated and exposed antislavery communities. These vulnerable places had been lightning rods for anti-abolition anger, and it did not take much to look across fields and down roads and imagine danger lurking in the shadows. Elvira Platt wrote in late July that word had come to Civil Bend that a company of Missourians would soon be coming their way. All able-bodied men mustered "in hot haste; arms were seized, ward-robes hastily arranged, requisitions made on our pantries, and by noon between twenty-five and thirty men were on their way to Sidney, our county seat, to join the company that would go out from there." Once the men were on their way, however, those who remained in the isolated antislavery hamlet felt unprotected, and "rumors came that the Secessionists in our midst are heard to whisper 'Now the Union men are all gone, it is our time to strike.'" Civil Bend, she wrote, "is more exposed than any other place; as we have twenty miles of uninhabited prairie just below us; and unless we have spies out, the enemy might come upon us without warning."[5]

On the Missouri side, slaveholders who had long worried about their slave laborers running off to Iowa only grew more fearful once hostilities began. Northwestern Missouri was rent by guerrilla warfare, with many incidents of murder, robbery, and arson occurring during vigilante ambushes and swift hit-and-run raids on farms and settlements. As the turmoil spread during 1862 and military deserters made occasional raids into southwest Iowa, reports came of both enslaved blacks and white refugees escaping north into the state.[6]

Hints that runaways were heading for Iowa quickly grabbed public attention. The "contraband" dilemma began shortly after secession and initially rose from arguments about whether the U.S. Army should return to their owners the people who escaped from slavery and flooded into their encampments. On July 9, 1861, Illinois congressman Owen Lovejoy introduced a resolution that eventually passed by a vote of ninety-three to fifty-five, stating that "in the judgment of this House, it is no part of the duty of the soldiers of the United States to capture and return fugitive slaves." One Burlington, Iowa, newspaper editor applauded, saying it would be a farce "for our troops to 'aid and comfort' the enemy by catching and restoring 'contraband.' The South should have thought of that (as well as many other things) before engaging in rebellion."[7] From this time forward, the wartime runaways were called "contrabands."

In November the same editor reprinted a long article from Illinois's *Springfield Republican*, which stated that "so far as soldiers or officers have lent themselves to the work of returning negroes to their claimants they have acted in defiance of the constitution and the laws," because according to the Fugitive Slave Act, such returns had to be performed by civil authorities (a U.S. marshal and commissioner). Individuals who returned enslaved people to their owners were engaged in slavecatching, the newspaper editor wrote, an activity that "is bringing disgrace upon our armies and disgusting the people." He concluded that "Gen. Jim Lane, in his rough way, has hit the exact line of duty for the army in this matter. It is 'to suppress the rebellion, and *let slavery take care of itself.*'"[8] And indeed, everywhere Union troops went in the South, slaves seized their freedom by flocking to the military camps, undermining the institution of slavery long before its legal abolition. But this military policy applied only to blacks who ran to military camps, not those taking flight to the free state of Iowa.

## Iowa's Response to Contrabands

In January 1862 the Iowa General Assembly considered a bill providing "that negroes coming and residing in the different counties in this State shall give security to the amount of $500 [about $11,500 in 2011] not to come upon the county for support &c." The bill's author claimed that although "his sympathies were all against the institution of slavery," they were also "against the association of white men with negroes," so he wanted "to prevent our State from being overrun with them." To block the bill, another legislator moved to indefinitely postpone it. In discussing the motion, a colleague drolly opined that this act conflicted with another statute that made it a crime to "place an obstruction upon railroads," because the proposed bill "would operate as an embargo upon what is well known as the 'Underground Railroad,' and thereby interfere with the business of some of our 'Abolition friends.'" Though the motion to postpone prevailed, the editor of Boone County's *Boonesboro Times* thought something needed to be done immediately rather than "postpone it till we are overrun by them [negroes] and then pass such a law" to keep them from coming here. He argued that "worthless as free negroes are in any country, the worst of all, are those who have just escaped from slavery, who have never had to provide for themselves the food they eat, or the clothes they wear." It was just such a class, he wrote, "that the war is throwing upon us" and that must be kept out of Iowa.[9] As ever, white Iowans' opposition to slavery did not mean that they accepted blacks as equals.

Mixed feelings were apparent even in strongly antislavery towns such as Amity. Here in this small border community, residents struggled to assist about seventy runaways between 1862 and 1864, this in the face of their neighbors' hostility. John Cross wrote letters to the American Missionary Association saying that "negro hate is a ruling passion" with many in the county seat of Clarinda (thirteen miles from Amity), and that some of the county farmers who employed African American girls in their houses had been threatened: "Send those 'niggers' back, or they would be burnt out." The farmers told the man who threatened them that any such acts would be reciprocated.[10]

The fugitives also actively defended themselves. When two kidnappers visited Amity disguised as "good union men" looking to buy horses, Cross was pleased to see some of the young contraband men gather about the two "with loaded muskets and fixed bayonets." Faced with this threat, the kidnappers' "slave driving bravado soon oozed out," and they pleaded with the approaching townsfolk not to let the blacks kill them. Local authorities released the two after getting from them a bond guaranteeing they would send free papers (paperwork emancipating slaves) for the runaways in Amity within ten days, plus delivering certain clothing and bedding the runaways had left behind, all of which was done.

Despite their goodwill toward the fugitives, however, Cross and friends were dismayed to find that "the evils of slavery [were] more deeply rooted" than they had supposed in the "colored element." For "almost every week, some new development is being made of their depravity the most prominent traits of which, are falsehood, and licentiousness." Especially bothersome to Cross was that "one great difficulty exists, in making parties, who have 'taken up' with each other, & have children." Because slaveowners neither recognized nor respected slaves' marriages, newly freed people in turn had little respect for the law, instead making and breaking their relationships according to personal feeling and community expectations. On the good side, in Cross's view, although the blacks needed "much instruction, both literary and moral," their Sabbath school numbers were increasing and the children were making "commendable progress."

As we have seen, many who had escaped slavery longed to free the relatives they had left behind, and they sought help in doing so. The story of Sam Scott and Reuben and Foster Griffith is a case in point. The two Griffith brothers, Quakers, had just come home to their folks' farm north of Indianola, in Warren County, after being in Kansas Territory. With the territory's free-state future no longer in doubt, they returned home in 1860 in time to vote in the presidential election. Reacquainting themselves with local news, they heard of a runaway named Sam Scott now living in their vicinity. Sam was known to be "a fine, quiet and congenial fellow" who "worked from house to house, helping with any task that came his way. All in the community liked him, adults and children alike." He would often say, "Some of these days I'll have my own little children here and live like white folks." The sympathy he aroused prompted various schemes to rescue his family from enslavement during the war years. Reuben Griffith eventually told his nephew, Edwin Hadley, what actually happened.[11]

Unlike Reuben, who was "not given to exaggeration and spoke in an easy quiet way," Foster, his "impetuous brother," was the leader of the plan to rescue Sam Scott's family. Other Griffith family members tried talking Foster out of the raid, saying it was far too dangerous. But seeing that their efforts were futile, George Griffith offered to help, saying: "I have a good nice team of young horses just broke to drive, and a new Studebaker Wagon. Take them and do what you can."

After making a cover for the wagon, Foster Griffith and Sam Scott headed south toward Maryville, Missouri, about 120 miles away, a journey that should have taken ten days to two weeks. It was later reported that "as they disappeared down the road George said, 'I never expect to see my team or their driver again. But they are risking their lives. I am only risking the loss of my team and wagon.'" Edwin Hadley wrote, "I remember Uncle Reuben saying, 'Every minute I could spare I watched the road running south of town.'" When they were long overdue, Reuben made up his mind "that if they did not return that night, [he] would mount [his] horse and set out on their trail."

But before Reuben could try to rescue the rescuers, he got word of what had happened. Walking down the road one evening, he said, "I thought I saw ahead of me someone move cautiously from bush to bush as if hiding. Another runaway slave I thought." He ambled over to where he last noticed movement and saw "a young Negro boy about fourteen years of age" hiding in the bushes. "He was trembling, scared as a rabbit. He was weary, dirty, and his clothes were in rags." Reuben, seeing the boy had been shot in the leg, "took him home, gave him something to eat, and then asked what happened."

The boy, whose name was Bill, said he had come a long way and gotten away from some men trying to take him back. But that desperate escape was his second; it happened after his father and a white man had rescued him, his siblings, and his mother from their master, hiding them in a wagon and heading north. Unfortunately, the slaveholder and his men caught up to them and, getting in front of the wagon, forced them to stop. Fearing for his life, Bill slipped out the back of the wagon and ran for the bushes. When they shot at him, he was hit in the leg and dropped to the ground to hide behind a log. He heard them say: "Don't waste time with him. We got to get out of here. We're on the wrong side of the line." Yanking the boy's father and his white companion from the wagon, the men threw a rope over a branch of a tree, intending to hang them. But the white man warned if they did that, they would "not live to get home." The men, after a brief talk among themselves, threw the two back into the wagon with the rest and headed south.

Reuben, asking Bill how he had managed to get to the Griffiths' farm, learned that the boy had been trying to reach it to tell the white man's friends what happened. After a brief rest, Bill gave Reuben more details about "where his mother and he were held as slaves, near Maryville, and he described the country and the prison near that town." By this time Reuben was convinced that the two men in the boy's story were his brother Foster and Sam Scott.

The next morning, Reuben "borrowed an officer's uniform from the Home Guard" and placed it in his saddlebag. He then "mounted [his] fastest horse" and "was on [his] way to Maryville," his wife and children waving goodbye. Fifty miles out, he stopped at the small Quaker settlement in Hopeville and got a fresh horse. By the third day, Reuben was at a Maryville hotel, with a room just across from the prison stockade. Next morning, though "under a great strain," he put on the officer's uniform with the thought that he "might have to act very un-Quaker like." He kept telling himself he "must show no fear to those people" and realized he "might have to do some bluffing."

He rode to the stockade gates and "demanded entrance and was, of course, refused." He later wrote, "without hesitation I drew my revolver and said, 'I have business inside. I will enter and if I am harmed, an army of federal men will be on you before you know it.' . . . With this, they drew back and allowed me to pass. Quietly I dismounted, tied my horse to a hitching rack just inside" and carried out "a tour of inspection." Most of those inside were "a motley crowd, desperate characters," though some were Northern soldiers in "ragged and dirty" uniforms. Then, near a group of men playing cards, Reuben spotted Foster and Sam looking on. They saw him at the same time. Completing his inspection, Reuben recalled, he then "with no show of hurry, untied [his] horse and rode toward the gate."

Reuben arranged to spend another night at the hotel, and as darkness came on, he rode slowly out of Maryville so he would not arouse suspicion. Reaching the outskirts, he took off as fast as possible for the U.S. Army encampment about ten miles away, riding "as [he] never rode before" until reaching the picket lines. He urged the commanding officer to make a company of soldiers available so Foster and Sam could be released. Though at first hesitant and fearing a general conflict, the commanding officer seemed to be "hoping for an excuse to march on the prison," and he ultimately responded: "I will have a group of soldiers there by morning, Captain. They will surround the prison. I will place you in command [for] you have shown great presence of mind and can handle the affair as well as I can."

Riding back on the fresh mount they had given him, Reuben "aroused the prison guard and officials at once and demanded the immediate release of the prisoners." When they refused, he told them, "'By morning your prison will be surrounded by Union soldiers.'" They laughed at him. "'By morning,' they said, 'the prisoners will be hung.' 'Do as you please,'" Reuben said, "'but there will not be one of you left to tell the tale. Your prison will be torn down and your city burned to the ground.' Their laughter ceased."

He returned to the hotel and after a bit of sleep, woke to the sun and walked down to where the troops awaited his orders. Standing at their head, he led them to the stockade, where he demanded the release of his brother and Sam, who were indeed scheduled to be hanged that morning. The guards acquiesced. To the prisoners' great relief, Reuben also demanded that all the military prisoners be released, which was done. On the way back to Indianola, Foster pointed out to Reuben the tree on which the slavecatchers had almost hanged him and Sam. As for the Scotts, they returned to Warren County. Not long thereafter, the reunited family had another child, whom they named Sam Jr., in addition to their two girls and Bill, the oldest. Bill later lived on a farm southeast of Indianola at Otter Creek.[12]

## War Weariness

As wartime contrabands straggled in, Iowa Democrats lost no time whipping up racial intolerance. People in the river towns were especially alert to black people moving upriver to find work. David Richardson of the *Davenport Democrat* complained that the blacks were not moving into areas where they were needed—namely, rural areas—but instead heading for towns, where they eked out a pre-

carious living. Democrats in the Burlington area seized on this issue before the 1862 local elections, hustling up laboring men's votes
by claiming that a great Negro emigration was coming their way.
The Republican editor of the *Burlington Daily Hawk-Eye* castigat-
ed such "dirty dogs who edit Secesh [secessionist] papers and make
secesh [*sic*] speeches throughout the country [and] are . . . trying
to convince themselves—for they can convince nobody else—that a
huge army of negroes are about to invade the north, and become
the competitors of white men in our field of labor." And yet, de-
spairingly, he admitted that the tactic was often successful, giving
as an example, "an Irish woman [who] yesterday expressed great
concern about the 'nagura.' Eleven 'Conservative' gentlemen had
been to see her husband to post him up. He wasn't afraid of the
'tame nagurs' who live in Burlington. But he didn't like the '4,000
wild nagurs' which the Black Republicans were bringing here to do
all the 'work!'"[13]

Farther inland, central Iowa residents in the capital city of Des
Moines also noticed incoming black refugees (twelve in 1860 rising
to seventy-two in 1865), and the local press reported on it, good
and bad. Although most runaways to Iowa remained anonymous
to nearly all but family and the census taker, one who settled in
Des Moines, Jefferson Logan, proved an exception (see figure 27).
In 1862 he and three other people enslaved in northwest Missouri's
Johnson County decided to slip north while their masters were
away in St. Louis. Taking some horses one night, they rode toward
the border. Along the way, they joined other northbound runaways,
becoming three of thirteen fugitives traveling in two double horse-
team wagons to Des Moines. There, Logan recalled that the city's
then small number of residents (fewer than four thousand) saw
them as "great curiosities." Finding odd jobs first at a hotel, then
on a farm, Logan finally went to work for the well-known Wesley
Redhead family. For the next twenty-one years, they entrusted him
with key tasks—overseeing the children's upbringing and managing the other hired laborers. Logan married and had two sons,
through the years saving and carefully investing until at age sixty-
five he was the richest black man in Des Moines. Upon his death in

1904 Des Moines's leading underground railroad operator, Isaac Brandt, served as one of the pallbearers.[14]

The editor of the Des Moines *Iowa State Register* feared that ultraconservative rhetoric "had vitiated the minds of the people," but he was relieved when, on January 5, 1863, four days after President Lincoln signed the Emancipation Proclamation (which freed slaves living in the states still in rebellion), Des Moines's Sherman Hall overflowed with an excited crowd. "The great meeting," reported the editor, "has given the loyal citizens of this community an unusual degree of confidence and encouragement." It showed "that an overwhelming majority of our citizens hail the Edict of Emancipation with joy," ranking it a "master stroke of policy" and a constitutional war measure "to knock away the corner-stone of Treason."[15]

Emancipation of the rebels' human property was one thing, but allowing African Americans in Iowa to become soldiers in the war effort was quite another. Some one hundred of Iowa's African Americans had found early wartime opportunities as servants to commissioned officers from the state.[16] Wanting to expand on these humble contributions to the war cause, Alexander Clark, a leader in Muscatine's black community (and the same man who had helped Jim White in 1848), wrote to Governor Kirkwood in the summer of 1862 asking for black companies to be made part of Iowa regiments. The governor was reluctant, for he knew that many white troops detested allowing black enlistment at all, let alone the prospect of fighting side by side with African American soldiers. The reply Clark got from Kirkwood's secretary was not encouraging. "You know better than I," he wrote, how "the prejudices of our people for you" are such that "your color would not be tolerated in one of our regiments. However wrong this may be, we cannot ignore the fact."[17]

Kirkwood and his fellow Iowa leaders, Sens. James Grimes and James Harlan, believed in general that blacks ought to serve, although their motives were dubious. Senator Grimes said to people in Dubuque that he would rather "see a Negro shot down in battle than the son of a Dubuquer." But the three men saw no way to achieve this goal in light of most white troops' racism. It was not until July 1863, after news came in of blacks' strong performance in battles elsewhere, that Kirkwood sought permission for Iowa to set up a black regiment. Secretary of War Edwin M. Stanton quickly agreed. The result was the Sixtieth U.S. Colored Infantry Regiment, six of whose ten companies were made up of men from Iowa and were known as the First Iowa Volunteers (African Descent). The regiment served in eastern Arkansas.[18]

Deep war weariness had set in by 1863, in Iowa and the rest of the nation. This weariness permeated politics, dampened Republican prospects in the 1864 election, and exacerbated divided loyalties. Democratic victories in midwestern elections in the fall of 1862 had strengthened those elements of the party that favored making peace with the Confederacy. In Iowa, peace meetings, mainly in the southeast counties, called for a negotiated reunion of the states to end the "abominable war for emancipation," and two large peace rallies of several thousand people occurred at Oskaloosa and Dubuque.[19]

If peace-minded newspaper editors criticized the war too strongly and too often, however, they risked a visit from a U.S. marshal or a vigilante mob. On August 14, 1862, U.S. Marshal Herbert M. Hoxie carried out the nighttime arrest of Dennis Mahoney of the *Dubuque Herald* and also nabbed David Sheward of the *Fairfield Constitution and Union*. Without benefit of a trial, both were hauled off to Old Capitol Prison in Washington, D.C., where they spent three months. Other offices of outspoken Democratic editors suffered damage or destruction at the hands of vandals or mobs at night. Soldiers marched on Thomas Clagett's *Keokuk Constitution* on February 19, 1863, and smashed presses and equipment; a group on May 23, 1863, entered and trashed the offices of the West Union *Fayette County Pioneer* after its owner, John Gharkey, wrote of his town being a "stinking hole of Abolitionism"; and in August 1863 several men broke up the operation of Joseph Shollenbarger's Sigourney *Keokuk County News*.[20] Given Iowans' divisions over the war and the role of African Americans in it, the state's Republican leaders especially worried about the southern tier of counties, with their strong anti-abolitionist feeling and weak support for the war. But trouble emerged elsewhere, too, such as in Madison County in south-central Iowa.

Unaware of Madison County's divided sympathies, four runaways went into the county in the fall of 1861. John Graves, Alec Nicols, Henderson Hays, and Anderson Hays made their way into Winterset to get Graves's horse shod on what was their second day of freedom since escaping from the vicinity around Maryville, Missouri.[21] They had run after learning that their slaveholder, James Graves, jittery about the war and the fate of his property, planned to send them all down to Texas. Deep in the Confederacy, that state seemed like a safer place to keep human property than in Unionist Missouri. Taking two mules and two horses, the men initially traveled during the night and hid in the woods during the day. On Saturday, October 26, thinking themselves safe in Iowa, they rode by daylight into the small town of Winterset.

At the blacksmith shop, John Graves was told it would take two hours before his horse could be shod. But when the four noticed the local militia drilling nearby and a crowd gathering about them, they got frightened and took off. No more than two or three miles out of town, however, several horsemen brandishing rifles and shotguns caught up with them. One man on a large white horse with a firearm across his saddle rode past and, stopping a short distance ahead, wheeled about and forced the runaways to halt.

Thus captured, the four were led back to Winterset, where their captors sought out an official to jail them. With these legal niceties under way, Graves recalled, the rest of the men "formed a ring around us boys to keep the crowd back. They got to talking pretty loud and some one dared any one to try to come inside that ring, and they hadn't more than said it than the coats began to fly and there wasn't any ring at all." This melee ended with the runaways being rescued by their defenders. "The men that took us out of the ring gave us something to eat and told us which way to go," said Graves, "and we wasn't long in getting out of there." Traveling east, by the next morning they had reached Indianola (Warren County), from where they soon left for Newton (Jasper County).

After finding work at the nearby farm of Richard Sherer, the twenty-two-year-old John Graves later joined the First Iowa Volunteers (African Descent) under the name of Sherer in October 1863. He served through the end of the war and then, adopting his father's name of Miller, returned to Newton before moving to Des Moines, where he spent many of his last years working at the Historical, Memorial and Art Building.

Madison County was a hot spot of worry for state officials. Although a series of raids by U.S. Marshal Hoxie in 1862 led to the arrests of seven people accused of organizing to "afford aid and comfort to the rebellion," overall his efforts simply stirred up the area's peace sympathizers.[22] Upon the release of the seven people three months later, two hundred peace advocates gathered in Winterset to welcome them home from Camp McClellan, a training and prison camp in Davenport. Seeing this celebration, a disgusted editor of the *Winterset Madisonian* wrote, "The Secesh Martyrs were escorted into town by a dismal group of Butternuts [a common slang term for rural proslavery people], some in Butternut wagons, some on Butternut horses, and others on Butternut feet," yelling out "'Three cheers for the Secesh Traitors!' 'Damn the Abolitionists!' 'To hell with the black Republicans!'" This editor considered it "a disgrace to Central Iowa . . . , a mixture of Treason, diabolism, drunkenness and insanity!" His comments spawned threats to demolish the editor's office, but nothing came of them.[23]

### An Important Judicial Decision

Next door in Polk County, antiblack Democrats turned to the law to gin up sentiment against contrabands. They looked to an unused and generally unenforced state act of 1851 that prohibited free "Negroes and mulattoes" from entering the state and found a local case to which to apply the law. Archie P. Webb had been enslaved from the time of his birth in Mississippi, then gained his freedom at about age twenty and, with the help of some friendly federal troops in 1861, had made his way from Arkansas to Polk County, Iowa. At a substantial farm in Delaware Township (a few miles northeast of Des Moines), Webb found work with Stephen Brooks, who was having trouble obtaining enough help with so many young men away at war.[24]

After Webb had been there for two years, a few of Brooks's neighbors came by one wintery day in early January 1863. They told the farmer that his black laborer had to go if they were to keep their good opinion of him. When he ignored them, before long the troublemakers—encouraged by some Democrats in the capital—took action. They got James L. West, one of three township trustees, to make an affidavit before notary public F. M. Hubbell (then clerk for the Casady and Polk law firm) stating that he had warned Webb to leave Iowa in accord with the 1851 law and the young man had not done so. With that, the township justice of the peace, Stephen Harvey, issued a warrant to arrest Archie Webb.

County sheriff I. W. Griffith took ten men with him, including Iowa secretary of state James Wright, to Brooks's place on Saturday, January 17, to make the arrest. The men surrounded Webb near a woodpile and captured him without resistance. When the case came before Justice of the Peace Harvey, he tried to get Webb to admit he was a slave so that he might be discharged, because the act of 1851 pertained only to free blacks and mulattoes, but Webb refused to do so, declaring he was a free man. So Justice Harvey fined Webb $12 (roughly $220 in 2011) and sent him back to Sheriff Griffith for detention in the county jail until the costs were paid.

Almost immediately, on January 20, Webb's defenders applied for a writ of habeas corpus to force a court decision about whether the man's arrest and detention were lawful. Their illegality, according to this petition and a second amended filing, lay in the fact that the sheriff had arrested a free black man without any warrant showing he had committed a crime. Meanwhile, some people who were furious about the antiblack tactic exposed it in the press. The editor of the *Iowa State Register* warned Sheriff Griffith that he would "bitterly repent the act which he yesterday executed" and two days later asked why the law firm of Casady and Polk had not also gotten up papers to eject from town the black friend of a local white, Democratic whiskey seller on Second Street.[25]

A very effective letter, published by the *Iowa State Register*, came from a Democratic neighbor of Brooks. "There are Democrats in this Township," he wrote, "who do not sympathize in any manner with the late movements against Archie P. Webb, a free Negro." This "villainous work" by "a set of Secesh scoundrels" ignored that labor was scarce, "and unless contraband laborers are permitted to be employed on Iowa farms," he warned, harvests would be scant in the coming year. Moreover, after seeing and talking with Webb, the writer found that "in point of native manliness, he is infinitely superior to those who persecute him" and "has no crime to answer for except the blackness of his skin." Finally, "before closing," the neighbor commented, "permit me, as a Democrat and in behalf of Democrats, to inform Sheriff Griffith through your columns, that many of his former party-friends in this neighborhood will remember him evermore for the part which he took in the disgraceful persecution of Webb. He knew better, but as for poor, stuttering, sputtering, imbecile [justice of the peace] Harvey, nature never intended that he should be responsible for his acts!"[26]

On Monday, February 2, a correspondent to the *Chicago Tribune* sat down in the courtroom "filled by an anxious audience" where "the reading of the decision was listened to with breathless attention." It had been nearly two weeks since the hearing before Judge John Henry Gray had taken place on January 21, at which J. S. Polk for the prosecution and S. Sibley for the defense had presented their arguments. Now Judge Gray was ready to give his opinion. What he said that day a listener described as a carefully prepared, "elaborate and forceful" statement.[27]

Reviewing facts of the case, he found that the 1851 state law had never been legally published; by oversight, it had been left out of the code and had instead been published later with a few other special laws. These omissions did not invalidate the law, however, so Gray addressed its status in relation to the constitutions of both Iowa and the United States. He found that Iowa's law conflicted with the right, granted by the U.S. Constitution, of citizens to live in any state. If a citizen was barred from enjoying the rights of life, liberty, and the acquisition, possession, and protection of property, and prevented from obtaining happiness and safety in the state of Iowa because he had been banished from it, then Iowa's law clearly contravened the guarantees in the nation's founding document. Further, Gray pointed out, the Bill of Rights guarantee that the people should be secure "against *unreasonable seizures* and *searches*" could not be met by a law "that *arrests* and imprisons a man where the only *crime charged* is that he is a freeman and has settled in the State of Iowa." The court's habeas corpus judgment, in sum, was that the 1851 state law was "inoperative and void; that the proceedings thereunder were therefore unauthorized, that the plaintiff herein is entitled to his liberty, and that he is hereby discharged from imprisonment."[28]

Newspapers generally applauded Gray's decision. "The people of Iowa," wrote a *Burlington Hawk-Eye* correspondent, "will thank Judge Gray," for he has thrown "the shield of the law over the weak and helpless who have sought a refuge in our midst." The *Chicago Tribune* correspondent applauded the habeas corpus decision as having "ended a wicked scheme of a gang of semi-traitors to inaugurate a general system of persecution against the free negroes in this State, and to that extent embarrass the execution of the President's Emancipation Proclamation in the Mississippi Valley."[29]

Nationally, after the Southern losses at the July 1863 battles of Gettysburg and Vicksburg, the air began to seep steadily out of efforts to make peace between the Union and the Confederacy, which had been based in part on the belief that the South could not be defeated. And yet, President Lincoln's chances to be reelected remained doubtful, blamed as he was for having suspended habeas corpus, employed the draft, and supposedly launched a war of emancipation. Lincoln and his armies had *"failed! Failed!! FAILED!!! FAILED!!!!"* yelled Henry Clay Dean, the powerful Iowa orator and Methodist preacher, to a Chicago crowd.[30] But those who called for making peace with the secessionists lost ground with each Northern battlefield success, especially after Sherman's army took Atlanta in the late summer of 1864. They ceased their intimidation at home and became increasingly humbled when they were charged with smelling of treason and undermining the Union.[31]

The more the Democrats stewed in losses and looked to revive themselves, the more they appealed to voters' basest fears and instincts, denigrating blacks and later working to deny black men the right to vote in Iowa and elsewhere. But men like Clark Dunham, Republican editor of the *Burlington Hawk-Eye*, saw the issue more broadly, pointing to everyone's complicity in slavery, which he believed to be the central evil of American society:

> There is no possibility of giving a sensible reason for talking about the rights of white men being superior to those of blacks or any intermediate shade. The simple fact is that white men had the *power* to make slaves of black men and they *did it*. It was wrong then, wrong now, and will be wrong to all eternity. We are now paying the penalty of that wrong. The civil war grew out of that wrong. The blood and treasure and cares and anxieties attending the war is our punishment for the outrage we have committed against the laws of reason, justice and humanity. And one of the worst penalties we are suffering under is that insane hate of the Negro, who is hated *because* he is wronged, which so blinds the madmen that they cannot see that freedom to *all*, is the only possible security for freedom to *any*.[32]

# 10

# Remembering and Forgetting the Underground Railroad

In Davenport, four months after Gen. Robert E. Lee's surrender at Appomattox on April 9, 1865, William H. Hildreth—a founder of what would become East Davenport—turned out of the family home the servant known as Old Aunty. In 1843 he had bought her as a slave and about 1850 moved her from the South to Davenport. There, she had remained a slave, working without wages and ignorant of her rights in this free state. By 1865, as she grew old and feeble, Hildreth saw her as a burden and "told her one day to leave 'his house and not show her d——d black face in his kitchen again.'" Too old to earn a living, she faced destitution and hunger in the few years remaining to her.[1]

Fortunately, she received support from kindhearted Davenport residents, and soon attorney Alfred Sully heard of her plight and "took up her cause." Sully, a "tall, rather slightly built, nervous, and energetic" twenty-four-year-old who worked for the old law firm of Corbin, Dow, and Browne, charged Hildreth with owing back wages, arguing that Old Aunty should receive "compensation for the whole twenty-two years' service." With little choice but to agree, Hildreth also provided his former servant with "a little old house to live in," and thereafter others also helped to make sure she spent her final years free of privation.[2]

These generous Davenport residents were not alone in their concern for African Americans after the Civil War ended. In the immediate aftermath of the war, many idealistic antislavery activists in Iowa, particularly the Quakers, turned to relief work among the newly freed people and organized schools for them. In 1866 Isaac T. Gibson of Salem, Iowa, reported that his group had established six such schools in Missouri, with nine teachers and 1,357 enrolled students. Some one hundred young Iowa teachers left their Quaker, Presbyterian, and Congregationalist families to work in difficult conditions among formerly enslaved people, helping educate them despite having few textbooks and few or no writing materials.[3]

As the years went by and the war faded in people's memories, former abolitionists naturally hoped people would remember the risks taken by both runaways and those who had assisted their escape efforts. In 1872 Ret Clarkson, publisher and editor of the Des Moines *Iowa State Register*, was already lamenting that "every day the various items and incidents of these historic facts, is rapidly being forgotten." This "most interesting chapter" of history, Clarkson urged, needed to "be written now while the actors are still living." It was they who carried the special distilled strength of "human sympathy, Christian sentiments and brave hearts," they who were the very "champions of the freedom of all men in a period when to be so was not only unpopular but also fraught with danger." In particular, "the good they did at the expense of personal profit and personal peril should never be lightly estimated."[4]

In places such as Henry County, formerly a hotbed of abolitionism, interest in what had gone before persisted. Mount Pleasant organizers brought in the famed abolitionist Frederick Douglass on February 28, 1867, for a lecture in Union Hall. At his Friday evening talk before a crowded house, white and black residents alike heard "the Cicero of the negro race" speak upon "the dangers of the Republic." Though a reporter thought it lacked "the fire of burning eloquence which was a marked characteristic of Douglass in his former days," even so his speech was "radical to the core," filled with "thought, logic, sarcasm, and sound statesmanship." It met with "demonstrations of the most enthusiastic applause from the vast audience."[5]

Some seventy miles west of Mount Pleasant in Oskaloosa, people began to talk of bringing together a local reunion of "old line abolitionists." In December 1868, at Judge Thompson's office in that town, several people agreed to hold such an event on the afternoon and evening of New Year's Day 1869. They sent a call out to all "who were abolitionists prior to the formation of the Republican Party in 1856," as well as inviting the public to attend. At the well-attended get-together, the two speakers were the Presbyterian minister R. A. McAyael and Methodist pastor L. B. Dennis. Within a few years, abolitionists' reunions throughout Iowa and Illinois mushroomed to grander proportions.[6]

The most widely publicized reunion of all took place in Chicago in 1874. Notice of the event had been circulated to four hundred newspapers, and many invitations went out to noted antislavery men requesting their attendance.[7] Iowans were well-represented there. Josiah B. Grinnell, in particular, chaired the second day's opening session and the evening session of the third day. Lester W. Platt from Civil Bend (Fremont County) was also there, as were William Leslie of Fort Madison, David Hardie (not to be confused with David Hardy) of Long Grove (Scott County), Charles Smith and his wife (Marion County), and Edward Turner. It was largely a gathering of elders: "Gray beards, bald heads, and spectacles, were the rule among the men," wrote a *Chicago Tribune* reporter, "and sober, Quakerish garbs among the women." There was also "a notable absence of colored people in the audience, though many invitations had been sent to representative men." For the next two days, addresses about noted organizations and leaders in the fight against slavery were interspersed with the singing of songs and the reading of poems (one by Woolsey Welles of Fort Dodge, Iowa) and letters from famous abolitionists unable to attend. A final portion of the third day was devoted to five-minute addresses by those present on "the dangers which were encountered in aiding fugitives to escape," as Mr. Turner of Iowa put it.[8]

African Americans held their own celebrations in the aftermath of emancipation. Five months after the Civil War's end, in September 1865, the town of Mount Pleasant treated itself to a "Proclamation Day" celebration. It began with a twelve-gun salute and a parade around the town square by members of local black churches, followed by an "experience meeting" and church dinner, with addresses by important white residents and formerly enslaved individuals who recalled their lives in bondage.[9] Most common among black Iowans were festivals every August 2, the anniversary of the abolition of slavery in the British West Indies in 1833. On that day in 1866 the African Americans of Keokuk, for example, "got up early in the morning, put on [their] holiday attire, prepared [their] dinner basket and took a special train to Sandusky [eight miles north] where [they] proposed to settle and make a day of it. [They were] resplendent with white and red and gay contrast of colors, and [were] as well appearing in [their] costume and deportment as any other public."[10]

In Des Moines the black citizens' celebration began with a procession on that same warm, breezy, sunny morning of 1866. "Stepping to the music of the free, and under many waving flags, the dusky ranks moved in perfect order down Court Avenue, across the bridge, wound up the road leading to the Capitol, and were soon assembled in the Capitol Square." In size, "the procession numbered almost the entire colored population of the Capital, and may be estimated at from four to six hundred. Perhaps two hundred and fifty white people, including many ladies accompanied the procession." A morning address by James Yancey of Fairfield, Iowa, whetted dinner appetites for all those assembled, after which four additional addresses occupied the afternoon.[11] Such celebrations took place in every town where lived a sizable black population (chiefly Davenport, Muscatine, Mount Pleasant, and Des Moines). The addresses dealt with the speakers' lives, their sacrifices, and black men's valor during the war, which evoked the war cry "Remember Fort Pillow," a Civil War battle after which surrendering black troops had been massacred by Confederate forces.[12]

Meanwhile, black communities grew in a northern subdivision of Newton and elsewhere. Mount Pleasant, a town of 4,000 people with 249 black residents in 1870, earlier had been a center of abolition radicalism. A man by the name of Lee, acting on his sympathies for freed blacks, established a subdivision in the northeast part of Mount Pleasant that has since disappeared. On it he erected a dozen small two- and three-bedroom dwellings soon filled by formerly enslaved tenants from Missouri. During the national debate on whether to ratify the proposed Fourteenth Amendment to the Constitution, intended to abolish discrimination on the basis of race, Mount Pleasant invited several civil rights advocates (Frederick Douglass, Wendell Phillips, Theodore Tilton, Anna Dickinson, and C. C. Burleigh) to speak on the question. Listening to Wendell Phillips lecture in March 1867 was Joseph Dugdale, who afterward proclaimed that Mount Pleasant's citizens "are fast being educated up to the type of radical anti-slavery, and are about to open the public schools for the reception of all the pupils of the city, irrespective of color!" And indeed, a school for blacks that had been set up in 1863 in a rented frame house closed in 1867 when townspeople integrated its students into the local schools.[13]

Dugdale, an antislavery and women's rights advocate much admired by Northern radicals, had moved with his wife Ruth to Mount Pleasant in 1861, when he was fifty-one, and he soon became active in social and political affairs. His progressive friends knew the Quaker as "a meek and gentle spirit" who in 1828 had courageously sided with the Hicksites, who split from the Society of Friends because they strongly opposed slavery and were willing to break the fugitive slave laws. His Mount Pleasant associates were also well aware of the aid he and his wife had given to runaways while in Ohio during the 1830s, and of his helping to organize Friends in Pennsylvania who had been discontented with, or disowned by, their conservative leaders.[14]

Dugdale received full thanks from Iowans for his abolitionist activities in 1875 at an underground railroad reunion at Salem, Iowa. At the Methodist Episcopal chapel on June 18, former abolitionists recalled past days of fearful and exciting events in Iowa. The two-day event interspersed talks with readings of letters from eastern abolitionists not able to attend, including William Lloyd Garrison, Lydia Maria Child, and Indiana's leading underground railroad Quaker, Levi Coffin. Salem's event, because it took place in a Quaker community, naturally attracted more Quaker attendees, and most of them were from southeastern Iowa, chiefly Henry, Lee, Scott, and Muscatine counties.[15]

Gradually overshadowing such reunions and abolitionists' stories of their fight against slavery, however, was a competing view of history that aimed to reunite the country by denying that slavery was the Civil War's root cause. In this view, the war was about preserving the Union, not abolishing slavery. People who endorsed this outlook tended to espouse a benign image of the Southern plantation as a pleasant place inhabited by happy slaves. Similarly, this point of view deemphasized Northern complicity in perpetuating slavery. This revisionist history left out the struggles of abolitionists and freed people, turning people's eyes away from the auction block and closing their ears to the lash at the whipping post. Stories that cast slavery as a sin and war as retribution were muffled and eventually drowned out by voices trumpeting white supremacy, stifling black hopes for civil rights and prosperity and discrediting abolitionists who wished to keep the emancipation flame alive.[16]

Abolitionists tried to counter such sentiments by publishing firsthand accounts by both former slaves and noted abolitionists of what life had really been like under slavery and how difficult and dangerous rescue efforts had been. But books and reunions radiating pride in emancipation and the goodness of the abolitionist cause dwindled before an irresistible postwar desire for national reconciliation. All over the United States, whites accepted measures to curb blacks' rights and proved ready to forget the past. As historian David Von Drehle wrote in 2011, "Forgetting was the price of reconciliation."[17]

But memories of the fight against slavery did not entirely vanish. Some twenty-five years after the Civil War ended, as the generation of aging underground railroad operators thinned, Ohio professor W. H. Siebert decided to write about these mostly obscure but passionate adventurers in the cause. He began by gathering their recollections. Beginning in 1892 until 1898, the year before his volume *The Underground Railroad from Slavery to Freedom* appeared, he pursued leads through correspondence, oral accounts, research, and travel. He managed to collect the names of some 3,200 people, 116 of them from Iowa, who had participated in the underground railroad.[18]

Siebert's work and the local conversations inspired by his queries helped renew public interest in the underground railroad. When, for example, Elvira Platt and others in Fremont County, Iowa, received Siebert's inquiry, they communicated with one another and then met at Tabor. There, wrote Elvira, "we arranged to apportion different cases to each. That of the Nuckolls's Girls fell to my lot, but before I had begun the report I learned that Hon. Sturgis Williams of Percival had already written and sent it on." Consequently, she instead jotted down "an incident connected with the Underground R.R. in which, as you will see, I was a principal actor." (Both tales are told in chapter 6.) Although many of the activists Siebert contacted had been willing "to care for passengers and help them on the way," Platt knew well that ultimate success had to be credited to each fugitive's "own wit and cunning and ability to find aid from friend or foe till he was in a safe place."[19]

During the first two decades of the twentieth century, Iowa newspapers blossomed with articles telling the stories of one or another underground railroad incident and people associated with it. Some appeared following the death of a local abolitionist or the destruction of a house associated with such past events; others were in response to the appearance of a fine article such as O. A. Garretson's "Travelling on the Underground Railroad in Iowa," which was printed in the *Iowa Journal of History and Politics* in 1924. Still others followed up on a new book or some national attention given to John Brown, which encouraged companion pieces on Brown's activities and connections in Iowa.

The next wave of public interest accompanied the civil rights movement of the second half of the twentieth century. This renewed struggle focused attention on African American history, including struggles against enslavement. Just as John Brown's reputation shifted from madman to martyr and murderer to hero, so too the image of the underground railroad operators improved, reflecting a growing appreciation for African Americans' resistance to slavery and the historical cooperation of black and white citizens in mutual opposition to human bondage. In the 1960s and 1970s numerous books and articles fed increased public awareness of the subject, and the accompanying growth of the historic preservation movement helped identify places where the underground railroad's conductors had lived and where those fleeing slavery had hidden.

Unfortunately, in Iowa entire town sites associated with underground railroad operations, places that prospered during the 1850s and the Civil War, had already nearly or completely disappeared by the time the public renewed its interest in them. Of the rural hamlet of Civil Bend (Fremont County), only the Blanchard Cemetery remains. Towns that show but traces of these years include Grove City (Cass County), Nevinville (Adams County), Dalmanutha (Guthrie County), Frankfort (Montgomery County), Quincy (Adams County), Pleasant Plain (Jefferson County), Clay and Wassonville (Washington County), and Yellow Springs and Kossuth (Des Moines County). Mostly these places declined because they failed to get a rail line or because their mill went under as local farmers ceased growing wheat in favor of other crops.

Of the individual homes, outbuildings, and public structures connected with the underground railroad, few remain in any condition that the original occupants would recognize. The oldest, in Salem (Henry County), stands as a mute witness to the Quakers' aid to Missouri runaways. The house of Henderson and Elizabeth Lewelling, a two-story stone house on the south side of Salem (see figure 7), is most notable for its direct connection to slaveholder Ruel Daggs's efforts to retrieve the Walker and Fulcher families in June 1848, which resulted in one of the last federal court cases under the Fugitive Slave Act of 1793 (see chapter 2). For the past fifty years, the property has been open to the public as a local history museum.[20]

In western Iowa two buildings from the 1850s that were associated with assisting runaways moving through the Kansas and Nebraska territories still stand. The 1853 house of John Todd stands on Park Street in what was then the staunchly antislavery Congregationalist town of Tabor (Fremont County) (see figure 28). In the basement of Todd's house were stored the arms and ammunition for the Kansas free-state cause that John Brown subsequently used in his raid on Harpers Ferry in October 1859. Todd's one-and-one-half-story frame house today is a museum operated by the Tabor Historical Society.[21]

Fifty-eight miles northeast of the Todd place is the house of Congregationalist minister George B. Hitchcock, which was a major stopping place on the underground railroad after the trains left Tabor (see figure 29). The 1856 two-story brown sandstone house stands on a hill above the East Nishnabotna River about a mile west of the town of Lewis (Cass County). Now restored, it is state-owned property—a designated National Historic Landmark—operated as a museum by the Friends of the Hitchcock House under a management agreement with the Cass County Conservation Board.[22]

Two additional buildings exist, but in altered condition or location, from the time when Kansas runaways came across Iowa. James Jordan's house, located in West Des Moines, is a museum operated by the West Des Moines Historical Society (see figure 30). This 1867 building represents an expansion of the house where John Brown rested overnight in 1859 with twelve people liberated from slavery. The museum includes information about the underground railroad.[23] The second property is a private residence east of West Branch (Cedar County) known in the 1850s as "Traveler's Rest." There John Brown stayed when stopping in the Springdale vicinity. Although the 1850s-era building is still largely intact, it has been moved a few hundred feet west from its original location to the east side of West Branch.

Other Iowa buildings lasted into the twentieth century but yielded to neglect before the renewed interest in the underground railroad could save them. Especially missed is the cement/gravel (also called "grout") house of William Maxson, just east of Springdale in Cedar County (see figure 17). It was built in 1848 and survived until 1938. It was there, during the winter of 1857–1858, that John Brown's men trained for battle. It subsequently became the subject of several articles and received many visitors, so its advancing deterioration during the early 1930s prompted discussion about its possible restoration. The state planning board identified it as a historic site worthy of state ownership, and it was documented for the Historic American Buildings Survey, but efforts to save it were in vain. The owner had it demolished during the fall of 1938 on the grounds that "it had become unsafe for the many visitors." All that remains today is a marker on a boulder at the roadside, placed there by the Daughters of the American Revolution in 1924.[24]

Forty-eight miles northeast of Springdale was Robert Lee Smith's place, one mile south of DeWitt in Clinton County. It was Smith who hid Eliza and Celia Grayson from men hired by the Nebraska slaveholder Stephen F. Nuckolls for several weeks before the women escaped to Chicago in the winter of 1858–1859. In 1970, 110 years later, the house became the victim of a highway expansion project.[25] The Horace Anthony house, however, where Robert Smith delivered the Graysons during their journey to Illinois, still stands at 1206 Anthony Place in Camanche, just downriver from Clinton. This private residence is listed in the National Register of Historic Places.

Southwest of Burlington are the ruins of another important underground railroad location, the house where Dr. Edwin James lived during the 1850s (see figure 11). He is best known for aiding the black man mistaken for a slave named Dick (see chapter 3). The building survived until it was largely demolished to make way for the U.S. Army Ammunition Plant sometime during the Second World War.

Each building's demise meant the loss of a visible monument to the clandestine system that assisted people seeking freedom from enslavement in the southern United States. To walk through and about these houses would have helped draw us from our current lives into the ones these long-ago activists and fugitives knew. Spaces, stair treads, layout, woodwork, floors, and ceilings would have helped take us back to a crucial era of our country's history. Nearly all are gone, and the few that remain reach us in ways that no book can convey.

In the absence of most of the old buildings, we can still learn from studies of the grounds on which they stood and the artifacts they contained. For instance, an archeological excavation of the onetime rural hamlet of Civil Bend was carried out in 2004. The researchers identified four sites: the 1849 schoolhouse thought to have been burned by people opposed to the enrollment of black children, Lester and Elvira Platt's nearby cabin, Ira Blanchard's house, and James Smith's house. But they were not able to locate the cabin where the Garner family lived and suffered so badly from proslavery violence. Shifts in the course of the Missouri River had scoured away the site and any artifacts the family might have left behind.[26]

Many of the remnants of the past detailed in these pages can no longer be seen today. Buildings are gone, trails are lost in undergrowth, sloughs are drained: all have disappeared beneath the sod, and only the sweeping landforms survive. People's memories disappeared along with the material signs of this history and the generation that made it. Still, plenty remains to be discovered. Important fragments of these exciting times survive in old newspapers, letters, and court documents concerning the people who participated in the political battles over slavery. Here are found their pleas, arguments, disputes, and reports of events that spread so quickly by telegraph and evoked immediate and increasingly intense responses.

In particular, there is much yet to be learned about individual Iowans who worked on the underground railroad. The State Historical Society's research identified some 180 of these courageous people, only a few of whom could be mentioned here. Most of them remain unstudied. The first step toward figuring out who they were is a close reading of old newspapers, for they reveal bits and pieces of information, such as church membership and economic activities, that help sketch the outline of a life. In particular, the stories of most of the black Americans who escaped into Iowa await their researchers. True enough, they and their families are less well-documented than many white Iowans, but census data from Missouri and Iowa often provide critical clues, as do county histories and newspaper obituaries. Exploring these sources will help shed light on the lives of Americans who risked everything to live free and unfettered in Iowa.

## ACKNOWLEDGMENTS

I came to this book not intentionally, but as an outgrowth of a related project. In 1999 the Iowa General Assembly directed that the State Historical Society of Iowa prepare a proposal for them on how best to commemorate places associated with the underground railroad in Iowa. Ultimately, the Iowa Department of Transportation kindly awarded federal matching Enhancement Funds under the Intermodal Surface Transportation Efficiency Act of 1991 (ISTEA; Public Law 102-240) and project work began, combining research, field work, and archeological investigation. When research and field work revealed that fewer than expected buildings survived of that history, project attention turned to preparing publications that could tell the stories and routes of escape across Iowa and convey the state's part in this pre–Civil War history, thereby adding to the stories associated with the few buildings that remain.

In directing this project and writing the book, I greatly benefited from the help of a number of wonderful researchers, local historians, institutions, and individuals. I am greatly obliged to and grateful for the exceptional research work carried out by John Zeller and Eric Lana. Working through all surviving Iowa newspapers dating from 1846 to 1863, they uncovered thousands of news items on antislavery debates and evidence of underground railroad activity in Iowa and combed through every county history to locate additional stories and background information on individuals. Augmenting the research was John Zeller's liaison activity with local historical organizations, which yielded considerable leads and new sources on places of interest. Also greatly appreciated was John's generously volunteered photographic and mapmaking skills, his donation of various secondary materials on these topics, and his own bighearted sharing of historical insights, along with his good humor and wealth of enjoyable stories.

I am indebted to Douglas Jones, staff archeologist with the State Historic Preservation Office, for his enthusiastic commitment to gathering information about eastern Iowa's antislavery story and helping me in my publication efforts. As he became increasingly engaged in the underground railroad project, he organized archeological investigations at underground railroad sites and made many public presentations. From these he drew in additional information from excellent local researchers Steve Hanken and Mike Boyle, and he also found additional clues in local historical society and library collections.

Special thanks go to James Hill, Midwest field representative of the National Park Service's National Underground Railroad to Freedom program. His ongoing encouragement and range of contacts within Iowa and in adjacent states brought forth important information. In particular, he shared important details gathered about underground railroad activity in Nebraska City, Nebraska, and what he had learned of the kidnapping and rescue of Maria and Henry Garner at St. Louis through the generous help of Kristian Zapalac, staff member of the Missouri State Historic Preservation Office.

To friends who graciously came to my aid in reading the manuscript, I owe more than thanks. G. Galin Berrier, who writes and lectures on Iowa's underground railroad, read the entire manuscript and, with insight and discernment, offered many helpful suggestions and improvements to the text and provided a valuable sounding board on the subject. I am grateful to Amanda Pirog, who read several chapters of the manuscript with clear-eyed talent for noting confused and overstated sentences; her numerous editorial and reading suggestions have been very useful.

I am grateful to the State Historical Society of Iowa and Division Director Gordon Hendrickson for providing me with three rich and rewarding years during which to write this manuscript. Its library and manuscripts staff were especially helpful in assisting me to locate material: especially, the interlibrary loan services of Shari Stelling; the manuscripts and photo expertise of Mary Bennett and Becki Plunkett; the archival aid of Sharon Avery; the editorial thoughts of Ginalie Swaim; the graphics assistance of Berry Bennett, Don Hirt, and Rick Dressler; and the photographic reproduction services of Charles Scott.

I have been fortunate to work with and benefit from the knowledge of numerous friends in towns and counties of Iowa interested in local underground railroad activity, including: Lewis Savage (deceased), Doug Hamilton, Dan Clark, Kent Sissel, Floyd Pearce, Max Bebout, Carol Carpenter Hanson, and, in particular, Jean Leeper, who kindly shared photos and archival material gleaned from her own research.

Finally, my dearest appreciation goes to my wife, Karen, whose companionship, love, and understanding included much patience for the many evenings and weekends taken up to complete the manuscript at home, time that invariably drew me away from our other enjoyments and comforts together.

NOTES

## Introduction

1 The description of Walker comes from the Affidavit of James McClure, taken at Farmington, Iowa, October 9, 1848, in *Daggs v. Frazier*, U.S. District Court Law Case files, U.S. District Court for the Southern Division of Iowa (Burlington), January Term, 1849, records of which are in U.S. Courts, Record Group 21, National Archives and Records Center, Central Plains Region, Kansas City, Missouri (hereafter cited as Daggs Case File).

2 The four-hundred-acre size of the farm is based on the probate record of Ruel Daggs's estate as of his death on December 16, 1862.

3 In 1992, the State Historical Society of the Iowa Department of Cultural Affairs received matching grant funds for the project from the Iowa Department of Transportation, under the Enhancement Fund grant program of the Federal Highway Administration.

4 For the interpretation of the underground railroad as a great force pushing the nation to Civil War, see Wilbur H. Siebert, *The Underground Railroad from Slavery to Freedom* (New York: Macmillan, 1899). Perhaps the leading writer to doubt that large numbers of slaves traveled to freedom on the underground railroad is Larry Gara, *The Liberty Line: The Legend of the Underground Railroad* (Lexington: University Press of Kentucky, 1961).

5 On abolitionists' mixed success in persuading Northern churches to adopt an antislavery stance, see John R. McKivigan, *The War against Proslavery Religion: Abolitionism and the Northern Churches, 1830–1865* (Ithaca, NY: Cornell University Press, 1984).

## 1 Iowa and the Politics of Slavery

1   The role of border states in the rising slavery controversy is detailed in Stanley Harrold, *Border War: Fighting over Slavery before the Civil War* (Chapel Hill: University of North Carolina Press, 2010). The place of border states in the unfolding debate is recognized in the two volumes of William W. Freehling's *The Road to Disunion*, vol. 1, *Secessionists at Bay, 1776–1854* (New York: Oxford University Press, 1990), 17–22, 473–474, 536–564; vol. 2, *Secessionists Triumphant, 1854–1861* (New York: Oxford University Press, 2007), 2–3, 63–65, 141–143.

2   *Burlington Hawk-Eye and Iowa Patriot*, October 24, 1839, a Whig newspaper.

3   Theodore Dwight Weld, *American Slavery As It Is: Testimony of a Thousand Witnesses* (New York: American Anti-Slavery Society, 1839), 7.

4   Henry Mayer, *All on Fire: William Lloyd Garrison and the Abolition of Slavery* (New York: St. Martin's Griffin, 1998), 217, 240.

5   On the various strains of and connections among religious evangelicalism and abolitionist reform and politics, see Douglas M. Strong, *Perfectionist Politics: Abolitionism and the Religious Tensions of American Democracy* (New York: Syracuse University Press, 1999).

6   On the efforts to move Northern churches to a strict antislavery stance, including failures and divisions within the movement, see McKivigan, *The War against Proslavery Religion*. See also Ian Frederick Finseth, "'Liquid Fire within Me': Language, Self and Society in Transcendentalism and Early Evangelicalism, 1820–1860" (master's thesis, University of Virginia, 1995), http://xroads.virginia.edu/~95/finseth/thesis.html.

7   See chapter 1 of Anne Farrow, Joel Lang, and Jenifer Frank, *Complicity: How the North Promoted, Prolonged, and Profited from Slavery* (New York: Ballantine, 2005).

8   Talk by Albert Pike at New Orleans, quoted from the *Chicago Daily Tribune*, January 29, 1855, in Elmer LeRoy Craik, "Southern Interest in Territorial Kansas, 1854–1855," *Collections of the Kansas State Historical Society 1919–1922*, vol. 15 (Topeka, KS: State Printer, 1923), 338–339.

9   Hinton Rowan Helper, *The Impending Crisis of the South: How to Meet It* (New York: A. B. Burdick, 1860), 23.

10  Burlington *Wisconsin Territorial Gazette and Advertiser*, October 5, 1837, quoted in Joel H. Silbey, "Pro-slavery Sentiment in Iowa, 1838–1861" (master's thesis, University of Iowa, 1956), 18; on antiblack sentiments, see Mayer, *All on Fire*, 217.

11  For discussion of these laws in midwestern states, see chapters 1 and 2 of Eugene H. Berwanger, *The Frontier against Slavery: Western Anti-Negro Prejudice and the Slavery Extension Controversy* (Urbana: University of Illinois Press, 1967).

12  *Statute Laws of the Territory of Iowa* (Des Moines: Iowa Printing Co., 1900; orig. Dubuque: Russell and Reeves, 1839), 69–70. All calculations to 2011 dollar amounts were figured using the Inflation Calculator website, www.westegg.com/inflation.

13  Twelve years later, in a test case, a district court judge ruled that the exclusion law violated both the state and national constitutions and was therefore not binding. The Case of Archie P. Webb, Polk County, Iowa, ruling by Judge John Henry Gray, February 2, 1863. One year later the legislature repealed it. See chapter 9 for the whole story.

14  Ward Robert Barnes, "Anti-Slavery Politics in Iowa 1840–1856" (master's thesis, University of Iowa, 1968), 63–64.

15  Barnes, "Anti-Slavery Politics," 63–64.

16  See William Lee Miller, *Arguing about Slavery: The Great Battle in the United States Congress* (New York: Knopf, 1996).

17  *The History of Clinton County, Iowa* (Chicago: Western Historical Co., 1879), 414.

18  *Iowa Territorial Gazette*, June 29, 1839, quoted in Joel H. Silbey, "Pro-slavery Sentiment in Iowa, 1838–1861," *Iowa Journal of History* 55:4 (October 1957), 293.

19  *History of Clinton County, Iowa*, 414.

20  Burlington *Wisconsin Territorial Gazette and Advertiser*, October 5, 1837, quoted in Silbey, "Pro-slavery Sentiment in Iowa" (master's thesis), 18.

21  *Davenport Gazette*, October 10, 1844, quoted in Barnes, "Anti-Slavery Politics," 12.

22  James Brewer Stewart, *Holy Warriors: The Abolitionists and American Slavery* (New York: Hill and Wang, 1997), 95–125.

23 Iowa's first local antislavery society had been formed in Denmark in January 1840. Others included the Washington County Anti-Slavery Society and the Salem Anti-Slavery Society, formed in 1841, and the Lee County Anti-Slavery Society, formed in September 1843. Barnes, "Anti-Slavery Politics," 13, 17, 20.

24 Barnes, "Anti-Slavery Politics," 68-69, 72, 74.

25 On Alanson St. Clair, see Robert R. Dykstra, *Bright Radical Star: Black Freedom and White Supremacy on the Hawkeye Frontier* (Cambridge, MA: Harvard University Press, 1993), 72-79, and notes on 304-305; Barnes, "Anti-Slavery Politics," 83-86.

26 From 1838 to 1845, St. Clair had been an abolition lecturer in New England. He spent his first two years as a traveling agent for the Massachusetts Anti-Slavery Society, led by William Lloyd Garrison. Then, purged from the organization after joining "church-oriented" opponents of Garrison, he eventually moved to the Chicago area. See Massachusetts Anti-Slavery Society, *Eighth Annual Report of the Board of Managers of the Mass. Anti-Slavery Society* (Boston: Dow and Jackson, 1840), xliii.

27 Other executive committee members, all from southeast Iowa, included Lewis Epps (Denmark), William Leslie (Fort Madison), William McClure (Yellow Springs), Adam Fordney (Burlington), Asa Calkin (Iowa City), William French (Birmingham), and Henry Ritner (Danville). This list is from Barnes, "Anti-Slavery Politics," 103.

28 Early Iowa has been called "proslavery," but that term is more a shorthand expression for Iowans who thought that slavery ought not be interfered with where it existed. Such views became less politically influential with increasing numbers of migrants into the state who did not accept slavery's legitimacy. The question of Iowans' sentiments toward slavery has received varying consideration by historians. Emphasis on the "proslavery" side is provided in David L. Sparks, "The Birth of the Republican Party in Iowa, 1854-1856," *Iowa Journal of History* 54:1 (January 1956), 1-34; and Silbey, "Pro-slavery Sentiment in Iowa" (*Iowa Journal of History*), 289-318. Another emphasis —viewing Iowans as hostile to slavery but as trying to avoid dealing with it or favoring noninterference—is presented by James Connor, "The Antislavery Movement in Iowa," *Annals of Iowa*, 3rd ser., Part I, 40:5 (Summer 1970), 343-376; Part II, 40:6 (Fall 1970), 450-479.

## 2   *Iowa Becomes Antislavery*

1   James E. Potter, "Fact and Folklore in the Story of 'John Brown's Cave' and the Underground Railroad in Nebraska," *Nebraska History* 83 (2002), 73–88; Byron D. Fruehling and Robert H. Smith, "Subterranean Hideaways of the Underground Railroad in Ohio: An Architectural, Archaeological and Historical Critique of Local Traditions," *Ohio History* 102 (Summer and Fall 1993), 98–117.

2   The main propagator of the quilt connection to the underground railroad is Jacqueline L. Tobin, *Hidden in Plain View: A Secret Story of Quilts and the Underground Railroad* (New York: Anchor, 2000). The main critic, Barbara Brackman, finds no evidence for secret codes in quilt patterns; see Barbara Brackman, *Facts and Fabrications: Unraveling the History of Quilts and Slavery: 8 Projects, 20 Blocks, First-Person Accounts* (Concord, CA: C & T, 2006).

3   See Howard Dodson, "Runaway Slaves—Fleeing Death, Seeking Life," *American Visions* 14:4 (August/September 1999), 18–25, an interview with John Hope Franklin and Loren Schweninger, authors of *Runaway Slaves: Rebels on the Plantation* (Oxford: Oxford University Press, 1999).

4   The story is drawn from Clark T. Smith, "Boyhood Recollections Connected with the Early History of Amity, Iowa, Now Known as College Springs," *College Springs Current Press*, November 24, December 8, December 15, and December 22, 1921. A photocopy of the manuscript that the author sent to the newspaper editor can be found in the Archives and Manuscripts Collection, Seymour Library, Knox College, Galesburg, IL.

5   Thomas P. Christensen, "Denmark—An Early Stronghold of Congregationalism," *Iowa Journal of History and Politics* 24:1 (January 1926), 37–50. On Asa Turner, see Dr. George F. Magoun, "An Iowa Missionary Patriarch," *Annals of Iowa*, 3rd ser., 3 (1897–1899), 53–62, and Magoun's *Asa Turner: A Home Missionary Patriarch and His Times* (Boston: Congregational Sunday School and Publishing Society, 1889).

6   Turner's friendship with David Nelson began at a camp meeting in Missouri, where Nelson persuaded Turner to adopt a more urgent abolitionism. See Hermann R. Muelder, *Fighters for Freedom: The*

*History of Anti-Slavery Activities of Men and Women Associated with Knox College* (Galesburg, IL: Knox College, 1950), 62–63, 139. For northeast Missourians' view of David Nelson, see Terrell Dempsey, *Searching for Jim: Slavery in Sam Clemens's World* (Columbia: University of Missouri Press, 2003), 22–26.

7   Magoun, *Asa Turner*, 156–157.

8   Magoun, *Asa Turner*, 162–164. Alton, consisting of but two or three dozen houses in 1832, had mushroomed into a town of three hundred houses by 1837. The emigrant guidebook *Illinois in 1837 & 8* stated, "A large proportion of the buildings are of the most substantial kind,—massive stone ware-houses," although "the larger portion of both business and dwelling-houses are temporary frames of one story." This portion of the guidebook is reproduced by the Illinois State Historical Library, "Sketches of the Cities and Principal Towns in the State of Illinois," http://www.state.il.us/HPA/lovejoy/alton.htm.

9   *Wisconsin Territorial Gazette and Advertiser*, October 5, 1837, 2. Elijah Lovejoy's controversial activities are noted in Harrison Anthony Trexler, *Slavery in Missouri 1804–1865* (Baltimore: Johns Hopkins University Press, 1914), 117–119; Muelder, *Fighters for Freedom*, 125–128, 132–133.

10  Barnes, "Anti-Slavery Politics," 17.

11  George C. Shedd, "Hibbard Houston Shedd," in *Nebraska State Historical Society Publications*, 2nd ser., vol. 10 (Lincoln, NE: Jacob North, 1907), 169.

12  Ephraim Adams, *The Iowa Band* (Boston: Pilgrim Press, 1902); Christensen, "Denmark—An Early Stronghold," 41–42; Magoun, *Asa Turner*, 226–230.

13  Augustine M. Antrobus, *History of Des Moines County Iowa and Its People*, vol. 1 (Chicago: S. J. Clarke, 1915), 524–525, 527–530; J. W. Merrill, *Yellow Spring and Huron: A Local History* (Mediapolis, IA: published by the author, 1897), 334–339; Barnes, "Anti-Slavery Politics," 18–19.

14  Two townships in particular, Washington and Crawford, drew the most Seceders. Barnes, "Anti-Slavery Politics," 23–25.

15  On the Aaron Street family, see Keith M. Street, *Descendants of Zadok Street and Eunice Silver, New Jersey Quakers through 10 Generations* (Wapello, IA: C. K. Casey Enterprises, 1996), 1–3, 9–11.

16 Most of the Friends living in the Cherry Grove Monthly Meeting area originally hailed from North Carolina.

17 Small Quaker communities soon also grew nearby. Four miles northwest of Salem was Lower Settlement on Cedar Creek, and twenty-one miles farther in the same direction was the Pleasant Prairie settlement. To the south and east were three rural Quaker neighborhoods, the most important being New Garden (located midway between Salem and Denmark), East Grove (five miles southeast of Salem), and Chestnut Hill (about five miles south of Salem). Louis Thomas Jones, *The Quakers of Iowa* (Iowa City: State Historical Society of Iowa, 1914), 51.

18 The most extensive treatment of immediate abolition as a divisive force in Quaker meetings is Ryan P. Jordan, *Slavery and the Meetinghouse: The Quakers and the Abolitionist Dilemma, 1820–1865* (Bloomington: Indiana University Press, 2007), but also useful is Ryan P. Jordan, "The Indiana Separation of 1842 and the Limits of Quaker Anti-Slavery," *Quaker History* 89 (Spring 2000), 1–27.

19 Elsewhere across northern Missouri slaveowners also remained watchful, hoping to assure others with slaves that there would be no trouble from nearby Iowa. Samuel R. Rolston, writing to a friend back in North Carolina from his two-year-old Jackson County farm in western Missouri, noted the rising number of enslaved African Americans brought there, assuring his friend that "we have had an active patrol established, [which] will encourage many persons to become citizens of our county who hitherto have been afraid in consequence of our border situation." Donnie Duglie Bellamy, "Slavery, Emancipation, and Racism in Missouri 1850–1865" (Ph.D. dissertation, University of Missouri, 1971), 32.

20 Bellamy, "Slavery, Emancipation, and Racism," 38–39; Russel L. Gerlach, *Settlement Patterns in Missouri: A Study of Population Origins* (Columbia: University of Missouri Press, 1986), 20–24, 28.

21 Craik, "Southern Interest in Territorial Kansas," 353–358.

22 Francis A. E. Waters, "Anti-Slavery Sentiment in Iowa," Washington, D.C., *National Era*, November 21, 1850.

23 Affidavit of James McClure, taken at Farmington, Iowa, Daggs Case File, October 9, 1848. Henry Brown, who worked for McClure, stated that he thought the four children were the Walkers', in the Deposition

of Henry Brown, taken at Fairfield, Iowa, Daggs Case File, March 22, 1850.

24 Mr. Way is mentioned in the subsequent court record in the Daggs case, but most likely the place where Slaughter and McClure stayed in Farmington was the house of Dr. A. Wayland, a proslavery sympathizer in town. See "The Negro Case," *Keokuk Telegraphic Weekly Dispatch*, July 13, 1848.

25 George Frazee, *Fugitive Slave Case, District Court of the Southern Division of Iowa, Burlington, June Term, 1850*, Ruel Daggs v. Elihu Frazier, et al. (Burlington, IA: Morgan and M'Kenny, 1850), 6.

26 Deposition of James McClure, Daggs Case File, October 9, 1848.

27 Deposition of Henry Brown, Daggs Case File, March 22, 1850.

28 Deposition of James McClure, Daggs Case File, October 9, 1848.

29 The way James McClure remembered it, "[Moses] Baldwin said he would wade in blood the depth I do not recollect before they should [be] taken from that place, and ordered me to leave or he would take my heart out and grind it in the dust." Deposition of James McClure, Daggs Case File, October 9, 1848.

30 Deposition of Henry Brown, Daggs Case File, supra note 18, March 22, 1850.

31 Deposition of James McClure, Daggs Case File, October 9, 1848.

32 Frazee, *Fugitive Slave Case*, 6.

33 Deposition of James McClure, Daggs Case File, supra note 18, October 9, 1848, and deposition of Henry Brown, Daggs Case File, March 22, 1850.

34 Deposition of Henry Brown, Daggs Case File, March 22, 1850.

35 The quotation comes from the deposition of Henry Brown, Daggs Case File, March 22, 1850; deposition of James McClure, Daggs Case File, supra note 18, October 9, 1848.

36 Frazee, *Fugitive Slave Case*, 6.

37 F. A. McElroy testimony in Frazee, *Fugitive Slave Case*, 6.

38 According to Rachel Kellum, who helped her father with the rescue, the Missourians also brought a cannon, which they placed in front of Henderson Lewelling's stone house. See her "Reminiscence," *Western Work* (August 1908), 5.

39 "The Salem Affair," *Burlington Hawk-Eye*, June 15, 1848. Hillsboro in

the early 1840s had been called Washington and was occasionally still referred to by this name in some sources.

40 "The Salem Affair," *Keokuk Telegraphic Weekly Dispatch*, June 15, 1848.

41 *Chicago Western Citizen*, July 11, 1848.

42 Kellum, "Reminiscence," 5. Nathan Kellum's mother was the sister of noted Indiana Quaker Levi Coffin, who is credited with assisting in the rescue of many slaves.

43 Kellum, "Reminiscence," 5. Julia Fulcher remained a slave in Clark County until the end of the Civil War. Then she married Hezekiah Hall and lived near Luray, Missouri, until 1875, when they moved to Attorney Givens's one-hundred-acre farm near Waterloo, Missouri, fourteen miles east of Luray, which they initially rented and then purchased. Lewis D. Savage, "Former Slaves, the Success Story of a Clark County Missouri Farm Family," at http://www.icelandichorse.info/daggsformerslavesuccessstory.html.

44 "Abduction of Slaves—Their Recovery, and Rescue by a Mob," St. Louis *Tri-Weekly Missouri Republican*, June 9, 1848; "Riot at Salem," *Keokuk Valley Whig and Register*, June 14, 1848; "The Negro Case," *Keokuk Telegraphic Weekly Dispatch*, June 15, 1848.

45 "Abduction of Slaves," *Keokuk Valley Whig and Register*, June 15, 1848.

46 "Salem—The Negro Case," letter to the editor signed by nine citizens of Henry County, *Keokuk Telegraphic Weekly Dispatch*, June 22, 1848.

47 "Abduction of Slaves—Their Recovery, and Rescue by a Mob," St. Louis *Tri-Weekly Missouri Republican*, June 9, 1848.

48 "The Negro Case," *Keokuk Telegraphic Weekly Dispatch*, July 13, 1848.

49 Those named in the suit included Elihu Frazier, Eli Jessup, John Pickering, Drury Overton, Elijah Johnson, Moses Baldwin, Thomas Clarkson Frazier, Moses Purvis, Franklin Street, Albert Button, William Johnson, Ruben Johnson, John Comer, Wyncoop Gilkinson, Paul Way, Isaac Frazier, John Ewing, Jesse Cook, and William Cook; see the September 1, 1848, summons by J. J. Dyer, Judge of the District Court of the United States for the District of Iowa at Iowa City, commanding the district marshal to summon these men to appear at the district court in Iowa City on January 1, 1849, Daggs Case File.

50 Frazee, *Fugitive Slave Case*. This report has also been reprinted in Paul Finkelman, ed., *Fugitive Slaves and American Courts: The Pamphlet Literature*, 2nd ser., vol. 1 (New York: Garland, 1988), 495–534. Subsequent citations refer to the original 1850 report by Frazee, which is available online via the Library of Congress's American Memory website at http://memory.loc.gov/ammem/index.html. See also chapter 5 in Dykstra, *Bright Radical Star*, 88–105, 306–309; Paul Finkelman, "Fugitive Slaves, Midwestern Racial Tolerance, and the Value of 'Justice Delayed,'" *Iowa Law Review* 78:1 (October 1992), 89–141; Robert J. Willoughby, "'I'll Wade in Missouri Blood': *Daggs v. Frazier*: A Case of Missouri Runaway Slaves," *Missouri Historical Review* 49:2 (January 2005), 115–138; and O. A. Garretson, "Travelling on the Underground Railroad in Iowa," *Iowa Journal of History and Politics* 22:3 (July 1924), 418–453.

51 See History of the Federal Judiciary, "Biographical Directory of Federal Judges, 1789–Present," at the Federal Judicial Center website, http://www.fjc.gov/public/home.nsf/hisj.

52 Though a former Virginian, Rorer could not be considered a proslavery man, for he had sold his Virginia farm in 1835 and freed his slaves. In 1839 he successfully won freedom for the slave Ralph in the Iowa Territory Supreme Court after slavecatchers had been prevented from returning the man to Missouri from the lead mines in Dubuque (this case is discussed in chapter 5). See also Connor, "The Antislavery Movement in Iowa," Part I; and James E. Connor, "The Antislavery Movement in Iowa, 1833–1860" (master's thesis, Drake University, 1970), 23–25.

53 Frazee, *Fugitive Slave Case*, 21.

54 Frazee, *Fugitive Slave Case*, 33.

55 Frazee, *Fugitive Slave Case*, 34.

56 Frazee, *Fugitive Slave Case*, 34–39, 40.

57 Frazee, *Fugitive Slave Case*, 40.

58 See Finkelman, *Fugitive Slaves*, for a comparison of the Daggs case and a South Bend, Indiana, fugitive slave case called *Norris v. Newton et al.* These cases constituted the last two federal court cases argued under the Fugitive Slave Act of 1793. In his *Slavery in the Courtroom: An Annotated Bibliography of American Cases* (Washington, DC: Library of Congress, 1985), 80, Finkelman noted that the Daggs case

"was one of the last cases argued solely on the basis of the Fugitive Slave Act of 1793. It was also one of the few fugitive slave cases heard in Iowa."

59 Muscatine *Iowa Democratic Enquirer*, June 27, 1850.

60 Dykstra, *Bright Radical Star*, 104–105, quoting from U.S. Senate, *Appendix to the Congressional Globe*, 31st Cong., 1st sess. (August 23, 1850), 22, pt. 2: 1623.

61 *Burlington Hawk-Eye*, July 11, 1850.

62 On the failed collection efforts, see Finkelman, *Fugitive Slaves*, 132–134. For evidence that the defendants divested themselves of real estate, see note 2 of the nomination for the National Register of Historic Places of the "Lewelling, Henderson and Elizabeth (Presnel) House," a property listed in the National Register on August 31, 2007:

Between the time of the incident in June 1848 and the time of the verdict in June 1850, land records and sales of the convicted defendants and the 1850 census support that they owned little if any property. John H. Pickering had also sold property on January 9, 1848, filed on September 13, 1849, in Salem (Town Lots Book H: 529). Thomas Clarkson and Lucinda Frazier transferred property south of town to his father Thomas Frazier on December 28, 1849 (Town Lots Book H: 41). William C. and Elizabeth Johnson sold property north of town on October 3, 1849, filed on November 3, 1849 (Town Lots Book H: 603). Paul Way sold numerous pieces of property from December 6, 1848 to December 6, 1849 (with some deeds not filed until February 5 and June 8, 1850), as well as platting an addition to Salem on July 27, 1849 (Town Lots Book H: 467). The 1850 census shows that Elihu Frazier (31) was a farmer with $0 in real estate, living with his wife Orpha and five children. Thomas Clarkson Frazier (37) also had $0 in real estate, and he worked as a carpenter and lived with his wife Ruth and seven children. John Pickering (40) was also reported as a farmer with $0 in real estate, listed as living with his wife Mary and a Hobson boy. The only William Johnson (21) identified was listed as a painter in the household of John Johnson. Likewise, John Comer (20) was a farmer listed in the household of James Comer (45). The only defendant to claim any real estate value was Paul Way (66), listed as a farmer with $200 in real estate, living with his wife and son (U.S. Census Bureau).

The official listing is at the National Register of Historic Places, National Park Service, Washington D.C. A copy of the nomination is available at the Iowa State Historic Preservation Office, State Historical Society of Iowa, Des Moines.

63 *Hannibal Journal*, reprinted in the *Keokuk Telegraphic Weekly Dispatch*, July 13, 1848. Evidently, the Hannibal editor was responding on June 29, 1848, to an editorial titled "Abduction of Slaves," in the *Keokuk Valley Whig and Register*, June 15, 1848; see Dempsey, *Searching for Jim*, 296.

## 3 The Struggle Intensifies

1 "Major William Williams' Journal of a Trip to Iowa in 1849," *Annals of Iowa* 12:4 (April 1920), 249.

2 The story as related here is reported in D. C. Cloud, "The Negro Case, For the Enquirer, Bloomington, November 8th, 1848," Bloomington *Iowa Democratic Enquirer*, November 11, 1848 (hereafter cited as Cloud, "The Negro Case").

3 D. C. Cloud, letter to the editor of the *Annals of Iowa*, December 3, 1897, which gives his recollections about the case of Jim. The letter is in the Des Moines Manuscript Collection of the State Historical Society of Iowa, CL6245, SM Box 17, Folder 5 (hereafter cited as D. C. Cloud letter).

4 D. C. Cloud letter.

5 All later attained legal and political prominence in the state. David C. Cloud was state attorney general (1853–1856); Ralph B. Lowe became governor (1858–1860) and an Iowa Supreme Court judge; Jacob Butler was speaker of the Iowa House of Representatives (1864–1865); and W. G. Woodward became clerk of the U.S. Circuit Court and then a judge on the Iowa Supreme Court.

6 When D. C. Cloud had arrived from Ohio nine years earlier, he was a carpenter. By fall 1839 he contracted with the young lawyer S. C. Hastings to make and install the windows and doors in his new house in exchange for using his law books and receiving instruction from him. Within three years Cloud had been elected justice of the peace. Admitted to law practice in early 1846, he continued to practice privately while also serving several terms as justice of the peace.

7 See Richard Acton, and Patricia Nassif Acton, *To Go Free: A Treasury of Iowa's Legal Heritage* (Ames: Iowa State University Press, 1995), 40–48; Richard, Lord Acton, and Patricia Nassif Acton, "A Legal History of African-Americans from the Iowa Territory to the State Ses-

quicentennial, 1838–1996," in *Outside In: African-American History in Iowa, 1838–2000*, ed. Bill Silag (Des Moines: State Historical Society of Iowa, 2001), 63–64; Robert R. Dykstra, "Dr. Emerson's Sam: Black Iowans before the Civil War," *Iowa Heritage Illustrated* 85:2–3 (Summer and Fall 2004), 55–56.

8   See Cloud, "The Negro Case"; J. P. Walton, "'Unwritten History of Bloomington (Now Muscatine) in Early Days,' read by J. P. Walton before the Muscatine Academy of Science, March 6, 1882," in *Annals of Iowa*, n.s., 1:2 (April 1882), 47–48, part of which is based on interviews with Sarah E. (Lowry) Hughes and Alexander Clark; "Samuel M. Hughes," biographical sketch in *History of Muscatine County Iowa: From the Earliest Settlements to the Present Time, Biographical*, vol. 2 (Chicago: S. J. Clarke, 1911), 597–598; "Mrs. Sarah Hughes/Well Known Woman Died Yesterday," *Muscatine News-Tribune*, August 27, 1913.

9   Walton, "'Unwritten History,'" 47.

10   Walton, "'Unwritten History,'" 47.

11   Cloud, "The Negro Case."

12   Cloud, "The Negro Case."

13   D. C. Cloud letter.

14   Walton, "'Unwritten History,'" 48.

15   Walton, "'Unwritten History,'" 48.

16   Dykstra, *Bright Radical Star*, 18, 296, quoting the *Bloomington Herald*, November 18, 1848.

17   Dykstra, *Bright Radical Star*, 18, 296; "The Negro Case—Again," Bloomington *Iowa Democratic Enquirer*, November 14, 1848.

18   Dempsey, *Searching for Jim*, 133, 137.

19   "The Underground Railroad," *Muscatine Journal*, September 2, 1854, reprinted in the *Quincy Daily Whig*, September 8, 1854.

20   Dempsey, *Searching for Jim*, 111.

21   The Pyles family story is based on the following sources: Mrs. Laurence C. Jones, "The Desire for Freedom," *Palimpsest* 8:5 (May 1927), 153–163; Betty DeRamus, *Forbidden Fruit: Love Stories from the Underground Railroad* (New York: Atria, 2005), 110–120; G. Galin Berrier, "The Underground Railroad in Iowa," in *Outside In: African-American History in Iowa, 1838–2000*, ed. Bill Silag (Des Moines: State Historical Society of Iowa, 2001), 47–48; and Jessie Carney

Smith, ed., *Notable Black Women: Book II* (Farmington Hills, MI: Thomson Gale, 1995), 535–536.

22 DeRamus, *Forbidden Fruit*, 110–112, 235.

23 DeRamus, *Forbidden Fruit*, 111.

24 DeRamus, *Forbidden Fruit*, 112–114.

25 Jones, "The Desire for Freedom," 159; DeRamus, *Forbidden Fruit*, 115–116.

26 Smith, *Notable Black Women*, 536.

27 "The Slave Dick," *Burlington Weekly Hawk-Eye*, June 25, 1855.

28 Thomas Rutherford is mentioned in the family genealogy of his wife, Eliza Terry, at the "Record of James Lawrence Terry—Son of James Terry, who was a son of Stephen Terry," *Terry Family Historian* 3:2 (June 1984), online at http://www.terry-family-historian.com/ TFHJUN1984.htm.

29 "A Fugitive Slave in Iowa: Correspondence of the N. Y. Tribune," reprinted in the *National Anti-Slavery Standard*, July 14, 1855.

30 George Frazee, "The Iowa Fugitive Slave Case," *Annals of Iowa*, 3rd ser., 4:2 (July 1899), 128.

31 L. H. Pammel, "Dr. Edwin James," *Annals of Iowa*, 3rd ser., 8:4 (January 1908), 292–293, 295.

32 Pammel, "Dr. Edwin James," 295.

33 Frazee, "Iowa Fugitive Slave Case," 129.

34 "The Slave Dick," *Burlington Weekly Hawk-Eye*, June 25, 1855.

35 Frazee, "Iowa Fugitive Slave Case," 128.

36 Frazee, "Iowa Fugitive Slave Case," 128–129.

37 On Milton D. Browning, see Edward Holcomb Stiles, *Recollections and Sketches of Notable Lawyers and Public Men of Early Iowa: Belonging to the First and Second Generations; With Anecdotes and Incidents Illustrative of the Times* (Des Moines, IA: Homestead, 1916), 295–296.

38 Frazee, "Iowa Fugitive Slave Case," 129–130, 133.

39 "A Fugitive Slave in Iowa," *National Anti-Slavery Standard*, July 14, 1855.

40 William Salter, *The Life of James W. Grimes, Governor of Iowa, 1854–1858; A Senator of the United States, 1859–1869* (New York: D. Appleton, 1876), 72–73.

41 Salter, *Life of James W. Grimes*, 73; Stiles, *Recollections and Sketches*, 240–249, 259, 281–291, 300–302. Formal thanks for the participation of Rorer, Warren, and others took place at a June 26 mass meeting in Denmark, the resolutions of which were printed in the *Burlington Daily Hawk-Eye & Telegraph*, June 30, 1855.

42 Frazee, "Iowa Fugitive Slave Case," 132.

43 On the life of Edwin James, see Maxine Frances Benson, "Edwin James: Scientist, Linguist, Humanitarian" (Ph.D. dissertation, University of Colorado, 1968); Pammel, "Dr. Edwin James."

44 Salter, *Life of James W. Grimes*, 73.

## 4  A Hole of Abolitionists

1 *History of Appanoose County, Iowa* (Chicago: Western Historical Co., 1878), 372.

2 From Calvert's place, the man was taken to Arthur Corner's, near Drakesville, who took him to Jacob Lamb's near Libertyville in southern Jefferson County. Lamb then escorted him to the Quaker settlement at Salem in Henry County. Erastus Nulton, Hartford, Missouri, to Professor Siebert, March 16, 1896, MIC 192, Box 45, Folder 11, Wilbur H. Siebert Collection, Ohio Historical Society Collections (hereafter cited as Siebert Collection).

3 Federated Women's Clubs of the County 1924–1927, *Pioneer History of Davis County, Iowa* (Bloomfield, IA: Bloomfield Democrat, 1927), 147.

4 *History of Appanoose County, Iowa*, 451–452, 92; L. L. Taylor, ed., *Past and Present of Appanoose County, Iowa*, vol. 1 (Chicago: S. J. Clarke, 1913), 365–379.

5 This is contrary to what is presented in the *Pioneer History of Davis County, Iowa*, 148–149, which attributes to Horatio A. Wonn a leading role in Drakesville underground railroad operations. However, none of the writings of people who lived through and participated in these events (for example, George Elliott's son, Arthur Corner, William E. Conner, Hiram Pagett, and John H. B. Armstrong) mentions Horatio Wonn, who eventually became a state senator. His 1871 obituary in the *State Register* claimed that Wonn had been "one of the original agents of John Brown's Underground Railroads." One can safely con-

clude that if Wonn did play some role in underground railroad events, it was not a part large enough to be remembered by those with proven connections. The writings of participants are contained in Box 4, Siebert Collection, which includes letters from Arthur Corner with W. E. Conner attachment, January 1, 1896; John H. B. Armstrong, December 10 and 12, 1895; H. Pagett, February 22, 1896; son of George Gilbert, November 18, 1895.

6   *History of Appanoose County, Iowa,* 372.

7   In fact, Appanoose County was organized and its lands claimed before Missouri's Putnam County, immediately to the south, opened to settlement; see Taylor, ed., *Past and Present of Appanoose County,* 365–379; *History of Appanoose County,* 372–373.

8   For John and Archie's escape, see *History of Appanoose County,* 373.

9   The story that follows is drawn from two accounts contained in Box 45, Siebert Collection: a letter from "Son of George Elliott," Cedarville, Iowa, November 18, 1895, and an account by W. E. Conner attached to an Arthur Corner letter from Drakesville, Iowa, dated January 1, 1896. W. E. Conner's description could not have been completed before early 1897, because in it he mentions the death of Mr. English "this winter," and that death occurred on January 18, 1897 (*Oskaloosa Weekly Herald,* January 21, 1897). Other supplemental information about individual participants is drawn from manuscript schedules of the 1860 U.S. Census. My thanks to researcher Dave Holmgren for sorting out the involvement of the Corner and Conner families in Drakesville's underground railroad activity.

10  Two years later, the father of the family returned to Missouri in the midst of the Civil War, attempting to find his daughter, who had been brought to the McQuitty farmhouse for nursing after having taken sick on the night of the family's escape. He made his way to the headquarters of Union Colonel David Moore, a forty-five-year-old Ohioan who had come to northeast Missouri in 1850 and in 1862 organized the Twenty-First Missouri Regiment. Recovering from the loss of his leg a few months earlier at the Battle of Shiloh, he was evidently touched by the father's plea, for the colonel sent a detail to McQuitty's house that found the child and delivered her to her anxious father waiting at camp. As William Conner described it, the father, now "the happiest man on earth . . . , thanked the col. over and over." With his

daughter, the father went north to Drakesville and stayed overnight with George Elliott, telling their host "all about his trip" and how the family was "doing well up in Canada and when he got home with the child their happiness would be complete." See the account of the family's rescue by W. E. Conner, attached to an Arthur Corner letter from Drakesville, Iowa, dated January 1, 1896, in Box 45, Siebert Collection.

11 "Kidnapped," reprinted from the *Page County Herald* in the *Albia Weekly Republican*, October 27, 1859.

12 "Outrage in Clark County," Des Moines *Iowa State Register*, August 15, 1860.

13 For examples of this, see "The Kidnapped Slave," reprinted from the *Cincinnati Gazette* in the *Burlington Daily Hawk-Eye*, October 30, 1857; "Kidnapping Case in Chicago," *Dubuque Weekly Times*, July 28, 1859; and William Elsey Connelley, *Quantrill and the Border Wars* (New York: Pageant, 1956), 136–137.

14 "Slave Stealing and Negro Hunting," reprinted from the *Chicago Tribune* in the *Dubuque Weekly Times*, April 18, 1861.

15 "Negro Stealing in Indiana," *Montezuma Republican*, December 27, 1856; see also "Organized Kidnappers," reprinted from the *Harrisburg Telegraph* in the *Burlington Daily Hawk-Eye*, April 24, 1860.

16 "Fugitive Slave Case in Cincinnati," *Dubuque Weekly Times*, April 14, 1857.

17 "An Outrageous Conspiracy—Attempt to Enslave a Family of Free Negroes," reprinted from the *Louisville Democrat* in the *Jasper Free Press*, November 3, 1859.

18 "An Act to Prevent Slave-Holding and Kidnapping in Ohio," *Burlington Daily Hawk-Eye & Telegraph*, April 28, 1857.

19 *Burlington Daily Hawk-Eye*, August 14 and 21, 1858. See also *Burlington Daily Morning News*, August 18 and 24 and September 2, 1858.

20 *Burlington Daily Morning News*, September 2, 1858.

21 See "The Curtis Affair," Iowa City *Iowa Weekly Republican*, February 22, 1860.

22 The man named Vincent may have been the outspoken antislavery preacher George C. Vincent, from southeastern Washington County.

23 The other two attorneys for the defense were J. B. Edmonds and U. D. McKay.

24  "The Kidnapping Case," Iowa City *Iowa Weekly Republican*, February 8, 1860.

25  "The Kidnapping Case," Iowa City *Iowa Weekly Republican*, February 8, 1860.

26  *Washington Press*, February 22, 1860, and "Finale and Farce of the Curtis Affair—The Negresses Adopted," in Iowa City *Iowa Weekly Republican*, February 15, 1860.

27  "Kidnapping at Iowa City—Great Abolition Hubbub—Nigger in the Wood-Pile," reprinted from the Iowa City *Reporter* in the *Davenport Democrat and News*, February 2, 1860, and "A Letter from Iowa City," *Davenport Democrat and News*, February 3, 1860.

28  "Effect of the Dred Scott Decision in Iowa," reprinted from the *Chicago Press* in the *Davenport Daily Gazette*, February 7, 1860; *Washington Press*, February 22, 1860; *Iowa Transcript*, February 16, 1860.

29  *History of Johnson County, Iowa* (Iowa City: 1883), 464; see also *Washington Press*, February 22, 1860, and "Finale and Farce of the Curtis Affair—The Negresses Adopted," in Iowa City *Iowa Weekly Republican*, February 15, 1860.

30  The main source of information about Jerry Boyd's kidnapping and murder is a single article comprising three reports from the *Chicago Tribune*, the *St. Joseph Gazette*, and the *Galena Advertiser*, all of which were published together in a number of papers, including the *Davenport Daily Gazette*, October 29, 1860. See also the Iowa City *Iowa Weekly Republican*, October 31, 1860; *Washington Press*, October 31, 1860.

31  Letter from Warner Spurrier, Solon, Iowa, to Governor Kirkwood, October 14, 1860. Samuel Jordan Kirkwood Papers, 1841–1894, State Historical Society of Iowa, Iowa City.

32  The amount of money raised was reported to be $500 in "The Galena Kidnapping Case: Return of the Negroes," *Davenport Daily Gazette*, October 29, 1860. A different amount—$1,000—is given in S. W. McMaster, *60 Years on the Upper Mississippi: Life and Experience* (Rock Island, IL, 1893), 174–175.

33  *Davenport Daily Gazette*, October 29, 1860.

34  *Davenport Daily Gazette*, October 29, 1860.

35  *Davenport Daily Gazette*, October 29, 1860.

## 5   The Kansas-Nebraska Act and
## Political Change in Iowa

1   For the history of the Kansas-Nebraska Act and its implications, see Freehling, *The Road to Disunion*, vol. 1, 536–565; John R. Wunder and Joann M. Ross, eds., *The Nebraska-Kansas Act of 1854* (Lincoln: University of Nebraska Press, 2008); Don E. Fehrenbacher, *The Dred Scott Case: Its Significance in American Law and Politics* (New York: Oxford University Press, 1978), 179–187; Robert R. Russel, "The Issues in the Congressional Struggle over the Kansas-Nebraska Bill, 1854," *Journal of Southern History* 29:2 (May 1963), 187–210; and P. Orman Ray, *The Repeal of the Missouri Compromise: Its Origin and Authorship* (Cleveland, OH: Arthur H. Clark, 1909).

2   The address is printed in Salter, *Life of James W. Grimes*, 33–50.

3   Salter, *Life of James W. Grimes*, 47.

4   Fears about the rising number of immigrants, especially Catholics from Germany and Ireland, were a major political issue during the 1850s.

5   Salter, *Life of James W. Grimes*, 39, 44–45. See also Craik, "Southern Interest in Territorial Kansas," 356–457.

6   F. I. Herriott, "A Neglected Factor in the Anti-Slavery Triumph in Iowa in 1854," "Deutsch-Amerikanische Geschichtsblatter," *Jahrbuch der Deutsch-Amerikanischen Historischen Gesellschaft von Illinois—Jahrgang 1918-19*. Vol. XVIII–XIX (Chicago, 1920), 279.

7   See, for example, an April 10 meeting at Kossuth (Des Moines County), reported in the Mount Pleasant *Iowa Weekly Observer*, April 20, 1854; a meeting of citizens of Morning Sun Township (Louisa County), reported in the *Wapello Intelligencer*, April 18, 1854; a July 8 "Anti-Nebraska Meeting in Warren County" reported in the *Ottumwa DeMoines Courier*, August 24, 1854; a July 15 Anti-Nebraska Convention of about two hundred people from fifteen townships, reported in the *Elkader Clayton County Herald*, July 21, 1854; a largely attended "People's Meeting," reported in the *Ottumwa DeMoines Courier*, July 27, 1854, reprinted from the *Burlington Telegraph*.

8   Walter Farwell, "Slavery in Fremont Co. 'til 1848 Iowa Boundary Was Moved South," *Sidney Argus-Herald*, February 10, 1977.

9   Dr. Ira D. Blanchard, a man of indomitable will and firm in his anti-

slavery convictions, also traveled to Kansas in 1856 to successfully urge using the overland trail built through Iowa for Kansas-bound settlers as an escape route for runaways. Blanchard harbored runaways, suffered threats and physical assaults, and in one instance, traveled to St. Louis to rescue two local free black people (Maria and Henry Garner) kidnapped to be sold into slavery (see chapter 8). This strong abolitionist did have his faults. In 1848 his philandering had cost him both his position and his Baptist ordination. His dismissal from the Kansas mission precipitated the family's move across the Missouri River to the farm in Civil Bend. See Kay McAlexander Kinnan, *Who Was Ira D. Blanchard?* (Dallas, TX: Legacy Printing, 2009).

10 What we know about frontier times in and about Civil Bend—the lives of Indian missionaries and underground railroad events—derives in part from the writings of Elvira Gaston Platt, who in 1842 married Lester Platt, a printer at the radically antislavery Oberlin College. Elvira had attended Oberlin in 1836–1837 and taught at a rural township school in Ohio before her marriage. When the young Congregationalist couple came west to live in Civil Bend and work with the Pawnees in Nebraska, Lester became a hustling farmer and later, an Indian trader, while Elvira during various periods taught at and operated Indian schools. Together at Civil Bend through the 1850s, they supported and participated in underground railroad and Kansas free-state activities. Both pursued ventures in common but also lived quite independent, almost separate, lives. Elvira was a well-liked and highly regarded teacher and beloved in her family. Lester was hard-working and enterprising and an inveterate reader, but he was also a self-contained person, not talkative, and "used to having his own way about things." See Mrs. Elvira Gaston Platt, "Reminiscences of a Teacher among the Nebraska Indians, 1843–1885," *Transactions and Reports of the Nebraska State Historical Society*, vol. 3 (Fremont, NE: Hammond Bros., 1892), 140; Aunt Elvira [G. Platt] letter, Keatskatoos, Nebraska, to Mrs. Lizzie C. Lehman, Percival, Iowa, October 11, 1875, and Lizzie [Mrs. C. B. Ricketts], letter to her mother in Monroe (Platte Co.), Nebraska, November 13, 1874, both in the Platt Family Papers, Series Two RG0907.AM, Nebraska State Historical Society, Lincoln.

11 John Todd, *Early Settlement and Growth of Western Iowa* (privately printed, 1905), 22.

12  This first instance of Tabor's involvement in underground railroad action is described in two reminiscences: a letter from S. H. Adams, Tabor, Iowa, to Professor Siebert, October 31, 1894, MIC 192, Box 45, Folder 11, Siebert Collection; and Todd, *Early Settlement* (1905), 59–60. The story is from these sources unless otherwise noted.

13  Among those helping S. H. Adams were John Hallam, James K. Gaston (George Gaston's son), and Irish Henry.

14  "The Under Ground Railroad In Iowa: A Story of Deacon Adams and John Brown," *Des Moines Register and Leader*, June 28, 1908.

15  W. E. Conner, Ottumwa, Iowa, undated letter to Prof. W. H. Siebert, Box 45, Folder 11A, Siebert Collection.

16  Samuel G. Wright, "Journal," 1839–1860, manuscript in Knox College Library, Galesburg, Illinois, as reported in Hermann R. Muelder, *Fighters for Freedom: The History of Anti-Slavery Activities of Men and Women Associated with Knox College* (New York: Columbia University Press, 1959), 200; letter from S. H. Adams to Professor Siebert, October 31, 1894.

17  Letter from S. H. Adams to Professor Siebert, October 31, 1894.

18  Iowa City *Iowa City Republican*, August 2, 1854.

19  Letter of William Salter to the *Chicago Tribune*, July 15, 1854, reprinted in the *National Anti-Slavery Standard*, August 5, 1854.

20  On the political situation in 1854, see F. I. Herriott, "James W. Grimes versus the Southrons," *Annals of Iowa* 15:2 (July 1926), 323–357, and 15:4 (October 1926), 403–432; Richard Lee Doak, "Free Men, Free Labor: Iowa and the Kansas-Nebraska Act" (master's thesis, Iowa State University, 1964); David S. Sparks, "The Birth of the Republican Party in Iowa, 1848–1860" (Ph.D. dissertation, University of Chicago, 1951), 59–117.

21  Salter, *Life of James W. Grimes*, 54.

22  George W. Martin, "The First Two Years of Kansas," *Transactions of the Kansas State Historical Society, 1907–1908*, vol. 10 (Topeka, KS: State Printing Office, 1908), 122.

23  For the movement of people toward Kansas Territory and the resulting turmoil, see Nicole Etcheson, *Bleeding Kansas: Contested Liberty in the Civil War Era* (Lawrence: University Press of Kansas, 2004), 28–138; William Elsey Connelley, *A Standard History of Kansas and Kansans* (Chicago: Lewis, 1919); Gunja SenGupta, *For God and*

*Mammon: Evangelicals and Entrepreneurs: Masters and Slaves in Territorial Kansas, 1854–1860* (Athens: University of Georgia Press, 1996).

24 Martin, "The First Two Years of Kansas," 123; "Manifesto of the Border Ruffians: An Appeal from the People of Kansas Territory to the People of the Union," reprinted from the *Kansas City Enterprise Extra*, August 26, 1856, in the Columbus *Ohio State Journal*, August 27, 1856, clipping in Webb Scrapbooks, vol. 16, 165, Microfilm Roll #4 of LM 92, Kansas State Historical Society, Topeka (hereafter cited as "Manifesto of the Border Ruffians").

25 The *Platt Argus*, November 6, 1854, reprinted in Daniel W. Wilder, *The Annals of Kansas* (Topeka: Geo. W. Martin, Kansas Publishing House, 1875), 40.

26 "Kansas Legislature," *Fairfield Ledger*, August 16, 1855.

27 Webb Scrapbooks, vol. 5, 157, Microfilm Roll #1 of LM 90, Kansas State Historical Society, Topeka.

28 J. N. Holloway, *History of Kansas* (Lafayette, IN: James, Emmons, 1868), 340.

29 On Charles Lenhart's activities, see William A. Phillips, *The Conquest of Kansas, by Missouri and Her Allies* (Boston: Phillips, Sampson, 1856), 357–358; G. W. Brown, *Reminiscences of Old John Brown: Thrilling Incidents of Border Life in Kansas* (Rockford, IL: Abraham E. Smith, 1880), 9, 11, 62; Todd Midfelt, *The Secret Danites: Kansas' First Jayhawkers* (Winfield, KS: Central Plains Book Manufacturing, 2003), 88–98.

30 On Lane's persuasive style and actions, see Wendell Holmes Stephenson, *Publications of the Kansas State Historical Society Embracing the Political Career of General James H. Lane*, vol. 3 (Topeka: Kansas State Printer, 1930), 69, 74, 161.

31 Glenn Noble, *John Brown and the Jim Lane Trail* (Broken Bow, NE: Purcells, 1977), 32. Feelings about Sidney began to shift when newspapers published warnings to "beware of the town of Sidney in Fremont County, Iowa, and of the ferry across the Missouri at Nebraska City, for Sidney is a violent proslavery town, and this ferry is kept by a proslavery man." Better, the correspondent recommended, was for settlers to "go to Tabor and cross at the Wyoming ferry between Plattsmouth and Nebraska City. Tabor is a Free State town . . .

and the Wyoming ferry is kept by a Free State man." As for Sidney, he could "assure emigrants that it is no place for them." The warning, signed F., was written by Franklin Benjamin Sanborn from Oska-loosa, under the headline "Southern Iowa—Oskaloosa—Information for Emigrants—Beware of Sidney," *Boston Evening Telegraph*, August 29, 1856, in Webb Scrapbooks, vol. 16, Microfilm Roll #4 of LM 92, Kansas State Historical Society, Topeka; also reprinted in Sanborn's report, "To the Kansas State Committee of Massachusetts and the Committee for Middlesex County," Springfield, Massachusetts, August 29, 1856, published in the *Boston Evening Telegraph*, September 1, 1856, in Webb Scrapbooks, vol. 16, 214, Microfilm Roll #4 of LM 92, Kansas State Historical Society, Topeka.

32  "Very late from Kansas . . . Convention at Topeka," *Cleveland Daily Herald*, July 14, 1856, a clipping from Webb Scrapbooks, vol. 17, 70, Microfilm Roll #4 of LM 92, Kansas State Historical Society, Topeka. The best description of conditions for setting up the land route and organizing emigrant companies is by one of the Kansas National Committee line leaders heading the operation, Shalor Winchell Eldridge, in *Publications of the Kansas State Historical Society Embracing Recollections of Early Days in Kansas*, vol. 2 (Topeka: Kansas State Printing Plant, 1920), 69–87. See also Noble, *John Brown*, 29–42; Dykstra, *Bright Radical Star*, 136–139.

33  Dykstra, *Bright Radical Star*, 138. Emigrant companies heading for Iowa City by rail got delayed at Davenport. One month after the new Mississippi River bridge there had opened, it had to be closed because a span burned after being struck by the *Effie Afton* steamboat. Until the bridge reopened in the first week of September, settlers had to wait in line to get across via steam-driven ferry. See "Letter from Iowa," *Boston Evening Telegraph*, August 14, 1856, in Webb Scrapbooks, vol. 16, 48, Microfilm Roll #4 of LM 92, Kansas State Historical Society, Topeka; correspondence from Davenport, May 26, 1856, to the *New-ark Daily Advertiser*, May 31, 1856, in Webb Scrapbooks, vol. 12, 261, Microfilm Roll #3 of LM 91, Kansas State Historical Society, Topeka; David A. Pfeiffer, "Bridging the Mississippi: The Railroads and Steamboats Clash at the Rock Island Bridge," *Prologue* 36:2 (Summer 2004), http://www.archives.gov/publications/prologue/2004/summer/bridge.html.

34 TYPO [pseudonym], "Letter from Nebraska," *Boston Daily Evening Traveler*, August 7, 1856, in Webb Scrapbooks, vol. 15, 240–241, Microfilm Roll #4 of LM 92, Kansas State Historical Society, Topeka.

35 The trail was dubbed the "northern" or "Iowa" route by free-state emigrants. Proslavery foes claimed it was used by "Lane's Army of the North," a term designed to impugn the assembling newcomers as a hostile invading force. Over the years, the route through Iowa became known as the "Lane Trail," in part to acknowledge Lane's early advocacy for it. See "Correspondence of the *St. Louis Gazette*" from Iowa City, June 16, 1856, clipping in Webb Scrapbooks, vol. 1, 127, Microfilm Roll #4 of LM 92, Kansas State Historical Society, Topeka; unsigned letter [by Dr. S. G. Howe] dated July 26, 1856, from Tabor to *Boston Atlas*, August 12, 1856, clipping in Webb Scrapbooks, vol. 16, 14, Microfilm Roll #4 of LM 92, Kansas State Historical Society, Topeka; "Manifesto of the Border Ruffians."

36 T. W. H. [Thomas Wentworth Higginson], July 24 letter titled "Authentic from Kansas," from Afton, Union County, Iowa, printed in the *Boston Journal*, August 9, 1856, clipping in Webb Scrapbooks, vol. 15, 250, Microfilm Roll #4 of LM 92, Kansas State Historical Society, Topeka; "Manifesto of the Border Ruffians."

37 Richard J. Hinton, *John Brown and His Men*, rev. ed. (New York: Funk and Wagnalls, 1894), 56; Robert Morrow, "Emigration to Kansas in 1856," *Transactions of the Kansas State Historical Society, 1903–1904*, vol. 8 (Topeka: Geo. A. Clark, State Printer, 1904), 305; Shalor Winchell Eldridge, *Recollections of Early Days in Kansas*, Publications of the Kansas State Historical Society, vol. 2 (Topeka: Kansas State Printing Plant, 1920), 77, 210; Frank W. Blackmar, *Kansas*, vol. 2 (Chicago: Standard, 1912), 618; W. M. Paxton, *Annals of Platt County, Missouri* (Kansas City, MO: Hudson Kimberly, 1897), 209; and "From Kansas," *Boston Daily Advertiser*, January 1, 1856, clipping in Webb Scrapbooks, vol. 8, in Microfilm Roll #2 of LM 90, Kansas State Historical Society, Topeka. The finest overall discussion of Governor Grimes and the missing arms appears in Dykstra, *Bright Radical Star*, 139–143.

38 Noble, *John Brown*, 37. Lists of the various companies and aspects of their character are in a memorandum attached to S. G. Howe and Thaddeus Hyatt, "Report of the Buffalo Convention Committee: To

the National Committee for Aid of Kansas," *New York Daily Tribune,* August 13, 1856, in Webb Scrapbooks, vol. 16, 39–40, Microfilm Roll #4 of LM 92, Kansas State Historical Society, Topeka. A portion of this list is also printed in Eldridge, *Publications of the Kansas State Historical Society,* vol. 2, 85.

39 Howe and Hyatt, "Report of the Buffalo Convention Committee," 39–40.

40 Unsigned letter from Tabor dated July 26, 1856, to *Boston Atlas,* August 12, 1856, clipping in Webb Scrapbooks, vol. 16, 14, Microfilm Roll #4 of LM 92, Kansas State Historical Society, Topeka.

41 TYPO [pseudonym], "Letter from Nebraska," *Boston Daily Evening Traveler,* August 7, 1856, in Webb Scrapbooks, vol. 15, 240–241, Microfilm Roll #4 of LM 92, Kansas State Historical Society, Topeka.

42 "Need of Relief for Kansas," *Boston Daily Advertiser,* August 15, 1856, reprinted in the *Boston Daily Courier,* August 18, 1856.

43 By this time Tabor numbered twelve families, according to John Todd, though he also accounts for another two dozen who had come to the Tabor area between 1852 and 1856, apparently settling beyond the outskirts of the town proper. Using names of families known to have settled in Tabor, the 1856 census lists roughly twelve households in the town, including about twenty-four men and forty-six women and children. See John Todd, *History of Fremont County, Iowa* (Des Moines: Iowa Historical Co., 1881), 588–589; Todd, *Early Settlement* (1905), 45–47; and manuscript schedules of the Iowa Census, Scott Township, Fremont County, 1856. The village was but four years old when, in May 1855, a new settler stepped off the stage in front of Jesse West's hotel. What L. E. Webb saw was not storefronts but a town "comprised of about a dozen houses, most of them being log huts, while a few were of sod"; L. E. Webb, "Tabor 45 Years Ago," *Tabor Beacon,* May 11, 1900, reprinted as "Memories," *Tabor Beacon-Enterprise,* February 21, 1985.

44 Gaston's recollections are recorded in Todd, *Early Settlement* (1905), 53–54; see also Oswald Garrison Villard, *John Brown, 1800–1859: A Biography Fifty Years After* (Boston: Houghton Mifflin, 1910), 267–268.

45 Letter of Thomas Wentworth Higginson, September 12, 1856, to the *New York Tribune.* His dispatches were published as "A Ride through

Kanzas [*sic*]," under the signature of "Worcester." Higginson later became one of the so-called Secret Six supporters of John Brown and during the Civil War commanded the first federally authorized Union regiment of freed African Americans, the First South Carolina Volunteers.

46 Eldridge, *Publications of the Kansas State Historical Society*, vol. 2, 75.

47 T. W. H. [Thomas Wentworth Higginson], "Authentic from Kansas," *Boston Evening Telegraph*, August 8, 1856, clipping in Webb Scrapbooks, vol. 15, 250, Microfilm Roll #4 of LM 92, Kansas State Historical Society, Topeka; "Latest News from the West," *Chicago Daily Tribune*, July 28, 1856, clipping in Webb Scrapbooks, vol. 15, 148, Microfilm Roll #4 of LM 92, Kansas State Historical Society, Topeka; Todd, *History of Fremont County*, 588–590; Todd, *Early Settlement* (1905), 45–47, 53.

48 Todd, *History of Fremont County*, 590. Sharps rifles were fast-firing, breech-loading rifles accurate over long distances—better weapons than the muskets many locals bore.

49 Todd, *Early Settlement* (1905), 54.

50 Villard, *John Brown*, 254–255; David S. Reynolds, *John Brown, Abolitionist* (New York: Alfred A. Knopf, 2005), 202–204.

51 John Todd to William Salter, September 17, 1856, William Salter Papers, Box 1, Folder 4, State Historical Society of Iowa, Des Moines.

52 William Elsey Connelley, "The Lane Trail," in *Collections of the Kansas State Historical Society, 1913–1914*, vol. 13 (Topeka: Kansas State Printing Plant, 1915), 270–275.

53 Noble, *John Brown*, 55; John Speer, *Life of Gen. James H. Lane* (Garden City, KS: John Speer, Printer, 1897), 128.

54 Noble, *John Brown*, 56–57; Eldridge, *Publications of the Kansas State Historical Society*, vol. 2, 100–101; Morrow, "Emigration to Kansas in 1856,", 304–306.

55 Todd, *Early Settlement* (1905), 57; Todd, *History of Fremont County*, 591.

56 Todd, *Early Settlement* (1905), 58; Todd, *History of Fremont County*, 591.

57 Villard, *John Brown*, 262; Reynolds, *John Brown*, 207.

58 Villard, *John Brown*, 262–268; Reynolds, *John Brown*, 207.

59  Villard, *John Brown*, 268–270.

60  Watson Brown to Dear Mother [Mary Brown], Brother and Sister, October 30, 1856, John Brown Collection, #299, Box 1, Folder 17, Item Number 102557, Kansas State Historical Society, Topeka; available on the Territorial Kansas Online website, http://www.territorialkansasonline.org.

61  Villard, *John Brown*, 270.

62  Irving B. Richman, *John Brown among the Quakers, and Other Sketches* (Des Moines: Historical Department of Iowa, 1904; orig. Chicago: R. R. Donnelley and Sons, 1894), 16.

## 6  Escapes and Rescues

1  John Todd, *Early Settlement and Growth of Western Iowa, or Reminiscences* (Des Moines: Historical Department of Iowa, 1906), 65–66; also James Patrick Morgans, *John Todd and the Underground Railroad: Biography of an Iowa Abolitionist* (Jefferson, NC: McFarland, 2006), 5–6; Morgans's book includes a letter from Martha Todd to Q. F. Atkins, December 25, 1856, reprinted on 179–181.

2  Connelley, "The Lane Trail," 269–270.

3  "'U.G.R.R.' in Iowa," *National Anti-Slavery Standard*, November 21, 1857 (hereafter cited as "'U.G.R.R.' in Iowa").

4  "'U.G.R.R.' in Iowa." Although the author is not named, it was probably Elvira Gaston Platt, sister of Tabor town founder George Gaston. She lived with her husband, Lester, in Civil Bend. Elvira is the only Civil Bend resident known to have written for the newspapers, and the writing style here closely resembles that of news stories signed by her.

5  "'U.G.R.R.' in Iowa"; Morgans, *John Todd and the Underground Railroad*, 180.

6  "'U.G.R.R.' in Iowa."

7  Todd, *Early Settlement* (1906), 66.

8  "'U.G.R.R.' in Iowa."

9  On George Clarke and Judy Clarke, see John H. Gihon, *Geary and Kansas: Governor Geary's Administration in Kansas* (Philadelphia: Chas. C. Rhodes, 1857), 66; *Lawrence Herald of Freedom*, January 3, 1857; advertisement of a reward for Judy Clarke's return in *Lecomp-*

*ton Union*, December 11, 1856. Judy Clarke's story as told to Mrs. S. R. Shepardson at Tabor is contained in Shepardson's attachment to "Reply of Mrs. E. G. Platt of Tabor, Iowa, to the U.G.R.R. Circular," Tabor, Iowa, sent to W. H. Siebert, Columbus, Ohio, Box 45, Siebert Collection. On John Armstrong's involvement, see John Armstrong, "Reminiscences of Slave Days in Kansas," collected by Miss Zu Adams in 1895, in History Slaves Collection, Kansas State Historical Society, at Territorial Kansas Online website, http://www.territorialkansasonline .org.

10 The story of this young man's escape, including all the quotations, is from Mrs. E. G. Platt, Tabor, Iowa, letter to W. H. Siebert, Columbus, Ohio, November 6, 1894, Box 45, Folder 11A, Siebert Collection (hereafter cited as Platt to Siebert letter).

11 Blacksnake whips, a traditional western whip six to twelve feet long and often used by army drivers during the Civil War for six-mule teams, carried a heavy shot load in the core to balance the lash. Some also contained a concentrated load (a lead ball or steel ball bearing) so that they could be used as improvised blackjacks. See http://www .answers.com/topic/whip#Snake_whips, and also John D. Wright, *The Language of the Civil War* (New York: Greenwood, 2001), 30.

12 Platt to Siebert letter.

13 On the relevance of the Dred Scott case to Iowa, see Dykstra, "Dr. Emerson's Sam," 51–52; and Fehrenbacher, *The Dred Scott Case*, 243–246.

14 William E. Gienapp, "'Politics Seem to Enter into Everything': Political Culture in the North, 1840–1860," in *Essays on American Antebellum Politics 1840–1860*, ed. Stephen E. Maizlish and John J. Kushma (College Station: Texas A&M University Press, 1983), 15–69; letter from Amos Bixby, Sugar Grove, Poweshiek County, Iowa, to his brother Lewellyn (possibly in Maine), April 30, 1855, in "Letters from Iowa," an unpublished report by Stephen B. Dudley, transcribed with comments and notes by Stephen B. Dudley, Wilsonville, Oregon, 1992, a copy of which is in the Amos Bixby folder of the Underground Railroad project files, State Historical Society of Iowa, Des Moines.

15 Howard A. Burrell, *History of Washington County, Iowa*, vol. 1 (Chicago: S. J. Clarke, 1909), 445–446; Dan Elbert Clark, *Samuel Jordan Kirkwood* (Iowa City: State Historical Society of Iowa, 1917), 139–141;

Louis Pelzer, *Augustus Caesar Dodge* (Iowa City: State Historical Society of Iowa, 1909), 243–244.

16  Locations for the debates included, among others, Washington, Bloomfield, Albia, Chariton, Tabor, Glenwood, Council Bluffs, Sioux City, Oskaloosa, Iowa City, Newton, Tipton, Anamosa, Maquoketa, Dubuque, Davenport, Muscatine, Wapello, and Fairfield. Clark, *Samuel Jordan Kirkwood*, 132–141.

17  Kirkwood hailed from Maryland, where his father and brothers owned slaves; see "First Nomination of Abraham Lincoln," *Annals of Iowa*, 2nd ser., 9 (1909–1910), 189.

18  Clark, *Samuel Jordan Kirkwood*, 134–135; Pelzer, *Augustus Caesar Dodge*, 240–241.

19  Clark, *Samuel Jordan Kirkwood*, 136. Kirkwood may have based his example on the experience of Margaret Garner, who escaped from slavery in Kentucky with her husband and four children, as well as other relatives, by crossing the frozen Ohio River to Cincinnati in the winter of 1856. When slavecatchers stormed the house in which they were hiding, Garner killed one of her children and attempted to kill the others and herself to prevent their return to slavery. Harriet Beecher Stowe told a story similar to Kirkwood's in her best-selling novel *Uncle Tom's Cabin, Or, Life Among the Lowly* (1852), and Toni Morrison's novel *Beloved* (1987) also draws on Garner's life.

20  "Sam Kirkwood," Davenport *Daily Iowa State Democrat*, July 10, 1859; see also Pelzer, *Augustus Caesar Dodge*, 247; Clark, *Samuel Jordan Kirkwood*, 131 and n. 186.

21  On the Democratic attempt to use Prescott's activities to spread anti-black fears, see "The Niggers in Iowa," May 5, 1859, and "More about the Niggers," May 12, 1859, in the *Leon Pioneer*; "A Negro Exodus to Iowa," *Fort Dodge Sentinel*, May 14, 1859; "Dubuque Times on Negro Colonization in Iowa," Davenport *Daily Iowa State Democrat*, May 31, 1859; "Negro Colonization in Iowa," *Dubuque Weekly Times*, June 2, 1859; "Negro Colonization in Iowa," *Anamosa Gazette*, June 3, 1859; "Negro Colonization in Iowa," *Cedar Rapids Cedar Democrat*, June 4, 1859; "Black Emigrants," McGregor *North Iowa Times*, June 8, 1859; "That 'Nigger Colony,'" *St. Charles City Republican Intelligencer*, June 30, 1859; "Negro Colonization," *Anamosa Gazette*, July 15, 1859; "Negro Colonization," *Sioux City Register*, August 25, 1859; "The Negro

Hobby," *Waverly Republican*, September 6, 1859; "Colonizing Negroes in Iowa," Des Moines *Iowa Weekly Citizen*, September 14, 1859.

22 *History of Emmet County and Dickinson County, Iowa*, vol. 1 (Chicago: Pioneer, 1917), 372; Thomas Henry Ryan, *History of Outagamie County, Wisconsin* (Chicago: Goodspeed Historical Association, 1911), available online at Fox Valley Memory, http://www.foxvalleymemory.org/Ryans/indextext.html.

23 F. I. Herriott, "The Aftermath of the Spirit Lake Massacre, March 8–15, 1857 (Concluded)," *Annals of Iowa*, 3rd ser., 18:8 (April 1933), 611; *History of Emmet County*, vol. 1, 372; Ryan, *History of Outagamie County*.

24 "Negro Colonization in Iowa," *Oskaloosa Weekly Times*, March 24, 1859; "The Niggers in Iowa," *Leon Pioneer*, May 5, 1859.

25 "Negro Colonization in Iowa," *Oskaloosa Weekly Times*, March 24, 1859.

26 "The Niggers in Iowa," May 5, 1859, and "More about the Niggers," *Leon Pioneer*, May 12, 1859.

27 "Negro Colonization in Iowa," *Dubuque Weekly Times*, June 2, 1859; "Dubuque Times on Negro Colonization in Iowa," Davenport *Daily Iowa State Democrat*, May 31, 1859; "Negro Colonization in Iowa," *Cedar Rapids Cedar Democrat*, June 4, 1859; "Negro Colonization in Iowa," *Anamosa Gazette*, June 3, 1859.

28 "Black Emigrants," McGregor *North Iowa Times*, June 8, 1859.

29 "Democratic State Convention," *Charles City Republican Intelligencer*, June 30, 1859.

30 "Negro Colonization," *Sioux City Register*, August 25, 1859; Herriott, "The Aftermath of the Spirit Lake Massacre," 616.

31 E. S. Hill, Atlantic, Iowa, letter to W. H. Siebert, October 30, 1894, Box 45, Folder 11A, Siebert Collection (hereafter cited as Hill letter).

32 According to "Slavery in Nebraska," *New York Daily Times*, July 27, 1855, based on a notice in the *Nebraska City News*, Nuckolls and Hail were "owners of quite a share of the site of Nebraska City, and extensively engaged in business there," and they owned "quite a number of slaves in Atchison County, Mo; in fact, a majority of the [roughly thirty] slaves in that county." The notice stated that Nuckolls and Hail "have imported slaves from Missouri, and are offering them for sale."

33 For the quotations and more information on Nuckolls, see Raymond

E. Dale, "Otoe County Pioneers: A Biographical Dictionary, Part VII, 1926–1927, Me–Q" (privately printed, 1964), a copy of which is at the Nebraska City Public Library.

34 "Slavery in Nebraska," reprinted from the *Pacific City Herald* in the *Burlington Daily Hawk-Eye*, January 8, 1859.

35 "A Bill to Abolish Slavery in Nebraska," reprinted from the *New York Tribune* in the *National Anti-Slavery Standard*, January 1, 1859; J. Sterling Morton and Albert Watkins, *History of Nebraska* (Lincoln, NE: Western Publishing and Engraving, 1918), 458.

36 E. G. P. [Elvira Gaston Platt], "Nebraska Negro Catchers in Iowa, Western Iowa, Jan. 7, 1859," *Burlington Daily Hawk-Eye*, January 21, 1859 (hereafter cited as "Nebraska Negro Catchers in Iowa"); "Slavery in Nebraska," reprinted from the *Pacific City Herald* in the *Burlington Daily Hawk-Eye*, January 8, 1859; "Slavery in Nebraska," *New York Daily Times*, July 27, 1855; *Pictures from Nebraska City, 1906*, 5–6, available online at http://www.memoriallibrary.com/NE/Otoe/1906/.

37 Ellen Gaston Hurlbutt, Tabor, Iowa, "The Underground Railroad in Tabor and Vicinity," March 18, 1935, Box 45, Folder 2, Siebert Collection.

38 "Nebraska Negro Catchers in Iowa."

39 *Iowa Weekly Citizen*, February 2, 1859, 2–5.

40 Hill letter.

41 "Nebraska Negro Catchers in Iowa"; Civil Bender, "Correspondence for the Fremont Herald," submitted December 7, 1858, Sidney *Fremont County Herald*, December 11, 1858 (hereafter cited as "Correspondence for the Fremont Herald").

42 "Nebraska Negro Catchers in Iowa."

43 "Nebraska Negro Catchers in Iowa."

44 J. F. Merritt, Civil Bend (Fremont County), Iowa, letter to his Dear Brother, December 5, 1858, Merritt Collection, State Historical Society of Iowa, Iowa City (hereafter cited as Merritt letter).

45 "Correspondence for the Fremont Herald."

46 Sturgis Williams, Fremont County, Iowa, letter to Wilbur Siebert, October 27, 1894, Ms. 116AV, Box 45, Folder 1IA 025, Siebert Collection.

47 "Nebraska Negro Catchers in Iowa"; Sturgis Williams, Percival (Fremont County), Iowa, letter to Professor W. H. Siebert, Columbus,

Ohio, October 27, 1894, Box 45, Folder 11A, Siebert Collection; Merritt letter.

48 "Correspondence for the Fremont Herald"; Hill letter.

49 "Correspondence for the Fremont Herald."

50 Untitled, Clarinda *Page County Herald*, September 23, 1859.

51 Hurlbutt, "The Underground Railroad in Tabor and Vicinity."

52 Oliver Mills, Lewis, Iowa, letter to W. H. Siebert, Columbus, Ohio, October 18, 1894, Box 45, Folder 2, Siebert Collection. "Here I will say," adds Mills, in Lewis "the home of Rev. Geo. B. Hitchcock was one of the principal resting places as well as that of J. N. Coe, Amos Gridley, my own home and many others." Oliver Mills, then thirty-nine years old, had moved to Iowa from Gustavus, Trumbull County, Ohio, in March 1850. From 1840 to 1850 he had participated in underground railroad efforts in Ohio. For biographical details, see *Compendium of History and Biography of Cass County, Iowa* (Chicago: Henry Taylor, 1906), 435–436.

53 W. L. Smith, "A History of the Robert Lee Smith Family" (1923), manuscript at the DeWitt (Clinton County), Iowa, Historical Society.

54 "The Case of Chapman," Clarinda *Page County Herald*, June 3, 1859.

55 Untitled, Clarinda *Page County Herald*, September 23, 1859.

56 "Served Him Right," *Janesville Daily Gazette*, July 2, 1860; "Compromised," reprinted from the *Page County Herald* in the *Burlington Daily Hawk-Eye*, June 30, 1860; Todd, *Early Settlement* (1906), 62.

57 "Slavery in Nebraska," *Muscatine Weekly Journal*, December 23, 1859; Morton and Watkins, *History of Nebraska*, 458.

58 "The Union Clean Gone; More of the Eliza Grayson Case," *Chicago Tribune*, November 16, 1860 (hereafter cited as "Union Clean Gone").

59 Chicago's black population during this period is described in Christopher Robert Reed, *Black Chicago's First Century*, vol. 1, *1833–1900* (Columbia: University of Missouri Press, 2005), 51–52, and in his article "African American Life in Antebellum Chicago, 1833–1860," *Journal of the Illinois State Historical Society* 94:1 (Winter 2001), 359–360.

60 "Great Fugitive Slave Excitement—A Colored Girl Rescued," *Chicago Daily Evening Journal*, November 13, 1860 (hereafter cited as "Great Fugitive Slave Excitement").

61  Paul Finkelman, "Slavery, the 'More Perfect Union,' and the Prairie State," *Illinois Historical Journal* 80:4 (Winter 1987), 267–268.

62  "Great Fugitive Slave Excitement." Jake Newsome's physical description comes from a Chicago paper's comment on the two rival Democratic state conventions, reprinted in the *Utica Daily Observer*, April 27, 1858.

63  "Great Fugitive Slave Excitement"; "The Union Again Threatened, the Colored Person Loose," *Chicago Tribune*, November 13, 1860 (hereafter cited as "Union Again Threatened").

64  "Great Fugitive Slave Excitement."

65  "Union Again Threatened."

66  "Union Again Threatened."

67  " Union Again Threatened"; "Great Fugitive Slave Excitement."

68  "Union Clean Gone"; "Slave-Hunting in Illinois," *National Anti-Slavery Standard*, November 24, 1860; three items titled "The Eliza Grayson Case" from the *Chicago Daily Evening Journal*: November 14, 16, and 20, 1860.

69  "Negro Rescue Case," reprinted from the *Chicago Journal* in the *Burlington Daily Hawk-Eye*, November 16, 1860.

70  Quoted in Morton and Watkins, *History of Nebraska*, 458. For the characterization of the *Times and Herald*'s antiblack attitudes, see "Union Clean Gone."

71  After the Civil War (during which he was a Southern sympathizer), Stephen Nuckolls lived in New York (1864–1867), getting rich by speculating on mining. Then he moved to Cheyenne in Dakota Territory and operated a mercantile business until the organization of Wyoming Territory, whereupon voters elected him in 1869 for one term to Congress. He continued to be important in Wyoming politics until departing for Salt Lake City, Utah, in 1872, where he engaged in milling and railroads until his death in 1879. See Dale, "Otoe County Pioneers," 1926–1927; *Biographical Directory of the United States Congress*, available online at http://bioguide.congress.gov/scripts/biodisplay.pl?index=N000166; J. Sterling Morton and Albert Watkins, *Illustrated History of Nebraska*, vol. 1 (Lincoln: Western Publishing and Engraving, 1911), 106–107.

72  Amity (later renamed College Springs) was a recent frontier settlement, a cooperative effort that came out of Knox College at Gales-

burg, Illinois. In 1855 three Galesburg men had selected the site after scouting southern Iowa, Kansas, and northern Missouri for suitable government land. The most complete overview of Amity and its early history is in Muelder, *Fighters for Freedom* (1959), 315–321. The moving spirits behind the Amity colony were B. F. Haskins and William J. Woods of Galesburg, but by the time of actual settlement they shared leadership with the prominent Illinois abolitionist and underground railroad operator John Cross. He and his family settled in Amity in 1857 and influenced antislavery work in the community. Cross remained in Amity until 1883, when he moved to Wessington Springs, South Dakota, where as a widower he lived with his son and daughter-in-law until his death on December 1, 1885. His wife had died in 1875 and is buried in the rural College Springs cemetery. Cross and his daughter, Alice Swatman Cross, were buried south of his house and then removed to Hope Cemetery upon its establishment. Biographical sketches of John Cross are provided in *Golden Jubilee: Fifty Years of Community Service, Templeton Congregational Church* (Wessington Springs, SD, 1937), 13–14; *History of Page County, Iowa* (Des Moines: Iowa Historical Co., 1880), 622.

73 The following account is from Smith, "Boyhood Recollections" (see chapter 2, note 4). Ammi Smith, Clark's father and the third arrival to the Amity settlement, came with his family of seven from Wheaton, Illinois (just west of Chicago), in September 1856.

7   *Iowa and the Martyrdom*
*of John Brown*

1   Villard, *John Brown*, 289–299.

2   Villard, *John Brown*, 308; Edward Payson Bridgman and Luke Fisher Parsons, *With John Brown in Kansas* (Madison, WI: J. N. Davidson, 1915), 36; Alberta Pantle, ed., "The Story of a Kansas Freedman," *Kansas Historical Quarterly* 11:4 (November 1942), 365–368.

3   George B. Gill, account of December 20, 1858, Missouri raid to free slaves, correspondence with Richard J. Hinton, July 4, 1895, in MC384, Box 8, Richard J. Hinton Papers, Kansas State Historical Society, Topeka (hereafter cited as Gill account). Nearly all of Gill's manuscript is contained in chapter 8 of Hinton, *John Brown and His Men*, 217–277.

4 "From Kansas. Old John Brown under Siege," correspondence from Lawrence, Kansas Territory, February 1, 1859, to the *St. Louis Democrat*, reprinted in the Des Moines *Iowa Weekly Citizen*, February 23, 1859.

5 F. B. Sanborn, *Life and Letters of John Brown: Liberator of Kansas, and Martyr of Virginia*, 2nd ed. (Boston: Roberts Bros., 1891), 485–487; Villard, *John Brown*, 381–382; L. L. Kiene, "The Battle of the Spurs and John Brown's Exit from Kansas," *Kansas Historical Collections*, vol. 8, *1903–04*, 443–449.

6 George B. Gill, "Biographical notes on Coppoc, Edwin and Barclay, Taylor, Hazlett, Leaman, J. G. Anderson, Kagi, Stevens, Tidd, Cook and Brown; prepared for R. J. Hinton about 1893," Box 8, 1,M,2, Richard J. Hinton Collection, Kansas State Historical Society, Topeka (hereafter cited as Gill, "Biographical notes").

7 Villard, *John Brown*, 384.

8 The note continues with "'Oh give thanks unto the Lord; for he is good: for his mercy endureth forever." The note is preserved in the Tabor Historical Society's archives.

9 Villard, *John Brown*, 384–385; Todd, *Early Settlement* (1906), 70. Todd was out of town that night, so H. D. King moderated the meeting.

10 Villard, *John Brown*, 385.

11 The resolution and Adams quotation are from Sanborn, *Life and Letters of John Brown*, 488. Samuel Adams identified the three men voting against the resolution: "E. S. Hill, who afterwards for thirty-five years or more was pastor of the First Congregational church at Atlantic, Ia.; James Vincent, Sr., late editor of the *Nonconformist*, and Augustus Reed"; see "The Under Ground Railroad In Iowa: A Story of Deacon Adams and John Brown," *Des Moines Register and Leader*, June 28, 1908, Section 3, 8.

12 Maria C. Gaston, "Reminiscences," in John Todd, comp., "Records of Public Meetings in Tabor, Fremont County, Iowa," 1877, located at the Tabor Historical Society.

13 Charles and Sylvia Case Tolles both had worked for Ira Blanchard at a Baptist Delaware Indian mission in Kansas ten years earlier, before Blanchard went to Civil Bend. At various times runaways arriving at Tabor were taken to the Tolles's farm on Silver Creek, a mile north

of present-day Malvern, where they would be hidden in the timber and brush until Charles Tolles could guide them at night to the next stop east. David C. Mott, "Charles Wesley Tolles," *Annals of Iowa*, 3rd ser., 14:8 (April 1925), 629; "C. W. Tolles," Glenwood *Mills County Tribune*, June 16, 1908. (This 1908 article indicates that when C. W. Tolles visited the old cabin site with the writer, "A small opening at the south edge of the timber marked the cabin's spot. A few bricks lay in a depression. The bricks were a part of the old cabin hearth. The depression marked the place of the cellar under the cabin.") Calvin Bradway's house was in the southeast quarter of Section 36 in Grove Township, Pottawatomie County, Iowa, according to F. G. Weeks (Carson, Iowa), "Weeks Writes on Underground Ry.," *Council Bluffs Nonpareil*, August 22, 1920.

14  "Obituary, Hon. Oliver Mills," *Lewis Standard*, July 11, 1907; *Compendium of History and Biography of Cass County Iowa* (Chicago: Henry Taylor, 1906), 435–436; Oliver Mills (Lewis, Iowa), letter to W. H. Siebert, Ms. 116AV, Box 45, Folder 11A, Siebert Collection.

15  Little is known about David A. Barnett. On the story of Grove City development, see the *Des Moines Register*, June 11, 1867.

16  *Past and Present of Guthrie County, Iowa*, vol. 2 (Chicago: S. J. Clarke, 1907), 240–241; Dalmanutha in Thompson Township, Guthrie County, Iowa, manuscript schedules of the U.S. Census, 1860.

17  Murray's farm was a mile east of what is today Redfield, Iowa. Darius B. Cook, *History of Quaker Divide* (Dexter, IA: Dexter Sentinel, 1914), 204–205; Union Township, Guthrie County, Iowa, manuscript schedules of the U.S. Census, 1860.

18  James Jordan's 1867 house, still standing at 2001 Fuller Road in West Des Moines, is operated as a historic site by the West Des Moines Historical Society. For biographical information about Jordan, see Johnson Brigham, *Des Moines . . . Together with the History of Polk County, Iowa*, vol. 2 (Chicago: S. J. Clarke, 1911), 1044–1048; *The History of Polk County, Iowa* (Des Moines: Union Historical Co., 1880), 825–827; "Death of Father Jordan," Des Moines *Iowa State Register*, March 3, 1891; "Death of a Pioneer: James C. Jordan of Walnut Township, Passes Suddenly Away," *Des Moines Leader*, March 3, 1891.

19  Letter to the editor from John Teesdale, "Old John Brown: Mr. Teesdale Supplements Our Last Sunday Story of the Old Hero's Visit to

Des Moines—Smuggling a Load of Slaves Through this City," Des Moines *Iowa State Register*, April 2, 1882.

20  "Death of Brian Hawley," Des Moines *Iowa State Register*, September 30, 1873, and October 7, 1873.

21  The Dickinson farm where Cornwall and his family of six lived was located where the eastbound Interstate 80 rest stop now stands (at about milepost 180). U.S. Census 1860 schedules for Rock Creek Township, Jasper County, Iowa; U.S. Census 1850 schedules for Johnson Township, Trumbull County, Ohio.

22  "Grinnell," *Montezuma Weekly Republican*, February 10, 1859; "The Village of Grinnell," *Montezuma Weekly Republican*, October 27, 1859.

23  Full of life, with a ready wit, ceaseless energy, ever seeing the pleasant side of things, and always an able promoter, Grinnell planted a town at age thirty-three, leveraged its railroad connection, and got it a college. More a publicist of reform causes than an original thinker, he certainly was, as one who knew him wrote, "decidedly a man of action," "constantly busy," and "prompt to express himself" (Stiles, *Recollections and Sketches*, 136). His promotional gifts bore fruit. Settlement in the prairie village grew to six hundred by 1859, aided by its location on the main stage route from Iowa City to Des Moines. The moral fervor of Grinnell and other leading citizens made the town noted for its opposition to saloons and its uncompromising stand against slavery. These men and women were true abolitionist agitators. Over the next forty years, Grinnell's restless spirit drew him into railroad development, the study of law (he was admitted to the bar in 1858), and politics (he was elected to the state senate in 1856 and to Congress in 1862 and 1864). See Stiles, *Recollections and Sketches*, 136–137; "Hon. J. B. Grinnell," *Grinnell Herald*, April 7, 1891; L. F. Parker, *History of Poweshiek County, Iowa*, vol. 1 (Chicago: S. J. Clarke, 1911), 351–352; and *Portrait and Biographical Record of Johnson, Poweshiek and Iowa Counties, Iowa* (Chicago: Chapman Bros., 1893), 137–138.

24  Josiah Bushnell Grinnell, *Men and Events of Forty Years* (Boston: D. Lothrop, 1891), 210–211.

25  Grinnell, *Men and Events*, 211.

26  Remarks of Colonel Cooper (Grinnell's first newspaper editor) at me-

morial services for "Hon. J. B. Grinnell," *Grinnell Herald*, April 7, 1891.

27 Grinnell, *Men and Events*, 207.

28 Grinnell, *Men and Events*, 210–213.

29 Grinnell, *Men and Events*, 213.

30 Letter from [Amos] Bixby, Grinnell, Poweshiek County, Iowa, to his brother Lewellyn (probably in Maine), February 22, 1859, in "Letters from Iowa," an unpublished report by Stephen B. Dudley in which he transcribed and annotated six original letters by Amos Bixby that were in his collection, Wilsonville, Oregon, 1992, a copy of which is in the Amos Bixby folder of the Underground Railroad project files, State Historical Society of Iowa, Des Moines, Iowa.

31 "Captain Brown at Grinnell," Des Moines *Iowa Weekly Citizen*, March 2, 1859; the editor of the *Des Moines Statesman* was quoted in "Hon. J. B. Grinnell and the Des Moines Statesman," *Montezuma Weekly Republican*, March 31, 1859.

32 Report of Mrs. Cornelius Devore (daughter of Draper B. Reynolds) in 1917, Marengo, Iowa, "WPA Iowa Federal Writers' Project 'The Negro in Iowa' Collection (unpublished), 1935–1942," 75–76, copy on file at the State Historical Society of Iowa Library, Des Moines; U.S. Census 1860 schedules for Marengo Township, Iowa County, Iowa; Gill account, repeated in Hinton, *John Brown and His Men*, 226–227.

33 Villard, *John Brown*, 387; Hinton, *John Brown and His Men*, 226–227.

34 Grinnell, *Men and Events*, 216; Villard, *John Brown*, 390. For slightly different versions of the boxcar arrangements, see Frederick Lloyd, "John Brown among the Pedee Quakers," *Annals of Iowa* (April 1866), 716–719; Erik McKinley Eriksson, "William Penn Clarke," *Iowa Journal of History and Politics* 25:1 (January 1927), 43–44.

35 Wm. P. Wolf, Tipton, Iowa, letter to Narcissa Macy Smith, April 10, 1895, published in her article "Reminiscences of John Brown," *Midland Monthly* (September 1895), 233–234 (hereafter cited as Wolf letter). When Wolf met Kagi and Brown, he was reading law with Rush Clark, a twenty-five-year-old Iowa City lawyer who, according to Wolf, fretted that "the sentiments and doings of John Brown should be charged up to the republican party, thereby convicting it of being composed of abolitionists, and so when I arrived at his office that morning, he seemed very much excited, and said he thought it the

duty of the republican party to have Brown and his men arrested and punished, and the negroes sent back to their masters." See biographical sketch of "Judge William P. Wolf" in C. Ray Aurner, ed., *A Topical History of Cedar County, Iowa*, vol. 2 (Chicago: S. J. Clarke, 1910), 368.

36 Wolf letter.

37 Wolf letter. The wagon remained in the Smith family until March 1882, when at a general sale the John Brown Wagon, as it was then known, was purchased by H. S. Fairall of the *Iowa City Republican*. A report of its auction is in "The Underground Railroad: John Brown's Old Wagon," *Des Moines Daily Iowa Capital*, September 3, 1883. What happened after Fairall made the wagon part of "his office relics at Iowa City" is unknown.

38 The return of Sam Tappan's wagon is noted in his April 17, 1859, letter to Thomas Higginson, Worcester, Massachusetts, in Thomas W. Higginson Collection, Box 1, Folder 8, Kansas State Historical Society, Topeka, available online at http://www.territorialkansasonline.org.

39 *History of Muscatine County, Iowa* (Chicago: Western Historical Co., 1879), 555–570; Volney B. Cushing, "Albert F. Keith" obituary, *West Liberty Index*, March 24, 1910; Villard, *John Brown*, 389.

40 Villard, *John Brown*, 389–390; George Gill, Springdale, Iowa, letter to Richard J. Hinton, June 15, 1860, MC 384, Box 2, Correspondence, June 1860, Richard J. Hinton Papers, Kansas State Historical Society, Topeka (hereafter cited as Gill letter).

41 Gill letter; Gill account, repeated in Hinton, *John Brown and His Men*, 227.

42 On William Penn Clarke, see Eriksson, "William Penn Clarke,", 3–11; Stiles, *Recollections and Sketches*, 767–768; "William Penn Clarke," *Proceedings of the Ninth Annual Meeting of the Iowa State Bar Association Held at Des Moines, Iowa, July 16–17, 1903* (Tipton, IA: Conservative, 1903), 35; Benjamin F. Gue, *History of Iowa from the Earliest Times to the Beginning of the Twentieth Century*, vol. 4 (New York: Century History Co., 1903), 52–53; Tyler Anbinder, "William Penn Clarke and the Know Nothing Movement: A Document," *Annals of Iowa* 53 (Winter 1994), 43–55; Robert R. Dykstra, "The Know Nothings Nobody Knows: Political Nativists in Antebellum Iowa," *Annals of Iowa* 53 (Winter 1994), 10–12.

43 Excerpts from William Penn Clarke's letter to the *Des Moines Register* in Harry E. Downer, *History of Davenport and Scott County, Iowa*, vol. 1 (Chicago: S. J. Clarke, 1910), 622.

44 J. C. Burns, Iowa City, to Laurel Summers, March 3, 1859, Summers Papers, Putnam Museum, Davenport, Iowa; Downer, *History of Davenport and Scott County*, vol. 1, 622; *The History of Cedar County with a History of Iowa*, vol. 2 (Chicago: Historical Publishing Co., 1901), 16. Summers, a contractor by trade, had become U.S. marshal in 1853. He revealed his views on slavery—opposing the government's constitutional power to enact the Wilmot Proviso or establish the Mason-Dixon line—in a letter he sent to John C. Calhoun from Parkhurst, Scott County, Iowa, on October 21, 1848, which was printed in the *Iowa Journal of History and Politics* 29:3 (July 1931), 420–421.

45 Christopher R. Reed, "African American Life in Antebellum Chicago, 1833–1860," *Journal of the Illinois State Historical Society* 94:1 (Winter 2001), 371; Villard, *John Brown*, 389–390. For Pinkerton's involvement in slave and runaway matters, see "Slave Hunt in Chicago! Arrest of an Alleged Fugitive by the United States Marshal," *Chicago Western Citizen*, June 10, 1851; "Great Excitement in Chicago—Supposed Fugitive Slave Case," *Dubuque Daily Republican*, September 3, 1857.

46 By fall, a report on the status of the twelve runaways noted that seven of them lived in Windsor. Two men "teamed," sawed wood, and "job[bed] around"; a boy of twelve did general help; and two women were hired as field hands to spade land for corn and potatoes. At their homes, they had planted gardens with onions, carrots, parsnips, and cabbages for winter, and among them they had three hogs, which they fed on swill (kitchen waste mixed with water or skimmed or sour milk) provided by neighbors. Five of the twelve, comprising a father, mother, and three children, lived about nine miles out in the country, working a farm on shares with about sixteen acres of corn and potatoes, some for their own use. According to the report, "all are anticipating the day when they can get a piece of land of their own." The report appeared as correspondence to the *New York Tribune*, November 6, 1859, a clipping of which is in the Webb Scrapbooks, vol. 17, 126, Microfilm Roll #4 of LM 92, Kansas State Historical Society, Topeka; the letter is also reprinted in James Redpath, *The Public Life of Capt. John Brown* (Boston: Thayer and Eldridge, 1860), 228. In 1894 Sam-

uel Harper told a writer that only he, his wife, and the Daniels's son, thirty-five-year-old John Brown Daniels, still survived of the group of fugitives who had arrived with John Brown in Windsor, Canada, in March 1859. Harper and his wife were "in a comfortable cottage on Bruce Avenue in Windsor," while their son "lives at Detroit." James Cleland Hamilton, "John Brown in Canada," *Canadian Magazine* (December 1894), 4–5.

47 On Luke Parsons's perspective and Kagi's recruiting efforts, see the reprint of a letter from Luke F. Parsons to C. Ray Aurner in *A Topical History of Cedar County Iowa*, vol. 1 (Chicago: S. J. Clarke, 1910), 438. Also, among the letters of Brown's men captured at Harpers Ferry, selected and published as Document No. 1, Appendix to [Governor Wise's] Message 1 to Virginia Legislature, December 1859, are a few related to Kagi's recruitment efforts and the responses he received. One from Luke F. Parsons (item 15) to Kagi is dated May 16, 1859; another from C. W. Moffett (item 22) is dated June 26, 1859. See also Villard, *John Brown*, 344.

48 Villard, *John Brown*, 344; John Brown letter to "Dear friends all," Washington County, Missouri, August 6, 1859, published as item 70 in Document No. 1, Appendix to [Governor Wise's] Message 1 to Virginia Legislature, December 1859; Gill interview with Katherine Mayo, November 12, 1908, Villard Collection, Columbia University Rare Book and Manuscript Library, New York. Ultimately, after his school term ended, Gill decided to join his comrades at the Kennedy farm in Maryland, but he had just started on his way when he heard the news about the raid at Harpers Ferry.

49 Gill, "Biographical notes."

50 Villard, *John Brown*, 405–414.

51 Benjamin Gue, "Iowans in John Brown's Raid, and the Author of the Mysterious 'Floyd Letter,'" *American Historical Magazine* 1 (1906), 164–169; and "John Brown and His Iowa Friends," *Midland Monthly* 7:2 (February 1897), 110–111.

52 Gue, "Iowans in John Brown's Raid," 165; Gue, "John Brown and His Iowa Friends," 110.

53 Gue, "Iowans in John Brown's Raid," 168; Gue, "John Brown and His Iowa Friends," 112.

54 George Gill commented that John Brown "was awful cautious for a

very brave man. He would turn aside where [Aaron] Stevens would go straight through," Gill interview with Katherine Mayo, November 12, 1908. This caution was a concern to his sons and the other men, who feared it could ruin the plan. On the internal dispute over capturing and holding Harpers Ferry, see Villard, *John Brown*, 423–424; Hinton, *John Brown and His Men*, 258–260; Richard J. Hinton, "John Brown and His Men, Before and After the Raid on Harper's Ferry, October 16th, 17th, 18th, 1859," *Frank Leslie's Popular Monthly* 27:6 (June 1889), 698–699; Ralph Keeler, "Owen Brown's Escape from Harper's Ferry," *Atlantic Monthly* 33:197 (March 1874), 343; Stephen B. Oates, *To Purge This Land with Blood: A Biography of John Brown* (New York: Harper and Row, 1970), 276–280.

55 "John Brown," *Lyon Weekly Mirror*, December 8, 1859; staff editorial on public observations for John Brown, *Burlington Weekly Hawk-Eye*, December 17, 1859.

56 "The Slavery Agitation, John Brown Sympathy Meeting at the Cooper Institute," *New York Times*, December 16, 1859; Villard, *John Brown*, 559–560; "John Brown's Sympathizers," *Staunton Spectator*, December 6, 1859, available online at "The Valley of the Shadow: Civil War–Era Newspapers," http://valley.lib.virginia.edu/news/ss1859/va.au.ss .1859.12.06.xml.

57 See comments under columns titled "The Rock Island Rail Road Bridge," "Grand Brown Sympathetic Meeting!," and two articles titled "Disgusting" in the December 3, 1859, issue, and "The Desecration of the American Flag" in the December 8, 1859, issue of the *Davenport Democrat and News*. See also Hildegard Binder Johnson, "German Forty-Eighters in Davenport," *Iowa Journal of History* 44:1 (January 1946), 45–46. German expressions of respect included "lowering the flag to half mast on Lahrman's hall, and drap[ing] it in mourning; a number of stores had crape attached to the doors, and some Germans wore crape on their hats," noted in *History of Scott County, Iowa* (Chicago: Inter-state Publishing Co., 1882), 673.

58 "The Desecration of the American Flag," *Davenport Democrat and News*, December 8, 1859.

59 "A Brown Sympathizer," Muscatine *Iowa Democratic Enquirer*, December 22, 1859.

60 Keeler, "Owen Brown's Escape," 342–366.

61  Keeler, "Owen Brown's Escape," 342–366.

62  C. B. Galbreath, "Barclay Coppoc," *Ohio Archaeological and Histori-cal Publications* 30 (1921), 467–469; Downer, *History of Davenport and Scott County*, 621–622; Gue, "John Brown and His Iowa Friends," 273; handwritten copy of article from James Thompson, *Davenport Gazette*, August 7, 1877, contained in Ms. 103, Dr. August P. Richter Papers, 1884–1925, Davenport, State Historical Society of Iowa, Iowa City.

63  Galbreath, "Barclay Coppoc," 469.

64  Richard Acton, "The Story of Ann Raley: Mother of the Coppoc Boys," *Palimpsest* 72:1 (Spring 1991), 27.

65  "Governor Kirkwood's Inaugural Address, Delivered to the Eighth General Assembly of Iowa," *Charles City Republican Intelligencer*, January 26, 1860.

66  The four flaws are noted as follows in Clark, *Samuel Jordan Kirk-wood*, 156–157:

    1st—The affidavit presented, was not made before "a magistrate," but be-fore a Notary Public.

    2nd—Even had the law recognized an affidavit made before a Notary Pub-lic, the affidavit in this case was not authenticated by the Notary's seal.

    3rd—The affidavit does not show, unless it be inferentially, that Coppoc was in the State of Virginia at the time he "aided and abetted John Brown and others," as stated therein.

    4th—It did not legally "charge him" with commission of "treason, felony or other crime."

    The most extensive treatment of the extradition issue is Thomas Teakle, "The Rendition of Barclay Coppoc," *Iowa Journal of History and Politics* 10:4 (October 1912), 503–566.

67  Gue, "John Brown and His Iowa Friends," 273–274.

68  Gue, "John Brown and His Iowa Friends," 273–274; S. C. Trowbridge, "Famous Fast Mail: The Historic Iowa Underground Railway, Furi-ous Riding to Save the Life of One of John Brown's Quaker Boys," *Des Moines News*, January 13, 1899.

69  Trowbridge, "Famous Fast Mail."

70  Trowbridge, "Famous Fast Mail."

71  *History of Cedar County, Iowa* (Chicago: Western Historical Co., 1878), 373.

72 Teakle, "The Rendition of Barclay Coppoc," 529–530; *History of Cedar County with a History of Iowa*, vol. 2, 33; "Barclay Coppic," *Muscatine Weekly Journal*, February 3, 1860. On Barclay Coppoc's visit to Jefferson, Ashtabula County, Ohio, see "Coppoc in Ohio," *Muscatine Weekly Journal*, April 6, 1860; and "A Douglas Editor among the Brownites," *Boone County News*, April 11, 1860.

73 "Requisition for Coppic—His Flight," *Davenport Daily Gazette*, January 31, 1860; "Governor Kirkwood and Young Coppic," *Davenport Democrat*, February 1, 1860; "Our Republican Neighbor on Disunion," *Davenport Democrat*, February 1, 1860; "The Requisition for Coppic," *Davenport Daily Gazette*, February 1, 1860; "The Coppic Requisition," *Davenport Daily Gazette*, February 6, 1860; "Excitement in Springdale," reprinted from the *Tipton Cedar Democrat* in the *Davenport Democrat and News*, February 13, 1860.

74 "The Mother of Coppic," Des Moines *Iowa Weekly Citizen*, December 21, 1859; Acton, "The Story of Ann Raley," 27–29.

## 8   Fearless Defiance

1   Mrs. E. G. Platt, Oberlin, Ohio, letter to William E. Connelley, Topeka, Kansas, October 1, 1900, in Platt Family Papers, Series Two RG0907.AM, Nebraska State Historical Society, Lincoln, referring to the help given to Kansas-bound settlers by residents of Civil Bend and Tabor.

2   "A Kidnapping Case," *Pacific City Herald*, February 9, 1860, identifies the four men as having lived in the Choctaw Nation. Connelley, *Quantrill and the Border Wars*, 146–147, claims that they had run away from Cherokee owners. One proslavery correspondent writing from Glenwood, Iowa, to the *St. Joseph Gazette*, February 29, 1860 (reprinted in the *Pacific City Herald*, March 8, 1860), incorrectly claimed that three runaways went to Tabor, where they joined a fourth fugitive, and that the three were those reported in the *St. Joseph Gazette* as having escaped from Mount Vernon, Missouri. The ages and look of the four fugitives are noted in Thomas A. Lucas, "Men Were Too Fiery for Much Talk: The Grinnell Anti-Abolitionist Riot of 1860," *Palimpsest* (Spring 1987), 16.

3   Connelley, *Quantrill and the Border Wars*, 146–147.

4 "A Kidnapping Case," *Pacific City Herald*, February 9, 1860; Jonathan Spikes, "Kidnapping and Rescue," Des Moines *Iowa State Register*, February 14, 1860.

5 "A Kidnapping Case," *Pacific City Herald*, February 9, 1860.

6 Joe Foster recruited Jim Gardner to drive the wagon and four others: Castle, W. K. Follett, Wyatt, and George Linville. Todd, *Early Settlement* (1906), 64; "A Kidnapping Case," *Pacific City Herald*, February 9, 1860.

7 "Tabor," *Pacific City Herald*, March 8, 1860, in which the editor reprints comments of another writer, followed by his own remarks about what actually happened.

8 Hill letter, October 30, 1894; Todd, *Early Settlement* (1906), 64; letter to the editor from "One Who Knows" to "Friend Shoemaker," Clarinda *Page County Herald*, February 24, 1860. The reference to the rescued men shooting two shots in the air is from Spikes, "Kidnapping and Rescue," Des Moines *Iowa State Register*, February 14, 1860.

9 Todd, *Early Settlement* (1906), 64.

10 Hill letter, October 30, 1894; see also Todd, *Early Settlement* (1906), 65, for a somewhat different account of this rescue.

11 The Grinnell portion of the story that follows relies on two principal sources: Lucas, "Men Were Too Fiery," 12–21; and manuscript notes compiled by Leonard F. Parker in preparing to write his *History of Poweshiek County*, file Ms.01.51, "1856–1860: The Grinnell Public School and the Superintendent," Grinnell College Libraries, Department of Special Collections, Grinnell, Iowa (hereafter cited as Parker manuscript notes).

12 Parker manuscript notes; Parker, *History of Poweshiek County*, 222–223.

13 Parker manuscript notes.

14 Ransom L. Harris, "Kansas to Honor John Brown: Will Celebrate 50th Anniversary of Battle of Osawatomie," *San Francisco Call*, August 12, 1906, 4; J. J. Lutz, "Quantrill, the Guerilla Chief: Quantrill and his Base Betrayal of the Iowa Slave Liberators," *Midland Monthly* 7:6 (June 1897), 509–520; Connelley, *Quantrill and the Border Wars*, chapters 9 and 10. Connelley's study contains the most detailed research, including letters of contemporaries on the Morgan Walker raid; modern biographical treatments of this event—including Ed-

262 :: NOTES TO PAGES 176-179

ward E. Leslie, *The Devil Knows How to Ride: The True Story of William Clarke Quantrill and His Confederate Raiders* (New York: DaCapo, 1998), chapter 4; and Duane Schultz, *Quantrill's War: The Life & Times of William Clarke Quantrill, 1837–1865* (New York: St. Martin's, 1997), chapter 4—are derived from Connelley's work.

15 Information about these events comes from Harris, "Kansas to Honor John Brown." For an account of the three black men from the Indian Territory joining up with the Quaker men in Pardee, Kansas, see Connelley, *Quantrill and the Border Wars*, 146–149.

16 It is unclear whether John Dean and Albert Southwick actually participated in the raid. The account given here follows those provided by Harris, "Kansas to Honor John Brown," and Connelley, *Quantrill and the Border Wars*, 154–157.

17 On Morgan Walker and his farm, see Pearl Wilcox, *Jackson County Pioneers* (Independence, MO: Jackson County Historical Society, 1975), 313–314; *The History of Jackson County, Missouri* (Kansas City, MO: Union Historical Co., 1881), 317; and Connelley, *Quantrill and the Border Wars*, 154–157.

18 Harris, "Kansas to Honor John Brown"; Connelley, *Quantrill and the Border Wars*, 156, 160; John J. Lutz, "Quantrill and the Morgan Walker Tragedy," *Transactions of the Kansas State Historical Society*, vol. 6 (Topeka, KS: W. Y. Morgan, State Printer, 1904), 326–327.

19 Connelley, *Quantrill and the Border Wars*, 154–159.

20 Connelley, *Quantrill and the Border Wars*, 159–160, especially n. 6.

21 Connelley, *Quantrill and the Border Wars*, 174–177.

22 The coroner's verdict appears in Wilcox, *Jackson County Pioneers*, 314–315; Morrison's burial is noted in Connelley, *Quantrill and the Border Wars*, 174.

23 Parker manuscript notes; OPPOSITION [pseudonym], "More Trouble at Grinnell," Des Moines *Iowa State Journal*, October 27, 1860. The trip back to Kansas is described in Connelley, *Quantrill and the Border Wars*, 132–133, 146–149.

24 On Majors and the shipping firm, see Raymond W. Settle and Mary Lund Settle, *War Drums and Wagon Wheels: The Story of Russell, Majors and Waddell* (Lincoln: University of Nebraska Press, 1966); Alexander Majors, *Seventy Years on the Frontier: Alexander Majors' Memoirs of a Lifetime on the Border*, ed. Colonel Prentiss Ingraham

(Lincoln: University of Nebraska Press, 1989; orig. 1893); "Alexander Majors," *Dictionary of American Biography*, vol. 12 (New York: Charles Scribner's Sons, 1933), 214–215.

25  Majors, *Seventy Years on the Frontier*, 72.

26  The most strident proslavery man among the three was William Russell. In 1856, as a leading merchant living at the Missouri River town of Lexington, Russell was a founding member of the "Law and Order Party" and helped lead the effort to close the Missouri River to free-state traffic bound for Kansas. See Raymond W. Settle and Mary Lund Settle, "Waddell and Russell: Frontier Capitalists," *Kansas Historical Quarterly* 26 (1960), 375. See also the William H. Russell sketch on the Kansas Bogus Legislature website, http://kansasboguslegislature .org/mo/russell_w_h.html. Russell, along with Sen. David Atchison and Benjamin Stringfellow, had led a group of armed men who boarded the *Sultan* (a steamboat), removed "provision, tents, &c., of the emigrants," carted them "to the storehouse of Majors & Russell," where they were "broken open" by some of the "ruffians" and items removed. "Russell & Majors have a quantity of arms and ammunition on hand," warned one Chicago emigrant, "and with their mechanics and teamsters—*all proslavery*—can bring out any time of day or night from two hundred to three hundred men." See R. Sheldon, letter to the editor on "The Missouri River Outrage Statement of Mr. Sheldon," *Chicago Democratic Press*, July 3, 1856.

27  Settle and Settle, *War Drums*, 86–87, 127–130; Morton and Watkins, *Illustrated History of Nebraska*, vol. 1, 92–93, 107.

28  J. L. Gibbs enumerated the slave inhabitants of Otoe County, Nebraska Territory, on June 1, 1860, as part of the eighth federal census, National Archives film series M653, transcribed and submitted to the USGen-Web Nebraska Archives, December 1998, by Ted and Carole Miller; see http://www.rootsweb.ancestry.com/~neotoe/otocensus.htm.

29  Morton and Watkins, *History of Nebraska*, 462. The $1,000 reward is mentioned in the *Nebraska City Conservative*, September 13, 1900, according to Olive Bigford, "Early History of Nebraska City," 2, Box 46, Folder 3, Siebert Collection.

30  "Mr. Grinnell Feels Aggrieved," Des Moines *Iowa State Journal*, August 4, 1860; OPPOSITION [pseudonym], "A Letter from Grinnell," Des Moines *Iowa State Journal*, September 29, 1860. The note about the

slaves being taken from Grinnell to Brooklyn, Iowa, is from the William Penn Clarke Papers, Des Moines manuscript collection, State Historical Society of Iowa. According to the *Andreas History of the State of Nebraska* (Chicago: Western Historical Co., 1882), "One was captured in Chicago a few months later but, it is believed, was never brought back." See the Kansas Collection, "Part 4: Nebraska City," http://www.kancoll.org/books/andreas_ne/otoe/otoe-p4.html#nebcity.

31 This, along with John Brown's liberation of the twelve Missouri slaves in December 1858, was the enterprise that inspired the three young Quakers originally from Springdale—Charles Ball, Ed Morrison, and Albert Southwick—to undertake their later suicidal mission to Morgan Walker's farm, as described in this chapter.

32 Todd, *Early Settlement* (1906), 66.

33 "Imprisoned," *Davenport Daily Democrat and News*, November 19, 1860; "Jail Delivery," Clarinda *Page County Herald*, December 7, 1860; "Jacob Hurd," St. Louis *Missouri Democrat*, December 7, 1860; *History of Pottawattamie County, Iowa* (Chicago: O. L. Baskin, 1883), 168; Todd, *Early Settlement* (1906), 67.

## 9 *War and Rebirth*

1 "Dubuque," Elkader *Clayton County Journal*, January 31, 1861.

2 "Missouri," reprinted from the *St. Louis Democrat* in the *Dubuque Daily Times*, March 17, 1861.

3 Bellamy, "Slavery, Emancipation, and Racism," 162–166.

4 "Iowa News," *Burlington Daily Hawk-Eye*, June 7, 1861; "The Missouri Border," *Charles City Republican Intelligencer*, July 25, 1861.

5 Correspondence dated July 28, 1861, from E. G. P. [Elvira Gaston Platt], to the *Burlington Daily Hawk-Eye*, July 31, 1861.

6 A few stories of "guerrilla raids and raiders" in Fremont County appear in *History of Fremont County, Iowa* (Des Moines: Iowa Historical Co., 1881), 481–485.

7 "Lovejoy and 'Contraband,'" *Burlington Daily Hawk-Eye*, July 19, 1861; "The War and Slavery," reprinted from the *Springfield Republican*, in the *Burlington Daily Hawk-Eye*, November 19, 1861.

8 "The War and Slavery," *Burlington Daily Hawk-Eye*, November 19, 1861.

9  "We Must Have Negroes in Iowa," *Boonesboro Times*, February 6, 1862; "The 'Nigger' in the Iowa Legislature," *Boonesboro Herald*, February 6, 1862.

10  The sources for all of the following events described by Cross are letters from John Cross, College Springs, Iowa, to S. V. Jocelyn, American Missionary Association Papers, for the following dates: April 6 and July 8, 1862; June 4, July 6, and September 9, 1863; March 7, April 4, and July 4, 1864; and also the October 1864 annual report form. All this material was generously provided by Leslie A. Schwalm, associate professor of history at the University of Iowa.

11  The following story comes from these two sources: "Sam Scott, Slave, Was Released by Warren Co. Man," *Indianola Record*, August 8, 1941; Edwin Hadley, "A Quaker Memoir: The Sam Scott Story," written about 1940 and posted on the family website: http://griffithfamilystories .blogspot.com/.

12  "Sam Scott," *Indianola Record*, August 8, 1941. As of this 1941 article, the following was known of Scott's children: "Included in the family was another son, Sam Scott Jr., who was born here. He and his brother Bill are both dead. The late Mrs. Henry Brown was a daughter of the Scotts. Another daughter married Jeff Irwin of Omaha. A third daughter married a cook who formerly worked at the old Todhunter hotel, now Hotel Warren. Henry Brown who may have heard much of this story from his wife has moved to Des Moines and was not available to verify statements with reference to this interesting bit of history."

13  "4,000 Niggers," *Burlington Daily Hawk-Eye*, October 16, 1862; *Davenport Democrat*, May 1, 1862, and *Burlington Daily Hawk-Eye*, October 10, 1862, articles discussed in Hubert H. Wubben, *Civil War Iowa and the Copperhead Movement* (Ames: Iowa State University Press, 1980), 79–80; Leslie A. Schwalm, "'Overrun with Free Negroes': Emancipation and Wartime Migration in the Upper Midwest," *Civil War History* 50:2 (2004), 160.

14  "Making the Most of Opportunity: The Story of Jeff Logan," *Des Moines Mail and Times*, December 3, 1904; "Jeff Logan, Ex-Slave Who Escaped from Bondage by the Aid of Isaac Brandt's Underground Railway Will Act as Pallbearer," *Des Moines News*, September 14, 1909; "Veteran Statehouse Negro Employee Dead," *Des Moines Tribune*, December 26, 1927.

15 "Des Moines and the Proclamation," Des Moines *Iowa State Regis-ter*, January 7, 1863; *Population of the United States 1860, Compiled from the Original Returns of the Eighth Census* (Washington, DC: Government Printing Office, 1864), 150; *Census Returns of the Dif-ferent Counties of the State of Iowa, as Returned in the Year 1865* (Des Moines: F. W. Palmer, State Printer, 1865), 41. On black arrivals, see "This Nigga!," Des Moines *Iowa State Register*, April 18, 1862; "John Ford, a Missouri Contraband," Des Moines *Iowa State Register*, May 17, 1862; "The Unprofitableness of Lying," Des Moines *Iowa State Reg-ister*, June 27, 1862; and "Ethiopian Hoe-Down!," Des Moines *Iowa State Register*, December 27, 1862.

16 This observation is from Sharon Avery, archivist at the State Histori-cal Society of Iowa, researching Pay Claims of Commissioned Officers (series) for newly mustered units in the records of the Iowa Adjutant General, at the State Historical Society of Iowa in Des Moines. The record series is incomplete, with no claims existing for many of the companies, and so the exact number of such servants is unknown.

17 Wubben, *Civil War Iowa*, 130, cites the response to Alexander Clark from Kirkwood's secretary, Nathan H. Brainerd, August 8, 1862, Mili-tary Letterbook (Kirkwood), 253.

18 Dykstra, *Bright Radical Star*, 196.

19 Though such gatherings ebbed after mid-1863, Democrats remained divided between war and peace elements. Democratic newspapermen in Dubuque, Muscatine, Council Bluffs, Burlington, and Keosauqua called loudly for peace, but war-Democrat editors in Davenport, Keo-kuk, Sioux City, Bellevue, and Des Moines refused to support a peace agenda premised on the idea of a needless war. Republican leaders and their war supporters in the press further tamped things down by intimidating peace promoters, charging them with disloyalty, and casting critics as Copperheads (supporters of the Confederacy) and traitors; see Wubben, *Civil War Iowa*, 93–95. On the rise and decline of anti-Republican and antiwar activity in Iowa, the most detailed and complete work is Wubben's book; for a regional perspective, see Frank L. Klement, *The Copperheads in the Middle West* (Chicago: University of Chicago Press, 1960); for a broad national viewpoint, see Jennifer L. Weber, *Copperheads: The Rise and Fall of Lincoln's Opponents in the North* (New York: Oxford University Press, 2006).

Two brief articles on Iowa peace advocates and Copperhead activity are Robert Rutland, "The Copperheads of Iowa: A Re-Examination," *Iowa Journal of History* 52:1 (January 1954), 1–30; and Frank L. Klement, "Rumors of Golden Circle Activity in Iowa during the Civil War Years," *Annals of Iowa*, 3rd ser., 37:7 (Winter 1965), 523–536.

20  Wubben, *Civil War Iowa*, 111–113; *Tipton Advertiser*, February 26, 1863.

21  The following story is from C. C. Stiles, "John Ross Miller," *Annals of Iowa*, 3rd ser., 19:5 (July 1934), 384–386; and "Former Slave Got Freedom by 'Underground,'" *Davenport Democrat and Leader*, April 15, 1923.

22  "The Madison County Arrests," *Keokuk Daily Gate City*, September 20, 1862.

23  In early 1863, the peace Democrats hounded out of Winterset one Lieutenant Henry. He had opened a recruiting office for Union troops and stood up to threats from a crowd demanding that he not display the American flag, but he left Winterset the next day. Also, of all the clusters of peace advocates in Iowa, only Madison County's called for the South to separate from the Union if a national convention could not agree on conditions for reunification. The strength of peace sentiment in Madison County was suggested by a report from the captain of the Clarke County guard stating that the secret society called the Knights of the Golden Circle intended to clear the abolitionists out of Osceola County with the help of two hundred partisans from Decatur County and five hundred from Madison County. On the Madison County situation, see Wubben, *Civil War Iowa*, 94, 118–121; "More Secession," Des Moines *Iowa State Register*, September 28, 1862; "Winterset Ovation," Des Moines *Iowa State Register*, December 16, 1862; "Madison Office to be Mobbed," Des Moines *Iowa State Register*, December 25, 1862; "The Winterset Disturbance!" Des Moines *Iowa State Register*, March 17, 1863.

24  The Archie Webb story, except where supplemented by additional notes below, is based on information contained in Nathan E. Coffin, "The Case of Archie P. Webb, A Free Negro," *Annals of Iowa*, 3rd ser., 11:2–3 (July–October 1913), 200–214.

25  "A Lawless Arrest!," Des Moines *Iowa State Register*, January 21, 1863; "Why Don't You Eject Him?," Des Moines *Iowa State Register*, January 23, 1863.

26 Letter from "Democrat of Delaware Township" in Des Moines *Iowa State Register*, January 25, 1863.

27 Coffin, "The Case of Archie P. Webb," 200–214.

28 Coffin, "The Case of Archie P. Webb," 201–213.

29 "From the Capital," *Burlington Daily Hawk-Eye*, February 6, 1863; the *Chicago Tribune* comment was quoted in Coffin, "The Case of Archie P. Webb," 214, and was reprinted in the *Janesville Daily Gazette*, February 4, 1863.

30 Weber, *Copperheads*, 167.

31 Violent talk and incidents persisted throughout 1863–1865. In South English (Keokuk County), Copperheads made a bold display of themselves, parading through the village in August 1863, an act that resulted in the killing of their leader, a Mr. Tally. Two months later near Sidney (Fremont County), when Provost Marshal Felix Van Eaton led some men to stop some suspects on the road, he was ambushed and murdered. Weeks later the county courthouse in Sidney suffered a blast of gunpowder that blew out windows and doors, lifted the roof out of place, and destroyed portions of walls; the building had to be torn down. In October 1864, fifteen miles south of Grinnell on the road toward Oskaloosa, three officers sent out to arrest deserters were intercepted and murdered. And during the same month in Davis County, twelve well-armed Missouri men disguised as federal troops robbed and killed three residents. All such incidents inflamed feeling against what were seen as disloyal citizens. S. H. M. Byers, *Iowa in War Times* (Des Moines, IA: W. D. Condit, 1888), 474–475; A. T. Andreas, *Illustrated Historical Atlas of the State of Iowa* (Chicago: Andreas Atlas Co., 1875), 505.

32 *Burlington Daily Hawk-Eye*, July 16, 1864, quoted in Wubben, *Civil War Iowa*, 157.

## 10 *Remembering and Forgetting the Underground Railroad*

1 News article from the *Davenport Gazette* reprinted in the Des Moines *Iowa State Register*, August 8, 1865; English translation of August Paul Richter, *Geschlichte der Stadt: Davenport und der County Scott*, *Davenport, Iowa, 1917*, online at "Scott Co, Iowa USGenWeb Project," http://www.celticcousins.net/scott/chpt52.htm.

2 For biographical information about Alfred Sully, who later became a leading Wall Street financier, see Henry Clews, *Twenty-Eight Years in Wall Street* (New York: J. S. Ogilvie, 1887), 553–554; Henry Hall, ed., *America's Successful Men of Affairs*, vol. 1 (New York: New York Tribune, 1895), 635–638.

3 Ronald E. Butchart and Amy F. Folleri, "Iowa Teachers among the Freedpeople of the South, 1862–1876," *Annals of Iowa*, 3rd ser., 62:1 (Winter 2003), 1–29; Jones, *The Quakers of Iowa*, 197–202.

4 Editor [Ret Clarkson], "Our Early Soldiers against Slavery," *Iowa Daily State Register*, December 22, 1872.

5 "Fred Douglass," *Mount Pleasant Journal*, February 13 and March 1, 1867.

6 "Reunion," *Oskaloosa Herald*, December 24, 1868; "Abolitionists," *Oskaloosa Herald*, December 31, 1868.

7 For the mention of advance planning arrangements, see "Local Miscellany," *Chicago Daily Tribune*, February 17, 1874; Larry Gara, "A Glorious Time: The 1874 Abolitionist Reunion in Chicago," *Journal of the Illinois State Historical Society* 65:3 (Autumn 1972), 280.

8 "The Abolitionists: First Reunion of the Old Guard," *Chicago Tribune*, June 10, 1874. For lengthy coverage of the second and third days, see "The Abolitionists: Proceedings of the Second Day of the Reunion," *Chicago Tribune*, June 11, 1874; and "The Abolitionists: Proceedings of the Third Day of the Convention," *Chicago Tribune*, June 12, 1874. Additional coverage in the form of an address delivered by William Goodell at the reunion appears as "The Slave Power," *Chicago Tribune*, June 15, 1874.

9 Peter H. Jaynes, ed., *Highlights of Henry County, Iowa, History, 1833–1976* (Burlington, IA: Doran and Ward Lithographing Co., 1977), 44.

10 "A Celebration," *Keokuk Daily Gate City*, August 2, 1866.

11 "The Colored People's Celebration," Des Moines *Iowa State Register*, August 2, 1866.

12 Others occurring during the 1860s included "Emancipation Day—Colored Folks Pic Nic," *Davenport Daily Gazette*, August 3, 1850; a Muscatine celebration of abolition in the West Indies noted in the Des Moines *Iowa State Register*, August 4, 1865; and "Emancipation Celebration," Des Moines *Iowa State Register*, August 2, 1867.

13  Robert K. Bower, "Joseph A. Dugdale: A Friend of Truth," *Palimp-sest* 56:6 (November/December 1975), 177; Jaynes, ed., *Highlights of Henry County*, 44; Teresa Federer, *Belle A. Mansfield: Opening the Way for Others* (Stanford, CA: Stanford Law School, 2002). On the black settlement in Lee's subdivision, see Carolyn Noon, "Lee Town Grows from Black Refuge," for the *Burlington Daily Hawk-Eye*, available online at "Healthy Henry County Communities," http://www.healthyhenrycounty.org/lee_town.htm. On Newton's black settlement, see "Slaves Find Refuge Here in Early Days," *Newton Daily News*, December 18, 1926; "Jasper County's Black Civil War Veterans," *Jasper County Gleaner* 18:2 (May 1996), 2–9; Stiles, "John Ross Miller"; Larry Ray Hurto, ed. and comp., *A History of Newton, Iowa* (Dallas, TX: Curtis Media, 1992), 78–79; "Clem Miller Died at Home Last Evening," *Newton Daily News*, February 11, 1914, reprinted in the *Jasper County Gleaner* 18:2 (May 1996), 6.

14  Bower, "Joseph A. Dugdale," 170–183; Federer, "Belle A. Mansfield," 164–167.

15  "Underground Convention," *Mount Pleasant Journal*, June 24, 1875.

16  On the drive for postwar reconciliation, see David W. Blight, *Race and Reunion: The Civil War in American Memory* (Cambridge, MA: Harvard University Press, 2001). For an excellent treatment of postwar abolitionist efforts to correct the historical record and fight what they judged as views promoting false historical understanding, see Julie Roy Jeffrey, *Abolitionists Remember: Antislavery Autobiographies and the Unfinished Work of Emancipation* (Chapel Hill: University of North Carolina Press, 2008).

17  David Von Drehle, "The Way We Weren't: The Civil War 1861–2011," *Time* 177:15 (April 18, 2011), 40.

18  Wilbur H. Siebert, *The Underground Railroad from Slavery to Freedom* (New York: Macmillan, 1899). Siebert continued to correspond with interested parties and collect research for years after the publication of his book. His collection of forty-seven hundred items includes responses generated by his own seven-question survey as well as copies of and notes from a wide variety of sources: books, diaries, letters, photographs, newspaper articles, biographies and memoirs, state and local histories, annual reports, trial records, U.S. and Canadian census reports, legislation, and congressional speeches. It has

been digitized and is available at the Ohio Historical Society and State Library of Ohio collaborative Ohio Memory website, "The Wilbur H. Siebert Underground Railroad Collection," http://www.ohiomemory .org/cdm4/index_siebert.php?CISOROOT=/siebert.

19  Mrs. E. G. Platt, Tabor, Iowa, November 6, 1894, reply to W. H. Siebert, Columbus, Ohio, Box 45, Folder 11A, MIC 192, Siebert Collection.

20  For more information on the Henderson Lewelling House, see "Aboard the Underground Railroad," at http://www.nps.gov/nr/travel/ underground/ia3.htm.

21  For more information on John Todd's house, see Tabor Historical Society, http://www.taboriowahistoricalsociety.org/todd.html.

22  For more information on George Hitchcock's house, see http://www .hitchcockhouse.org.

23  For more information about James Jordan's house, see http://www .thejordanhouse.org/jordanhouse/.

24  On the fate of the Maxson house, see the following undated newspaper clippings from the Maude Stratton Scrapbooks at the Herbert Hoover Presidential Library, West Branch, Iowa: "Historic 'John Brown' House Is Rapidly Disintegrating" (scrapbook #3); "Old Gravel House of 'John Brown' Fame Torn Down" (scrapbook #1).

25  The demise of Robert Lee Smith's house is mentioned in James Ney, "121-Year-Old Slave Haven Being Razed," *Des Moines Register*, May 31, 1970.

26  Lowell Blikre, principal investigator, with contributions by David W. Benn, "Phase I Intensive Survey of Seven Potential Historic Archeological Properties in the Civil Bend Vicinity, Benton Township, Fremont County, Iowa," BCA Report 1237 (Cresco, IA: Bear Creek Archeology, 2005).

The best single account about the slavery issue's rise in Iowa is Robert R. Dykstra's *Bright Radical Star: Black Freedom and White Supremacy on the Hawkeye Frontier* (Cambridge, MA: Harvard University Press, 1993). Its first half, which covers the antebellum years, contains well-documented discussions of white-black relations, covers exclusionary laws and slavery politics, and includes a chapter on the controversial rescue of runaway Missouri blacks by antislavery citizens at Salem, a predominantly Quaker town in Henry County. See also Dykstra's two subsequent articles: "Dr. Emerson's Sam: Black Iowans before the Civil War," *Iowa Heritage Illustrated* 85:2–3 (Summer and Fall, 2004), 50–63; and "Race, Courage, and Discipline in Iowa's Heroic Age," *Iowa Heritage Illustrated* 88:1 (Spring 2007), 22–31.

Given Iowa's border state status with Missouri, a useful perspective on the tensions and conditions faced by such states, south and north alike, is Stanley Harrold, *Border War: Fighting over Slavery before the Civil War* (Chapel Hill: University of North Carolina Press, 2010). The author shows how pressures mounted along the border states from frequent cross-border clashes sparked by black escapes, kidnappings, vigilante apprehensions, and entanglements between antislavery and proslavery groups, which reveal the extent that runaways shaped slavery politics.

Direct underground railroad operations in the West commonly engaged members of strongly antislavery religious denominations. In particular, Congregationalists, Quakers, Wesleyan Methodists, and New School Presbyterian churches of antislavery bent stood in the forefront of lending assistance to runaways. The reader will learn a great deal about one such denomination in Ryan P. Jordan, *Slavery and the Meetinghouse: The Quakers and the Abolitionist Dilemma, 1820–1865* (Bloomington: Indiana University Press, 2007). See also his article "The Indiana Separation of 1842 and the Limits of Quaker Anti-Slavery," *Quaker History* 89 (Spring 2000), 1–27, the events of which involved the main Quaker settlement at Salem, Iowa.

The best comprehensive evaluation on the slavery issue's effect among Northern churches is John R. McKivigan, *The War against Proslavery Religion: Abolitionism and the Northern Churches, 1830–1865* (Ithaca, NY: Cornell University Press, 1984). Here he writes of the push for immediate abolition having slowly gained momentum despite timid, balking antislavery commitments of Northern churches generally, all of this amid dispute, schism, denunciation, and attempts to conciliate the issue. See also the worthy contribution by John R. McKivigan and Mitchell Snay, eds., *Religion and the Antebellum Debate over Slavery* (Athens: University of Georgia Press, 1998). In thirteen essays the book examines the slavery and sectional struggle through the divergent responses of antebellum Protestantism.

For Iowa's underground railroad story, the sweep of activity there is nicely covered in G. Galin Berrier, "The Underground Railroad in Iowa," in Bill Silag, ed., *Outside In: African-American History in Iowa, 1838–2000* (Des Moines: State Historical Society of Iowa, 2001). Joining Iowa's underground railroad events to those in other western states of the time, James Patrick Morgans details many escapes to freedom in *The Underground Railroad on the Western Frontier: Escapes from Missouri, Arkansas, Iowa and the Territories of Kansas, Nebraska and the Indian Nations, 1840–1865* (Jefferson, NC: McFarland, 2010). Morgans also contributes a fine account of one Iowa antislavery pastor and the aid given runaways by his Congregationalist community of Tabor in *John Todd and the Underground Railroad: Biography of an Iowa Abolitionist* (Jefferson, NC: McFarland, 2006).

Iowa's involvement in underground railroad actions was closely involved with parallel operations across the Mississippi River in Illinois. For these, see Owen W. Muelder, *The Underground Railroad in Western Illinois* (Jefferson, NC: McFarland, 2007) and Hermann R. Muelder, *Fighters for Freedom: A History of Anti-Slavery Activities of Men and Women Associated With Knox College* (Galesburg, IL: Knox College, 1950; New York: Columbia University Press, 1959). For coverage of slaves temporarily brought by vacationing Southern slaveholders into the upper Mississippi River Valley and instances when African Americans were held in Iowa as domestics or mine workers before the Civil War, see Christopher P. Lehman, *Slavery in the Upper Mississippi Valley, 1787–1865: A History of Human Bondage in Illinois, Iowa, Minnesota and Wisconsin* (Jefferson, NC: McFarland, 2011).

Concerning the various times John Brown and his men spent in Iowa, the best single source continues to be Oswald Garrison Villard, *John Brown 1800–1859: A Biography Fifty Years After* (Boston: Houghton Mifflin, 1910), reprint paperback copies of which remain available.

For people interested in delving further into contemporary sources on antislavery times in the state, a visitor to the State Historical Society of Iowa in Des Moines or Iowa City will find microfilm copies of numerous newspapers from the period, such as the *Burlington Hawk-Eye* and *Muscatine Journal*, and letters of Iowa abolitionists in the William Penn Clarke Papers or the John Todd Papers. Numerous materials also have been brought together in the Antislavery and Underground Railroad project at the Des Moines facility.

INDEX

## Iowa and the Midwest Experience

---